VISIONARIES AND SEERS

Other books by Charles Neilson Gattey

Social history
The Bloomer Girls (Femina Books)

Biographies
Gauguin's Astonishing Grandmother (Femina Books)
A Bird of Curious Plumage (Constable)
The Incredible Mrs. Van Der Elst (Leslie Frewin)

With Zelma Bramley-Moore

Historical Novel
The King Who Could Not Stay The Tide (Epworth Press)

Plays
The Eleventh Hour
Man in a Million
The Enemy of Time
A Spell of Virtue
True Love—or the Bloomer
The Colour of Anger

With Jordan Lawrence

Play
The White Falcon

VISIONARIES AND SEERS

THEY SAW TOMORROW

CHARLES NEILSON GATTEY

Originally published in Great Britain 1977 as *They Saw Tomorrow* by George C. Harrap & Co. Ltd.

This edition published in Great Britain 1988 by:
PRISM PRESS
2 South Street,
Bridport,
Dorset DT6 3NQ.

and distributed in the USA by:
AVERY PUBLISHING GROUP INC.,
350 Thorens Avenue,
Garden City Park,
New York 11040.

and published in Australia 1988 by:
UNITY PRESS
6a Ortona Road,
Lindfield,
NSW 2070

ISBN 1 85327 020 2

Reprinted 1988

Printed and bound in the Channel Islands
by The Guernsey Press Company Limited.

Preface

IN this book I have written about some of the strangest of those who have tried to 'look into the seeds of time, and say which grain will grow and which will not', as Banquo said to the witches. When making my selection I have been influenced not solely by their success as prophets, but also by the extraordinary tenor of their lives, their relevance to their times, and their influence then and since.

Many and devious are the methods that have been adopted in attempting to foretell the future—astrology, palmistry, crystal-gazing, numerology, divination through the Tarot and tea-leaves, and so on. All this inevitably lends itself to exploitation of the credulous by the charlatan. But the appearance of one black sheep does not mean that all white sheep are really black. Unfortunately, too, those who begin by displaying psychic gifts and then try to exploit them for personal prestige or financial gain often find that they cannot switch such powers on at will, and so resort to deception, which if discovered discredits all they have ever done.

Cagliostro comes under this category, and so in a way does Mlle Lenormand, who till now has been completely overlooked by writers in the English language, and who I am therefore particularly glad to include in my selection.

My grateful thanks are due to the following in particular for help in finding facts and rare illustrations—Mrs Margret Busse of Beverley Hills; Mr Ellic Howe; Mr K. Q. F. Manning, Cultural Attaché at the British Embassy, Sofia; Mr John R. Freeman; Mr Michael G. O'Brien of the Highland Regional Council; Mr John Watt, Director of Leisure and Recreation of the Ross and Cromarty District Council and Mr John Crawford, their Regional Adviser in Art; the staff of the Battersea, British, Edinburgh, and Westminster Libraries—and also to Mrs W. Corneck, my expert and ever dependable typist.

C.N.G.

Contents

1

2

I The Pythia of Delphi

Socrates described prophecy as 'a madness which is the special gift of heaven, and the source of the chiefest blessings among men', and added that 'the prophetess at Delphi and the priestess of Dodona when out of their senses have conferred great benefits on Hellas, both in public and private life, but when in their senses few or none'.

Originally omens had been found in what Plato in his *Phaedrus* calls the 'sane' form of divination based on observation and interpretation according to an established code of phenomena in the animate and inanimate world. Significance was found in eclipses and earthquakes, in thunder and lightning, the flight, cries and other behaviour of birds, and even the rustling of leaves. At the shrine of Apollo at Sura, it came from the way the sacred fish moved in the tank where they were kept, and in the grove dedicated to the same god in Epirus from the appetite or lack of it of tame serpents when fed by the priestess, which enabled her to predict a good or bad harvest.

In Boeotia during festival time the inhabitants hurled barley loaves into a small lake. If they sank it was a happy augury for those who flung them in, but if they floated on the surface it meant the opposite. The insertion of a piece of lead, it appears, would have secured good luck.

Similarly, in Sicily people cast in gold and silver vessels into the craters of Mount Etna: if the fire consumed them it was regarded as a fortunate omen, but if the volcano spewed them back the outlook for the thrower was hopeless.

The form of 'sane' divination that was most in vogue was known as haruspication, and entailed the examination of the

1 Delphi: ruins of the temple. *Photo Michael R. Carter*

2 Reconstruction of theatre and Temple of Apollo, Delphi. *Radio Times Hulton Picture Library*

entrails of an animal sacrificed upon an altar. It was believed that the gods marked them with the portents they desired men to know, and that the priests were divinely guided into choosing for sacrifice the animals containing these telltale markings. The liver was regarded as being of especial importance in this respect, the chief parts for careful scrutiny being the lobes, the bile-duct and the hepatic artery. If the 'head' of the liver were missing or had perished it signified ruin or death. Alexander the Great was warned in this way of his imminent end.

The other form of the mantic art was called by Plato the 'insane', or ecstatic or inspired kind, and involved a dedicated seer or seeress, who is possessed by a god and predicts under his control. This, a far more awesome form of divination, was chosen by the principal oracles of Apollo.

It is not surprising that Delphi, in the heart of Greece, became the country's foremost centre for prophecy. The setting alone, even today, is awe-inspiring. The ruins of the temple of Apollo, which was almost as large as the Parthenon at Athens, are imposingly situated on a plateau below the lower slopes of Mount Parnassus within the obtuse angle formed by the twin limestone cliffs, each a thousand feet high, known as the Phaedriades, the shining crags, because the sun at dawn makes them seem to radiate light. A deep and forbidding gorge rends them apart, and down this in winter a torrent rushes to join the waters of the perennial Castalian spring before plunging into a rocky glen and flowing into the river Pleistus. The latter resembles a gigantic silver snake as it twists and turns from east to west through the valley, thickly lined with hoary olive-trees. Perhaps its shape inspired the legend of the python that Apollo is said to have slain. Then farther to the west is another spring, the Cassotis, whose water used to be conveyed by a series of ducts to the temple of Apollo. Overhead eagles and vultures circle menacingly, and when thunder rumbles and roars in the mountains it is easy to imagine that this is indeed where Apollo spoke to his worshippers.

For over a thousand years Delphi's precise position was unknown, and until 1892 the mountain village of Castri sprawled over the site. Then, thanks to the excavations of French archaeologists, it was restored to view, and by 1899 the outline of the town and temple was revealed, corresponding in detail with Pausanias' description in the second century A.D.

Diodorus Siculus, the Greek historian who lived in the time of Julius Caesar and Augustus, gives this version of how the oracle came into being.

> In ancient times the goats first discovered Delphi, which is why in our day the people there still prefer such an animal when they offer sacrifice before consulting the god. The discovery is supposed to have occurred in this fashion. At the spot where the *adyton* of the present temple is, there was once a chasm in the ground where the goats used to graze. Whenever one of them approached this opening and looked down, it would begin skipping about in an astonishing fashion and bleating in a quite different voice to its normal one. And, when the herdsman, puzzled by these antics, went to try and discover the cause, he, too, was similarly affected and began to prophesy the future.
>
> Later, news of what happened to people who visited the chasm began to spread among the peasants, and they flocked to the spot in large numbers, eager to put the phenomenon to the test; and whenever one of them drew near, he fell into a trance.... Thus it was that the place itself came to be regarded as miraculous. For a time, those who came thither to seek advice used to proclaim oracles to one another. But, later on, when many people in their rapture had hurled themselves into the chasm and vanished, it seemed wise to those who lived in the locality that to save lives one woman should be appointed as the sole prophetess, who alone should pronounce the oracles. They therefore constructed a contraption so that she could sit in safety over the chasm and breathe in the entrancing vapours and utter her oracles to those who sought her counsel. This contraption was supported by three legs, which is why it was called a tripod, and indeed the bronze tripods that we have today are almost exact replicas of it.

Tradition has it that when Apollo became the god worshipped at Delphi the priestess was given the title of Pythia, said by some to be derived from his other name, Pythian, after the python he is supposed to have killed there. The first Pythia is believed to have been called Phemonoë, and she probably lived in the seventh century B.C.

Although archaeologists during their excavations have failed to discover any fissures in the locality through which natural gases could have escaped, they may have closed through earth tremors. It is most likely that some crevice existed, for all records of visitors to Delphi in ancient times mention that the tripod in the *adyton* stood over an opening from whence rose a vapour, which enveloped the Pythia and sent her into a state of ecstasy, so that she behaved and spoke as though possessed by Apollo.

An alternative explanation is that the intoxicating vapour may have been artificially produced by burning elsewhere herbs that were mantic stimulants and channelling them into the oracular chamber. Plutarch's description might perhaps support such a theory, for he writes, 'The room in which those who came to consult the god were seated is, not often but occasionally and at irregular intervals, filled with a sweet-smelling vapour, as though the *adyton* were emitting as from a fountain the sweetest and most precious perfumes'.

At the oracle of Apollo at Argos the priestess went into prophetic frenzy after drinking the blood of a lamb, sacrificed at night, while at Aegae this state was achieved through a draught of bull's blood. At Claros and Branchidae, in Ionia, holy water produced the same effect, but at the former place, according to Pliny, this came from an underground spring, and he alleges cut short the lives of those who imbibed it.

Originally Pythias had to be virgins, as it was held that physical purity rendered them readier to keep secrets. But later a man from Thessaly named Echecrates, consulting the oracle, was smitten by the virgin's beauty and raped her. As a result of this scandal the Delphians decided that for the future the prophetess should be a woman aged fifty and older. Nevertheless,

Pythias continued to wear the dress of a maiden. They were regarded as the unconscious instruments of divine revelation, and as persons counted for little.

From Plutarch we learn that, when he visited Delphi, the Pythia belonged to

> one of the soundest and most respected families and has always led an irreproachable life, although, having been brought up in the home of poor peasants, when she fulfils her prophetic role she does so quite witlessly and without any special knowledge or talent. . . . The woman is committed to a strenuous existence and for the rest of her days must remain pure and chaste.

He also mentions the custom of pouring cold water over candidates for the office, in order to ascertain by their healthy way of shuddering that they were sound in mind and body and not subject to hysteria.

When Delphi was at the height of its fame, in the fifth century B.C., two priestesses were kept constantly occupied, and relieved each other, while a third was in reserve, prepared to take over in an emergency. But in Plutarch's time, in the late first century A.D., clients were so infrequent that only one Pythia was employed.

According to Flavius Philostratus, the first temple was a primitive affair constructed from boughs taken from Apollo's sacred tree, the laurel, to which in time the bees contributed their wax and the birds their feathers. Then, thanks to the offerings left by the stream of visitors, a temple of stone was built by Trophonius and Agamedes, which was destroyed by fire in 548 B.C. The Amphictyons, who were then managing the sanctuary, called upon Hellenes everywhere to contribute to the rebuilding fund and there was a wide response; even Amasis, King of Egypt, sent a large donation. A new temple was then erected between 530 and 514 B.C., of which Spintharus of Corinth was the architect. It is believed that it was rebuilt at least twice after that, and pillaged and almost razed by the thirty-year-old Nero because when he consulted the

Pythia she shouted, 'Your presence outrages me. Begone, matricide! Beware of seventy-three!'

Enraged by these words, he had the priestess buried alive, together with the priests, whose hands and feet were cut off first. He consoled his injured pride with the thought that the prophecy meant he would live another forty-three years. But he died a year later, for it proved to allude to Galba, who succeeded him as Emperor when aged seventy-three (by some computations).

Nature has given the scene savage beauty, and the impression produced on the pilgrim must have been intensified in those days by the presence of the shrine of prophecy. The seeker after certainty in a world of doubt could not help but have his faith strengthened as he approached. If he travelled on foot for three to four hours from the Gulf of Corinth by the long, dusty way up from the port of Cirrha (now Itéa), passing first through the sea of olives in the Crisaean plain, superb views of Delphi met him unexpectedly at sudden bends in the winding road. If instead he took the overland route from Athens, which crosses Boeotia and at Lebadeia (today Livadia) begins to climb the lower slopes of Mount Parnassus through splendid scenery until it reaches Castalia, he would reach Delphi by crossing a bridge over the gorge.

The oracular temple must have been exceedingly impressive set against such a spectacular background. There were the treasuries, replete with riches contributed by cities and people from all over the Mediterranean, and the converging streets lined with monuments and trophies and over three thousand statues of bronze, marble and gold. On a column in the forecourt were carved the three celebrated maxims: 'Know thyself'; 'Nothing in Excess'; and 'Go surety, and ruin is at hand'. Over the temple's portico was engraved the admonishment 'Let no man enter here unless his hands be pure'.

For the pilgrim there was so much to see and to admire: the Hall of the Cnidians, in which hung *The Descent of Odysseus among the Dead*, by Polygnotus, which some regarded as the finest work of that great painter; and the Hall of the Amphictyonic Council, the political centre of Greece and the supreme authority whose decisions every Hellenic state had sworn to carry out.

And when the supplicant reached his goal it seems that he was rarely disappointed with the responses he received. Cicero, the Roman philosopher and orator, who was inclined to be sceptical, wrote, 'Never could the oracle of Delphi have been so overwhelmed with so many important offerings from monarchs and nations if all the ages had not proved the truth of its oracles'.

Originally consultations took place only once a year, at the beginning of spring on Apollo's birthday, but as the number of inquirers increased they were also given advice on the seventh day of every month, except in winter, as he was regarded as the seventh god. At other times the Pythia may have answered questions by lot, keeping a store of black and white beans with her for that purpose. At first payment was made in kind by gifts, but when running costs rose a fixed minimum fee was levied, and those in need of urgent guidance could obtain priority by paying more. A city was charged eleven times as much as individuals. For the benefit of the poor, a free open-air mass oracle took place once a year. The Pythia would sit on the temple steps and reply to problems put to her.

For private consultations, there was an elaborate ritual. After the Pythia had purified herself by fasting and bathing in the Castalian stream the presiding priest, known as the 'prophet', and the attendant priests called the *hosioi*, the holy ones, would accompany her to the temple. First, the she-goat intended for sacrifice would be led into a room where was kept the *omphalos*, or sacred navel, the elliptical stone supposed to mark the exact centre of the earth. This was symbolically true, for Delphi was for long the religious centre of the Hellenic civilization. The animal was then sprinkled with holy water. If she shuddered in the correct manner it meant Apollo approved.

Plutarch, who was a priest of Apollo, wrote, 'That she should twist her head about as at other sacrifices would not suffice: she must tremble all over and her limbs must twitch, otherwise they will say the oracle is not functioning and they will not bring the Pythia to the temple'. In such a case the consultation would be abandoned, but nevertheless the animal would be killed.

'Quite recently', continues Plutarch,

> some foreigners having come to consult the oracle, it seems that when the sacrificial goat was sprinkled with holy water she remained motionless and appeared to be quite unaffected. The priests therefore redoubled their efforts, with the result that the goat was completely drenched with water and finally died in great distress.

He goes on to say that this had an adverse effect upon the Pythia.

> She descended into the *adyton* in a state of dejection and with the greatest reluctance. As soon as she gave her first answer, it was clear from the harshness of her voice that she was wandering like a disabled ship, as though she was filled with a dumb and evil spirit. At last, in utter confusion, she sprang towards the door and with a wild and terrifying shriek threw herself to the ground, putting to flight not only the clients but also the prophet, Nicandros, and the *hosioi* who were attending him. Returning a few minutes later, they picked her up. But though she had come to her senses again, she only survived for a few days.

The Pythia's behaviour on this occasion has features common to all mediumship: the change of voice in a state of trance and the distraught demeanour when suffering from malefic possession.

If, as was normally the case, the goat shuddered, then the Pythia in her robes of office, her forehead bound by a woollen fillet, would be crowned with a wreath of laurel, Apollo's plant. The legend was that the god had fallen in love with the nymph Daphne, who evaded him by turning into a laurel-tree. The priestess would then go into the underground sanctuary, the *adyton*, where she would drink water which had been piped into it from the spring Cassotis and was thought to possess a mantic influence. After this barley meal and laurel leaves were burnt before her and she was given some of the latter to chew, probably because it was found that they helped to induce self-hypnosis. She would then sit on the tripod, which, according to all contemporary accounts, was over the fissure. This was probably covered by a stone slab, which was then pushed aside so that the mystic vapour could be released and breathed in by her.

While these preparations were in progress the inquirers would have been taken into the *chresmographeion*, a kind of office. Those with credentials showing them to be Greeks would be admitted before foreigners, and lots then drawn to decide the order in which they consulted the oracle. The same procedure was adopted with the rest of the waiting clients. Women were barred, but could appoint men to question the Pythia for them.

After purifying himself with holy water the supplicant would pay the required fee, in exchange for which he would be given a sacred cake to place on the main altar outside the temple. Then, accompanied by the priests and the local representative of his own city, he would sacrifice a she-goat on the inner hearth, where a fire always burned. A foreigner coming from a city or country without an agent in Delphi had to employ an interpreter to perform the necessary rites on his behalf.

Following this ceremony, the inquirer would be allowed to enter the *adyton*. He would see before him a statue of Apollo flanked by two eagles, all of solid gold and symbolic of the legend that Zeus had dispatched two such birds from the north and south to discover the centre of the earth, and that they had met and perched at the spot where the *omphalos*, or sacred navel, was kept. The room contained in addition the god's lyre and sacred armour, his tree (the laurel), votive ribbons and the tomb of Dionysus. In the other half of the room, hidden by a screen or curtain, the Pythia, already in a trance, sat on her tripod, while the priest known as the prophet put to her the question which had earlier been disclosed to him by the petitioner.

The Pythia's reply would vary as regards coherence and intelligibility, and it was the prophet's business to interpret her meaning to the inquirer, who could if he wished have a record of it in writing. This would be either in prose or in hexameter verse, according to the prophet's mood. If the stranger were acting for someone unable to travel to Delphi in person he would be handed a sealed tablet. He risked heavy penalties should it be discovered that he had opened this before delivery.

Responses would not be revealed by the priests to any other person. When in verse form they were occasionally clarified, if the matter were of sufficient importance, by an accompanying prose commentary provided by the prophet and the other priests.

Philostratus, in his life of the famous mystic, prophet and healer Apollonius of Tyana, has related how, accompanied by his disciple Damis, he visited Delphi to ask whether his name would be remembered by posterity. He described how, when the power of the god came upon the Pythia, her bosom heaved and she panted. Her face reddened, then was drained of colour. Her limbs jerked and quivered, and her eyes blazed. Saliva frothed on her lips, her hair stiffened and she snatched off her headband. She seemed possessed by some entity. Then she started to speak in a strange tone, and the priests on either side wrote down her words and gave Apollonius the inspired communication. It said that he would be remembered by posterity, but not for any good he had done; instead it would be for the bad.

This angered him. 'I tore up the paper as I was leaving the temple. That is what all suppliants do whose pride has been injured.' At least while Apollonius was alive he was highly regarded by his contemporaries, but following his decease he was denigrated by the early Christian Fathers, and for centuries this was to be his posthumous fate.

The reply received by Apollonius was a clear one, and so

was that which said of the poet Homer, 'He shall be deathless and ageless for aye'. But others were worded like riddles, requiring much puzzling out to understand, and occasionally they were so phrased that they might mean either of two things, each the opposite of the other, and this was why oracles were accused of ambiguity. Heraclitus the philosopher wrote, 'The god of Delphi neither reveals nor conceals, but hints'. This indeed applies to many prophets.

Epaminondas was warned by the Pythia to beware of *pelagos*—sea. He therefore feared to go aboard a galley or to sail in any ship, but it transpired that she meant not the sea but the oak wood with that name, where he met his fate.

And when the Siphnians, who were enormously rich thanks to their gold and silver mines, dispatched a representative to Delphi to ask whether their good fortune would continue the response brought back went, 'When the city hall is white and the market-place white-browed, then beware of an ambush of wood, heralded all red'.

The buildings round the main square had recently been gilded with gold and silver, and as a result in brilliant sunshine they appeared white from a distance. Shortly after the prediction was received in Siphnos the attention of pirates, in ships with ramming beaks painted red for luck, was thus drawn to the small island. They landed, took prisoners and only released them on payment of huge ransoms.

The fact that some mediums today have been detected in deception does not mean that all practise impostures, and this was no doubt true also of the priestesses and priests of Delphi. The women, being mostly simple peasants, selected because of their strong religious faith, may have been influenced by the priests, and as a result of the emotion-stirring ritual entered the trance state with facility. The Pythia's conscious mind lost control and a disassociated personality took its place and answered the questions.

Such self-hypnosis undertaken several times a day left the seeress exhausted, which explains why sturdy peasants were chosen for the office, but even so the life of a Pythia was a short one.

The priests too were carefully recruited, and usually came from noble families, but in their case the qualities primarily required were high intelligence, quick wits and psychological insight. All this was essential to enable them to frame an intelligible reply as they listened intently to the obscure and rambling remarks of Apollo's supposed mouthpiece. Here the danger lay that a 'prophet' might consciously or unconsciously let his mind add to or alter the Pythia's muddled message. In important cases, where it appeared wise for a specific reply to be forthcoming, this may have occurred. Some 'prophets' may even have used hypnotic suggestion to convey to her mind the answer they wanted given.

After study of the responses that have been preserved, one can detect evidence that a fixed policy lay behind the wording of a small number of them. Others are so obscure and involved that they could well be faithful reproductions of the Pythia's utterances. Ambiguity was also caused by the need to couch the verses in the first person, as though Apollo himself were speaking, which did not make for clarity.

Plutarch, who was a priest at Delphi, writing in the second half of the first century A.D., states that it would not have surprised him

> if in ancient times some measure of ambiguity was sometimes judged to be necessary, for it was not just a matter of some individual person consulting the oracle about the purchase of a slave or some other private matter, but of very powerful cities, kings and tyrants with ambitions, seeking the god's counsel on important questions. To anger such men by harsh truths that conflicted with their desires might have harmed the priests of the oracle.

So to protect them, continues Plutarch:

> Apollo, though not prepared to conceal the truth, by clothing it in poetic form removed what might in direct prose be harshly worded, causing offence.... As for the answers given

to ordinary people, it was also occasionally advisable that these should be hidden from their enemies. Thus these too were wrapped in circumlocution and equivocation so that the meaning of the oracle could always be understood by those whom it concerned, if they spent time unravelling it.

It was different in his time, the first century A.D., reveals Plutarch, for the oracle was no longer concerned with 'complicated or secret matters'. The questions the Pythia was asked had 'to do with people's ordinary day-to-day problems'.

'Greek oracles reflect for a thousand years (roughly speaking from 700 B.C. to 300 A.D.) the spiritual needs of a great people', wrote F. W. H. Myers, who added, 'the Delphian god became in a certain sense the conscience of Greece'.

Divination would seem to have flourished most up to the fifth century B.C., when belief in the gods and goddesses was strongest. All classes then resorted to it. There were oracles and soothsayers everywhere, and some were less reliable than others.

For example, Plutarch in his *Life of Nicias* mentions how Nicias was chosen to lead an expedition to Sicily, and when the Athenians were debating whether to go ahead with it he announced that he had received warnings from his soothsayers that the omens were bad. Then those who had sought advice from the oracle of Amen-Re at Thebes in Egypt returned with that god's prophecy, which was, 'The Athenians will capture all the Syracusans'. This ended the debate, and the people voted for the expedition to leave, and Nicias reluctantly gave way. But his doubts grew when further auguries of disaster occurred: crows defiled a statue of the goddess Pallas Athene, and a man mutilated himself on an altar.

Throughout the campaign, Nicias showed signs of lowered morale. He procrastinated before taking the offensive, with the result that the Greeks did not succeed in capturing Syracuse, and, after suffering heavy casualties, he decided to raise the siege and sail back to Athens. But there was an eclipse of the moon. The soothsayer he had brought with him warned that he must not weigh anchor for three times nine days.

Nicias stayed, and spent the time offering sacrifice after sacrifice in the hope of gaining the favour of the gods. This delay, however, enabled the enemy to seal his entire fleet in the port and destroy it. Unable to get away by land, he and his army were all vanquished by the Syracusans.

When news of the calamity reached Athens the people blamed Nicias not for obeying a signal from heaven, but for selecting as his diviner an unreliable soothsayer, who had incorrectly interpreted the eclipse of the moon, and who ought to have known that for an army in retreat it was a favourable omen for the moon to hide her face.

The lesson to be learned from this is a familiar one—it never pays in matters of major importance to consult anyone but the very best, which was why Delphi remained at the top of the oracular league because of its high reputation for accuracy. The well-known story of King Croesus certainly illustrates this. He ruled Lydia, which is now part of Turkey, in the sixth century B.C., and his security was threatened by the mounting strength of King Cyrus, his Persian neighbour. He was considering a surprise attack on Cyrus before he was completely outmatched, and was anxious to know what were his chances of success, so he decided to consult an oracle. The trouble was that all claimed to be infallible, and yet might contradict one another. How could he know in advance which of them would be proved correct?

Then he had an inspiration and sent emissaries to the oracles at Branchidae, near Miletus, Abae and Delphi in Phocis, of Amphiaraus at Boeotian Oropus, Trophonius at Lebadea, of Zeus at Dodona in Epirus, and Zeus-Ammon in Libya. To all the same question was to be asked—what was the King doing in his palace at Sardis one hundred days after his messengers had left?

Every reply proved wrong except the one from Delphi. This went, 'I know the number of the grains of sand, and all the measures of the sea. I understand the dumb, and the speechless I hear. The smell has come to my nostrils of a hard-skinned tortoise as it is boiled with lamb's flesh in a covered vessel, all of bronze'.

On hearing that Croesus was delighted, for on the day in question he had in secret cut up a lamb and a tortoise and had boiled them together in a bronze cauldron, covered with a lid of the same metal, so that no one could peer inside. It was the most unlikely thing for a king to do of which he had been able to think, and he was now firmly persuaded that the Pythia of Delphi had genuine psychic powers, so decided that he would follow whatever advice he received from her.

As this would be coming from Apollo, he ordered a huge sacrifice to the god involving the burning of three thousand animals together with gold and silver encrusted beds, cups of precious metal, robes of pearl and his own finest purple tunics. The molten gold and silver were poured into moulds, the ingots taken to Delphi and presented to the priests for Apollo, arranged as a glittering pyramid, with on its crest a lion of pure gold weighing ten talents. With this offering he also sent the gold and silver jars, bowls and vases he himself valued most, together with a life-size statue in gold of his woman pastrycook. According to Herodotus, who saw it all, one gold bowl weighed a quarter of a ton and could hold five thousand gallons of wine. Croesus' wife dutifully added her necklace and girdles.

Incidentally, over the centuries other rulers and governments gave similar gifts to Delphi, though on not so grand a scale, so that treasuries had to be built to house them. Even when later Nero robbed the place of five hundred statues and transferred them to Rome, at least three thousand remained.

Hoping that such lavish offerings would win Apollo's favour, Croesus dispatched his ambassador to Delphi to ask if he should attack Persia, and if so whether he should first find an ally.

The Pythia replied that if Croesus crossed the river Halys a great empire would be destroyed, and that he should ally himself with the most powerful of the Greek nations.

Next, the envoy inquired, 'Will King Croesus have a long reign?' The answer came, 'Nay, when a mule becomes King of the Medes, then flee, soft-soled Lydian, by the pebbly Hermus, and do not linger, nor feel ashamed at being a coward'.

This pleased Croesus, for he interpreted it as meaning that as a mule could never be a king, neither could his kingdom be conquered and wrested from him.

Later, he was also to ask the oracle whether his son, dumb since birth, would ever talk, and the priestess replied, 'Croesus, thou prince of fools, desire not to hear within your halls the voice long prayed for of your son speaking. It would be better for that to be far from you. For he will speak first on a day of ill-fortune.'

As advised, Croesus allied himself with the most powerful of the Greek nations, which was Sparta, but instead of his beating the Persians the reverse occurred, and it was his empire that was destroyed. Apologists for the Pythia pointed out that her reply had been that if Croesus crossed the Halys a great empire would be destroyed, but she had not specified which one.

His conqueror, King Cyrus, had a Persian father and a Mede mother, so could be regarded as a mule. When Cyrus' forces swept into Croesus's capital, Sardis, and, breaking into the palace, rushed menacingly towards him, the fear of seeing them slay his father restored the dumb son's speech and he cried, 'Wretch, would you slay Croesus?'

Cyrus is said to have ordered the vanquished king and fourteen Lydian youths to be chained and burnt alive. When on the pyre Croesus called on the name of Solon, and the Persian ruler asked why he did this. The prisoner replied, 'Because he told me to call no one happy till he is dead'.

The saying so impressed Cyrus that he ordered the fire to be extinguished, but this proved impossible. According to the legend, Croesus then appealed to Apollo, who rewarded him at last for his opulent offerings by sending a shower which put out the flames, thus saving all fifteen lives.

Alexander the Great also consulted the Pythia when he too planned to attack the Persians. In his life of the conqueror,

Plutarch says that, anxious to learn the prospects for this, Alexander went to Delphi, but arrived there on an unpropitious day when the priestess refused to prophesy. Nevertheless, he demanded to see her, and when she declined (as it was contrary to divine law) he went to where she lived and tried to drag her forcibly to the sanctuary. Whereupon, impressed by his authority, she told him, 'You are invincible, my son'. And the moment he heard her say this the conqueror cried that there was no need for him to question the oracle further, since she had given him the message he had hoped to receive.

The oracle of Delphi's advice was sought, as might be expected, by the Greek city-states themselves on all matters of public importance, ranging from religion and law, prospects for the harvest, natural disasters, the outcome of wars, and where and when to colonize. Several of them appointed officials whose duties were to visit the Pythia and ask questions, and also to keep old oracles under review that still awaited fulfilment. Weight was certainly attached to the replies received, as they affected the lives of everybody to a considerable extent. The oracle was a sort of national barometer, according to whose readings the Greeks could be swayed this way or that.

One thing cannot be disputed, however: that the Pythia's pronouncements had an influence on affairs which was mostly salutary. Delphi became the hub of the Hellenic wheel, and the fact that people came there from all parts gave the priests exceptional accessibility to news and opinions. In this fashion they acquired insight and knowledge which was of immense value when interpreting the Pythia's utterances.

The Pythia was invariably consulted when the Hellenes were threatened by war. Never were they in more peril than after Xerxes, King of Persia, acting on a dream, invaded their land with his hordes in 480 B.C. When, following his triumph over the Spartans at Thermopylae, he advanced towards Attica the Athenians in alarm sent envoys to Delphi to seek the advice of Apollo.

Hardly had they entered the sanctuary than the Pythia,

whose name was Aristonicê, chanted a response that filled them with despair. They were to flee their homes 'to earth's utmost bounds', for all would be destroyed, fire and 'swift Ares in Assyrian car' were about to bring ruin upon them and 'devouring flame' to the shrines of the Immortals. 'Hence from my temple!' she cried. 'Bow your hearts to doom!'

The Athenians could not believe that such a fate would be theirs, and they sent again to the oracle, imploring Apollo to grant them a less cruel future. A second answer came from the lips of Aristonicê which, though clouded with obscurity, at least gave some grounds for hope. The land where stood the fortress Cecropian must be conquered from them, as well as 'the deep valleys of sacred Cithaeron', but they would be permitted to keep 'walls of wood unshaken' to shelter them and their children.

Then came a warning:

Stay not to meet the advancing horse and foot
That swarmeth overland, but turn thy back
In flight: hereafter shalt thou face the foe.
O blessed Salamis! How many children of woman
Shalt thou slay at the sowing of corn or the ripening of
  harvest.

'This answer seemed to them (and was indeed) milder than the first', recorded Herodotus. 'So they wrote it down and went back to Athens.'

There they argued at length over the meaning of the oracle. Some held that the 'wooden walls' meant the Acropolis, because in former times the rock there had been fortified with a wooden palisade. Others, led by Themistocles, maintained that the words could only mean ships, and that they should send their families to a safe refuge out of Attica and go aboard their fleet.

Then the faint-hearted feared that the last lines presaged a calamitous defeat. But Themistocles stood up in the Assembly and insisted that had Apollo implied that he would have said,

'Salamis the wretched or the cruel', but since he had used the adjective 'blessed' the slaughter must refer to the foe and not to the Athenians. His view prevailed, and, leaving only a handful of men to guard the Acropolis, the warriors went aboard their vessels and anchored near the island of Salamis.

The Persians, after laying waste Attica, reached Athens, captured the lower city and after a hard-fought siege overran the Acropolis, massacred its defenders and set fire to it.

However, Themistocles was proved right in his interpretation of the Pythia's prophecy, for the sea battle off Salamis led to his overwhelming victory over the enemy. As Aeschylus wrote in *The Persians*, the sea was completely obliterated from sight by the wrecks and the limbs of slaughtered men, and 'never in one day died such a host'. Soon Xerxes' men had fled from Greece, and the Athenians returning to their ruined city were cheered when they discovered that the sacred olive-tree on the Acropolis, which the Persians had burnt, was not dead after all but had sent up fresh green shoots. Athena had not deserted them.

Perhaps the most useful advice given concerned Greek colonization. No would-be emigrants would dream of sailing without first obtaining the Pythia's directions. When the priestess directed the Spartans to southern Italy to found Tarentum in 796 B.C., Phalanthus, who had been appointed to lead the prospective colonists, was told by her that when rain fell on him from a clear sky he was to seize the country and the city. He assumed that the oracle had a literal meaning, and did not trouble to have it explained by a professional interpreter, as was customarily done.

On landing in Italy Phalanthus gained several victories over the inhabitants, but failed either to capture a town or control a district. 'Then, remembering the oracle', writes Pausanias, 'it occurred to him that what Apollo had predicted was impossible since it could never rain so long as the sky remained cloudless.

He was so disheartened that his wife sought to comfort him. She laid his head upon her knees and began delousing his hair. While she was thus engaged, convinced that her husband's position was likely to worsen, she began to weep. And when Phalanthus felt her tears, he suddenly understood the meaning of the prophecy, for his wife's name was Aethra—clear sky. The following night therefore he attacked Tarentum, the greatest and most prosperous of all the coastal towns, and captured it from the barbarians.

When one considers the course of Greek history as a whole one becomes aware of a progressive improvement in moral standards inspired to a large extent through the oracle at Delphi. Herodotus was certain that it was thanks to the oracle that respect for the lives of women and slaves and reverence for oaths grew in strength, while Plato maintained that it should play a major role in the affairs of the ideal city.

To our modern eyes, what is surprising and commendable so early in the development of moral philosophy was the freedom from bigotry displayed by the priests of Delphi. When an inquirer asked, 'How best are we to worships the Gods?' he was told, 'After the custom of your own country'. He then queried, 'What if these customs vary?' To which the answer was, 'Choose the best'.

The Pythia, assuming the identity of Apollo, spurned the ostentatious sacrifice of the rich Magnesian and preferred the cake and frankincense which the devout Achaean offered in all humility, cautioned the Greeks against making superstition a cover for cruelty, encouraged gentleness and self-control, and showed compassion for the crippled, the maimed and the blind.

Delphi was traditionally the source of guidance for Sparta, whose greatness, some say, owed much to Lycurgus' government and his laws. He was the brother of one of its kings, who died leaving a child as heir. Everyone believed that his uncle would seize the throne for himself, but he announced that he would only rule as regent during his nephew's minority.

Some, nevertheless, suspected that Lycurgus would in the end refuse to relinquish power, and plotted against him.

Wearying of opposition, he went into voluntary exile, and spent the time studying conditions in other countries with the aim of acquiring knowledge that might be of value to Sparta. He was soon missed by his fellow-countrymen and asked to return, which in due course he did.

On the way back he consulted the Pythia, who called him 'beloved of God' and predicted that his laws should be the best and 'the commonwealth which observed them the most famous in the world'. This encouraged him into reforming Sparta's government and drawing up model laws, thus fulfilling the prophecy.

The remarkable thing about the Delphic oracle was that it was consulted for nearly a thousand years. One of the chief causes for its decline was the suspicion that some prophecies were fabricated by its priests, afraid to offend powerful states able to blackmail them with threats.

Its influence first began to wane following Euripides' attack. Plutarch became a priest at Delphi in an unsuccessful attempt to restore its glory, but he failed, and recorded his regret in *On the Decline of the Oracles*.

In Plutarch's time the philosopher and cynic Oenomaus recorded his impressions of the oracle of Apollo at Colophon. He complained that the first reply he was given, though very elegantly phrased, was completely nebulous, and what particularly annoyed him was that he discovered later it corresponded word for word with the one given to a commercial traveller who had been slightly ahead of him.

He continues that when he asked, 'Where shall I go now?' the priestess answered, 'Draw a long bow and knock over green-feeding ganders'.

'And who in the world', comments the indignant Oenomaus, 'will tell me what these untold ganders may mean?'

But despite the polemics of philosophers and sophists, faith in oracles was eroded only very slowly. Tertullian and Pliny both state that the ancient world was still crowded with them in the first century A.D.

It is interesting to note that the early Fathers of the Christian

Church did not question the authenticity of the oracles, but suggested instead that devils were allowed by the true God to tell the Pythias what the future held in store so that mankind might be led astray into idolatry, and the need for a Saviour be made more apparent.

In fact, the priestess at Delphi continued to be consulted well into the Christian era. The last oracle recorded was given in the year A.D. 362 to the physician of the Emperor Julian, who had attempted to bring back paganism after Christianity had been established as the Byzantine Empire's official religion.

'Tell your master that the curiously built temple has fallen to the ground,' went the Pythia's pathetic plaint, 'that bright Apollo no longer has a roof over his head, a prophetic laurel, or babbling spring. Yes, even the murmuring water has dried up.'

The reason for the latter occurring was because when Hadrian, Roman Emperor from A.D. 117 to 138, was a young man he visited Delphi, and through drinking water from the Castalian spring received the foreknowledge that he would gain the Imperial throne. Once this prediction was fulfilled he ordered the flow of the 'prophetic water' to be stopped lest it put a similar ambition into the mind of another, who might then seek to overthrow him. Thanks to the visit of his physician, the Emperor Julian ordered the Castalian stream to be unblocked, but alas, it was too late to revive Delphi's glory.

Ex antiquitate renascor
Boulanger. fecit.
MICHAEL
Nostradamus salonæ petreæ prouinciæ faciebat per annos die prima martii
a virginis partu 1555.° a Cesare nostradamus filio suo prima minerua libera
et non inuita donauit.
Regnante Hanrico secundo Rege galliarum christianissimo
27. iunij 1558.° consacrauit Hanrico quarto
amplissimo galliarum Rege christianissimo
regnante, vincentius seue Occitanus die 19.
martii 1605. descripxit et
consacrauit

2 *Nostradamus*

Between the Pythias of Delphi and Nostradamus there is a gap of well over a thousand years. They were not lacking in prophets, seers and sorcerers, but their predictions were so often recorded after fulfilment that one must view them with some scepticism. It is only when one comes to Nostradamus that one is presented with evidence in the shape of prophecies printed in books long before they came true, and therefore meriting the epithet 'amazing'.

In recent years a great deal has been written about Nostradamus and his prophecies. Most of what we know about the man himself comes from his disciple, Jean Aimes de Chavigny, who wrote a *Brief Discourse on the Life of M. Michel de Nostredame formerly counsellor and doctor in ordinary of the very Christian Kings, Henry II, Francis II and Charles IX*. This was published in 1596.

He was born as Michel de Nostredame in the town of Saint-Rémy in Provence about noon on Thursday, 14th December 1503. His father practised there as a notary, and came of a Jewish family that had been converted to Christianity. He was fortunate in having a devoted maternal grandfather in Jean de Saint-Rémy, a physician and astrologer, who took his education under his personal charge, teaching him Greek, Latin, Hebrew, mathematics, the Humanities, and how to gather herbs, prepare medicines and unguents. He also taught the boy how to use the astrolabe, and fostered in him an enthusiasm for studying the stars in their courses. In those days astrology and astronomy were opposite sides of the same coin, and magic still held a grip on medicine. No doubt young Michel was

Nostradamus. *British Library*

taught not only the particular efficacy of each herb but also how important it was to gather them under the right aspects, and how the lives of human beings themselves were supposed to be influenced by the conjunction of heavenly bodies.

Jean de Saint-Rémy passed away when Michel was still very young. The child's grandfather on his father's side, who was a grain-dealer, then continued his education until he was sent to the university at Avignon, where from the first he proved their cleverest student. According to Chavigny, he taught his fellows the movements of the planets, claiming that the earth was round and revolved annually round the sun, which, when it appeared to set, lit up the other side of the globe. If this is true, then he was ahead of his contemporaries in scientific knowledge. Galileo, almost a hundred years later, was to be harassed for advancing identical views.

Michel's father decided that he should follow his grandfather's profession, and for that purpose transferred him to the university of Montpellier which was renowned for its school of medicine, where anatomy was first studied by dissecting corpses, owing to the Duke of Anjou having granted them the privilege of receiving once a year an executed malefactor's body.

Hardly had Michel qualified than a plague epidemic brought him into combat with that most feared of diseases. It was a cruelly virulent sort called *le charbon*, as black pustules formed on the bodies of those infected. Michel fought tirelessly to save lives with skill and courage. Chavigny claims that, using his own formula, he manufactured a powder which purified the air. News of his success soon spread, and other towns begged for his help.

Michel's travels took him to Toulouse, Narbonne and Bordeaux. Then, when the epidemic had died out, he went back to Montpellier to take his doctorate. But, having done so, he was expected to teach, and then found himself increasingly in conflict with orthodox tenets and methods of treatment, so in 1531 he left, and for two years led the life of an itinerant physician in Languedoc and Provence, ministering to all classes, including many notables in their castles and country houses. Among these was the Princess of Navarre, to whom he dedicated his verse translation of the *Book of Orus Apollo, Son of Osiris, King of Egypt*. The title is sufficient to indicate that he had become attached to the occult.

On a visit to Agen in the Garonne he became friendly with Julius Caesar Scaliger, who after Erasmus was regarded as the foremost European scholar of that epoch, and as a result he settled there in 1533 and soon married. When his wife and two children died in another outbreak of the plague he was broken-hearted and left to try and forget his sorrows.

The next eight years he spent wandering in France, Italy and Sicily. It was during these travels that his gift of second sight began making itself manifest, if we are to believe Chavigny's account. On one occasion when in the March of Ancona he passed on a road some friars. Among them was a youth of humble birth, Felice Peretti, who had been a swineherd until he joined a mendicant order. On seeing the young man Michel dismounted from his mule and knelt before him. The astonished monks asked why he did this. 'Because I must kneel before His Holiness', he replied. They were probably more astonished than ever. It seems that little attention was paid to such an unlikely prophecy. But it was remembered by those present when years later, in 1585, after Nostradamus himself had died, the former swineherd (then Cardinal Montalto) became Pope Sixtus V.

On another occasion, Michel happened to be staying at the château de Fains in Lorraine with its owner, the Seigneur de Florinville, whose mother he was tending in his capacity as physician. As they were crossing the courtyard the nobleman, having heard of the other's prophetic gift, pointed at two sucking pigs, a black one and a white one, and challenged him to foretell their future.

'Certainly I can,' Nostradamus is reputed to have returned. 'We shall eat the black one and a wolf will devour the white one.' De Florinville saw an opportunity to play a trick. Going secretly to his cook, he ordered him to kill the white pig and serve it for dinner. That evening when they were feasting, Michel's host told him that they were eating the white animal, and that the wolf would never do so. But he shook his head. 'No,' he insisted. 'What we have before us is the black one, as I said.'

The cook was finally summoned to settle the argument, and nervously he admitted that Nostradamus was right. Apparently the white sucking-pig had been prepared for roasting as instructed, but while the man's back was turned a wolf had stolen into the kitchen and had made off with the piglet. Horrified at what had happened, and not supposing that it would make any difference, the cook had quickly killed the black one, which he had roasted and served.

In 1544 Nostradamus went to Marseilles to help fight another outbreak of the plague, and two years later we find him doing the same in Aix-en-Provence. His unconventional methods, insisting on fresh air and all water being boiled, met with such success that the city fathers granted him a pension for life. Next Lyons, afflicted by rampant whooping-cough, called for his aid. Here too his treatment saved so many lives that the citizens rewarded him with a sack of gold which, characteristically, he gave away to the poor.

In 1547 he decided to settle in windswept Salon de Craux, midway between Avignon and Marseilles, where he married a wealthy and well-connected widow and went to live in a narrow impasse off the place de la Poissonerie, not far from the boulevard now named after him. The house can still be seen today, overshadowed by the gloomy thirteenth-century château de l'Empéri, with its dungeon and dark history, that is perched on the summit of a rocky hill, where in 1966 the first world conference of astrologers was held in commemoration of the four-hundredth anniversary of his death—an occasion that was also celebrated by the unveiling of a statue to him. At the very top of his house, reached by a spiral stone staircase, is the room where he read and wrote undisturbed and studied the stars.

The pension from Aix-en-Provence, together with his wife's

money, now gave him the financial security to enable him to devote much of his time to esoteric pursuits, though he still went on working as physician. In view of his future reputation it is surprising to find that the first book he produced as a result of his new way of life was a *Traité des Fardemens*, which was published in 1552 and included not only recipes for making jams and other preserves but also for beauty-creams and face-paints, the use of which the Queen of France, Catherine de' Medici, had rendered fashionable. Women would discover in its pages a mine of culinary and cosmetic gold, as well as instructions on how to prepare a love philtre.

For men there was a pomade compounded of lapis lazuli, coral and gold leaf, which he had once prescribed for the Bishop of Carcassonne. This, he asserted, restored youth and banished melancholia and timidity, replacing them with boldness and gladness.

> If a man's beard is turning grey, it retards that ageing process. It prevents headaches and constipation, and multiplies his sperm to such an extent that a man may enjoy marital pleasures as frequently as he desires without impairing his health. It keeps the four humours in such health that were a man to take it from birth, he could live for ever.

Michel's scholarship had won for him many admirers, and foremost among them was Jean Dorat, a classical scholar, who taught Greek and who also often praised Nostradamus to his students, with the result that one of them, Jean Aimes de Chavigny, travelled to Salon to meet him. Apparently he fell so much under the sage and seer's spell that he became his pupil and disciple.

Chavigny, in his life of Nostradamus, paints a colourful and affectionate portrait of him.

> He was of little less than middle height, robust, cheerful and vigorous. His brow was high and open, the nose straight, the grey eyes gentle, though in wrath they would flame, a severe

and laughing face, so that one saw allied with the severity a great humanity. His cheeks were ruddy even into extreme age, his beard long and thick, his health good . . . and all his senses alert.

As for his mind, it grasped and understood easily all he wished. His judgment was subtle, his memory admirable, his nature was taciturn, thinking much and speaking little, discoursing well in due time and place; for the rest vigilant, alert, occasionally unexpectedly choleric, patient in his work. He slept only four to five hours, loved and praised liberty of speech; a happy man addicted to pleasantry whose wit was biting. He approved the ceremonies of the Roman church, and held the faith of the Catholic religion; outside of which he believed there was no salvation. . . . I must not forget to say that he willingly practised fasts, orisons, alms, patience: he abhorred vice and punished it severely. . . . He was very generous and charitable to the poor.

During his travels he had come across a rare book, *De Mysteriis Egyptorum*, and guided by its contents he set about developing his occult powers. It was in the quiet seclusion of his study that he began to record his famous prophecies, the *Centuries*, on which he spent some four years. The first edition of these, printed in Lyons by one Macé Bonhomme, was published on 4th May 1555. Chavigny says that Nostradamus,

foreseeing the signal mutations and changes which should come throughout Europe, and even the bloody civil wars and pernicious troubles of this Kingdom of France which inexorably drew near, full of enthusiasm and as it were rapt in a new madness he set himself to write his *Centuries* and other *Présages*. . . . He kept them a long time without wishing to publish them, believing that their controversial nature would undoubtedly attract derisive criticism and abusive attack as indeed happened. In the end, swayed by the desire which he had to be useful to the public, he published them; and immediately they became the talk of France and of the rest of Western Europe.

The published work contained only three complete *Centuries* and fifty-three quatrains of the fourth, and not one of the predictions had yet been fulfilled; moreover, the language was involved and obscure. It is therefore remarkable that they should have attracted much attention from the start, making it necessary for a second edition to be published in 1558 containing further *Centuries* (up to *Century VII*, quatrain 42).

Even today, when one first reads the original French edition, one's initial reaction is of perplexed disillusion. The language is enigmatic, at times almost unintelligible, as if written in code. The verses are not in chronological order, and jump about in time and subject. Strange sobriquets of Nostradamus's own coining are used for famous personalities. Everywhere we find mystifying puns and anagrams.

The book begins with a preface in the form of a letter from the seer to his baby son, César. He wrote that although for years past he had predicted well in advance what had later come to pass, and in certain cases had attributed this gift of his to divine power and inspiration, he had considered it wise not to reveal any foreknowledge that, if recorded, might prove harmful.

Such revelations concerned not only the immediate future but also the remoter reaches of time. He knew that the present kingdoms, religions and sects of the world would suffer many vicissitudes and changes and be completely transformed, but if he were to relate what would happen rulers, sectaries and ecclesiastics would find it so little in accord with their private fancy that they would at once condemn as false what future centuries would know to have been true prophecy. He had at first thought it wise to follow the counsel given in St Matthew's Gospel, Chapter VII, verse 6, warning him not to cast his pearls before swine, lest perhaps they trample them under their feet and turning upon him, tear him apart.

'That is why I have withheld my tongue from the vulgar, and my pen from paper', he claimed. 'But later on I thought I would for the common good describe the most important of the revolutionary changes I foresee, but that so as not to upset my present readers I would do this in a cloudy manner with abstruse and twisted sentences rather than plainly prophetical.'

Thus Nostradamus himself states that he (like the Delphi oracle at times) is being deliberately obscure so as to avoid trouble with his contemporaries. The inference is that most of his predictions would become clear only after the event, and this has been largely borne out. Many commentators, as I shall illustrate later, have assumed quatrains foretold certain future events, frequently by means of reasoning as tortuous as the seer's own language, and by mistranslation to support this. But when the event Nostradamus himself had in mind has occurred, then curiously enough his original meaning is no longer clouded and becomes remarkably clear.

Nostradamus gave actual dates for some of the happenings he foretold, and in his Preface claims that he could have dated them all. He then proceeds to mention one which he states will particularly affect his fellow-countrymen—1792. This, he says, is when the common man will come to power—'a year that shall be marked by a far worse persecution of the Christian Church than ever was in Africa, and which everyone will think an innovation of the age'. The French Revolution was at its height in that year, which makes this a noteworthy prophecy.

Anxious, no doubt, to run no risk of denunciation as a sorcerer, Nostradamus goes on to warn his son against 'the execrable magic forbidden by the Holy Scriptures and by the Canons of the Church'. This he must abhor.

The seer of Salon continues:

> Many occult volumes, which have been hidden for centuries have come into my possession, but after reading them, dreading what might happen if they should fall into the wrong hands, I presented them to Vulcan, and as the fire devoured them, the flames licking the air shot forth an unaccustomed brightness, clearer than natural flame, like the flash from explosive powder, casting a peculiar illumination all over the house, as if it were wrapped in sudden conflagration. So that you might not in the future be tempted to search for the perfect transmutation, lunar or solar, or for

uncorruptible metals hidden under the earth or the sea, I reduced them to ashes.

The modern materialist will dismiss all this at once as moonshine, written perhaps with the intention of impressing the credulous in a superstituous age, and may scoffingly suggest that Nostradamus did not even possess the rare works mentioned, and that this preface was a clever sixteenth-century exercise in self-advertisement to gull the public and sell the book. On the other hand, addicts of all matters occult will speculate as to what he destroyed. Could he have owned a copy of the legendary *Keys of Solomon* or some even more mysterious grimoire? One thing, however, is obvious: Nostradamus in this fashion was absolving himself from possible accusations of practising the black arts.

He ends the Preface with the declaration that he is not vain enough to call himself a prophet. He is a mortal man and 'the greatest sinner in this world, and heir to every human affliction'. But 'being surprised sometimes by a prophetical mood, amid prolonged calculation, while engaged in nocturnal studies of sweet odour, I have composed books of prophecies, containing each one a hundred astronomical quatrains which I have joined obscurely and are perpetual vaticinations from now to the year 3797'. He has obtained these prophecies in two ways; through divine inspiration and through astrology.

The most renowned astrologer of the first half of the sixteenth century was probably the Neapolitan mathematician Luca Gaurico, who after casting the horoscope of the fourteen-year-old Giovanni de' Medici said the youth would one day be Pope (which occurred in 1513, when he ascended the papal throne as Leo X); he also accurately predicted that another successor of St Peter, Paul III, would die in November 1549.

It is not always wise for a fortune-teller to pass on dread portents to his clients. Gaurico was rash enough to inform Giovanni Bentivoglio that he would die in exile, for which prediction the tyrant of Bologna as punishment had him tortured, but it did not stop the prophecy being fulfilled.

Neither did this deter Gaurico from telling Catherine de' Medici, after she had married Henri, that the talk of France when the latter succeeded to the throne would be a duel between two of his Court. This came to pass when on 10th July 1547 the new King Henri II witnessed the slaying of François de Vivonne de la Châtaignerie by Guy Chabot de Jarnac.

Gaurico also warned of danger from blindness or death caused by a head wound if the monarch were to fight a duel in an enclosed space. The risk would be greatest when he was forty-one.

So dread a message from the stars concerning her husband King Henri had haunted Queen Catherine, and when Nostradamus's fame reached her she sent for him to obtain a second opinion. The journey took him a month, and he arrived in Paris on 15th August and lodged, by a strange coincidence, at an inn resembling his own name, the Auberge St Michel by Notre-Dame. M. le Constable Montmorency himself came specially from Saint-Germain-en-Laye to take him to the Court's summer quarters there, which showed what prestige the *Centuries* had already gained for him. It was not as if he were the only astrologer practising in France. Catherine had four always at her beck and call, while in Paris it is estimated there were some thirty thousand fortune-tellers of all kinds, astrologers, sorcerers and alchemists.

Catherine, obsessed as she was by the occult, was well primed by her spies with news of the few whom time had proved accurate. It seems that she was impressed with her visitor the moment she saw him. He looked distinguished with his beard and wearing a doctor's square cap and long gown. There were no cabalistic signs, no zodiac motifs on his dress, no chain round his neck laden with charms and amulets, in an attempt to impress by outward trappings. But his eyes—these, she felt, were those of a true prophet. However, her character made her avoid mentioning the real purpose behind her summons. Instead she questioned him about his treatise on cosmetics and his medical remedies. As a mark of approval she arranged for him to stay in the Archbishop of Sens's town residence, where, once the Court knew his address, a constant stream of visitors descended upon him every day, seeking diagnosis of complaints and nostrums to cure them, prescriptions to preserve and restore beauty, and, of course, horoscopes. His journey had cost him a hundred écus, and he had received only a hundred and thirty from the royal purse, but the gifts and the gold his unsolicited clients left behind soon compensated him for the fatigues of travel, and a severe attack of gout which lasted for twelve days.

One night a page came knocking at the door of the library where Nostradamus was studying. A prized hound left in the boy's care had escaped, and he feared punishment when this was discovered. Before he had time to speak, the seer is said to have answered his unspoken question. 'You are worrying about a lost dog. Go and search on the road to Orleans. You will find him there, on a leash.' The page raced off as directed, and found the animal being led towards him by a servant. News of this incident, if authentic, must have soon spread round the capital, bringing more clients to the seer's door.

Suddenly there came a royal command for him to visit Henri and Catherine's children at Blois and cast their horoscopes. This placed him in an awkward position, knowing that the Queen had great ambitions for them all. He was of a more cautious disposition than Gaurico, and remembered how the latter had been condemned to the agonizing torture of five turns of the strappado. And he himself had actually already recorded in the nebulous phraseology of the *Centuries* the misfortune to which they were fated: the eldest, François, aged thirteen, would wed Mary from Scotland and die before he had reigned a single year; his twelve-year-old sister Elizabeth would become the child wife of Philip, the old Spanish monarch, and die young; her ten-year-old sister Claude would not live to see the age of thirty. Then there was the six-year-old who as King Charles IX would stain the earth of France with the blood of the massacred Huguenots; the five-year-old Henri, destined to be both King of Poland and of

France before assassination; his youngest sister, the adulterous Marguerite, wife of Henri of Navarre, known to history as *la reine Margot*; and the last born, another François, the frog-like rejected suitor of England's Virgin Queen.

It would have been heartless, tactless and dangerous to have explained to Catherine those quatrains in which he had already obliquely—and later, it proved, accurately—described their destinies, so he limited himself to assuring her that they would all be kings. She was pleased, assuming that he meant of different countries, whereas he had read in their horoscopes that they would succeed each other to the throne of France—a prediction that was fulfilled, except in the case of the youngest, François. And when she asked what he thought of Gaurico's prophecy concerning her husband he laconically answered that the King should never engage in duels, a warning that was not to be heeded.

When he returned to Salon, Nostradamus must have felt relieved that to protect himself he had cloaked the meaning of his verses and had nowhere mentioned the ruling King of France by name, for one of them actually confirmed the prediction in question. Translated, it went:

> The young lion shall overcome the old
> In warlike field in single combat
> In a cage of gold he will pierce his eyes,
> This is the first of two wounds, then he dies a cruel death.
>
> (CENTURY I, Quatrain 35)

If vague before the event, this quatrain reads astonishingly accurate after it. In July 1559, in celebration of two royal weddings, tournaments lasting three days were held in Paris. On the last day King Henri jousted with Montgomery, the Captain of his Scottish guard, and both men happened to bear the emblem of a lion on their armour. When they rode against each other for the third time the contestants correctly shattered their lances, but Montgomery failed to lower the haft quickly enough as they passed, and the splintered end of his weapon struck first against the King's throat and then, knocked away by the royal lance, flew up, pushing open the protective vizor of Henri's cage-like gilded helmet and piercing his eye. He was carried away in agony, and died ten days later.

Other quatrains of the *Centuries* read like a fancifully phrased history in verse of France in the second half of the sixteenth century. Mary, Queen of Scots married the Dauphin, later Francis II of France, in 1558, when he was fourteen. He died six weeks before his seventeenth birthday without issue. As a result Mary returned to Scotland, where her relations grew strained with Elizabeth, Queen of the other island kingdom. The quatrain that has been assumed to predict this reads:

> The eldest son unhappily married leaves a widow
> Without children, two islands in discord,
> Before eighteen, an incompetent age.
> The younger earlier shall be the betrothal.
>
> (X, 39)

The next King of France was Charles IX, and the last line has been regarded as a veiled reference to his betrothal at the age of eleven. He was responsible for the Massacre on St Bartholomew's Eve, which this quatrain seems to foretell:

> The cruel king, when his blood-stained hand
> Shall have done its worse with fire, sword and bows
> Then will his people be terror-stricken
> At the sight of nobles hung by the neck and feet.
>
> (IV, 47)

(The last line is remarkable when one recalls that Admiral Coligny was hung by one foot from a gibbet.)

Quatrain 63 of Century VI was regarded by early commentators as referring to Catherine de' Medici because she wore mourning seven years for her husband, but one would hardly regard her Regency as fortunate one for France, marred as it was by the Massacre of St Bartholomew's Eve. But a later nineteenth-century commentator thought it foretold Queen Victoria's grief over the death of the Prince Consort. The verse translates:

> The lady left to reign alone
> Her one husband dying first at his post of honour
> Seven years deep in mourning shall be spent
> Followed by long life and a great reign.

In the spring of 1564 Catherine took her fourteen-year-old son, the new King Charles IX, on a provincial Royal progress to promote support for the dynasty. They reached Provence in the autumn, and the Queen-Mother, remembering that Nostradamus lived in Salon, suddenly ordered a call to be made there. On the afternoon of 17th October the Court's cavalcade entered the gateway of St Lazare and made its way through hastily erected triumphal arches in the narrow streets, from the houses of which tapestries and carpets hung like gigantic speechless tongues awed into stupefied amazement by this unexpected honour.

From a dais covered with white and violet damask, the chief magistrate, supported by the local worthies, obsequiously read a fulsome oration welcoming the King. When it came for the latter to respond he said, with the ingenuous frankness of youth, 'I have come to see Nostradamus'. Then turning to one of his retinue, he ordered him to give the old man a horse so that he could ride with them.

Among the royal party was the ten-year-old Henri of Navarre. Nostradamus asked his tutor if he could see him, stripped of his clothes, but the boy, apprehensive that he might be beaten, stubbornly shook his head, so the seer left him in peace. In those days it was the custom to sleep naked, and early next morning, while Henri still slumbered, Nostradamus entered his chamber, then stealthily drawing back the bedclothes he examined the Prince's body and found the birthmark he sought. This prompted him to prophesy that one day the boy would have 'the whole inheritance'.

On the afternoon of 18th October the royal visitors departed. When they reached Arles, finding the Rhône in flood, they remained in the town for some days, and Catherine, missing Nostradamus's company, sent a messenger to Salon to bring him to stay with her until they were able to resume their journey. It was said by a Spaniard, Francisco de Alova, that whenever she quoted the seer's words she had an air as confident as if she were citing 'St John or St Luke'.

It is possible that on this occasion Nostradamus may have prescribed medically for her with success, for when he eventually left her she gave him a hundred gold écus, and the King not only added two hundred but appointed him his Physician-in-Ordinary and Counsellor, with the appropriate emoluments, which must have comforted the old man, for his health was failing fast.

He had now the further satisfaction of being consulted by the most respected men of learning as well as the nobility, who came from afar as if to an oracle. 'As St Jerome remarks of Livy, so may we remark of him,' wrote Chavigny with loyal pride, 'that those who came to France sought Nostradamus as the only thing to be seen there.'

Long study had aged him and he suffered severely from gout which turned to dropsy. Shortly after journeying once more to Arles as Salon's representative, on 1st July 1566, he sent for a priest, who heard his confession and administered to him the last rites. In the evening he told Chavigny, 'You will not see me alive at sunrise'.

Not many prophets have foretold the manner of their dying. But if we can regard his *Présages*, printed in 1568, as not having been added to after his death, then the following quotation would suggest that he foresaw the manner of it:

On returning from an embassy, the King's gift safely
stored,
No more will I labour for I will have gone to God,
By my close relations, friends, and brothers
I shall be found dead, near my bed and the bench.

The bench in question was one which he had made to assist him in getting in and out of bed, for his body had grown heavy. He must have tried hard to rise during the night, for he was discovered in the morning lying across the bench.

He had confided to Chavigny that he did not wish to be disturbed by the sound of feet passing over him when he fell asleep for the last time, so he was buried in an upright position within a recess made in the wall of the Church of the Cordeliers between the great door and the altar of St Martha.

On the stone marking the place was engraved:

> Here lie the bones of the most illustrious Michel Nostradamus, the only one, in judgment of all mortals, worthy to write with a pen almost divine, under the influence of the stars, of events to come in the whole world.
>
> He lived sixty-two years, six months and seventeen days. He died at Salon in the year 1566. Posterity disturb not his repose.
>
> Anne Ponsart Gemelle, his wife, wishes her spouse true felicity.

There is a tradition in Salon that half a century or so later they thought it would be more fitting if his remains were moved to a more prominent position in the church. It was wondered whether other prophecies might have been buried with him. According to this story, probably apocryphal, round his neck was found a metal disc marked with the date on which he had foreseen that his resting-place would be reopened.

In the seventh quatrain of *Century IX* he had written that evil would befall any man who violated his tomb. In 1793, during the French Revolution, one of the men pillaging the church smashed his way into it, pulled off the seer's skull and drank out of it. Then, as he emerged from the building, a burst of gunfire killed him. Though the building was destroyed, Nostradamus's remains were later recovered and reinterred in the Church of St Laurent in 1813.

In the year of the seer's death a further edition of his prophecies appeared, printed by Pierre Rigaud of Lyons, containing three hundred further unpublished verses, making ten *Centuries*, one thousand quatrains in all. The first French commentary of importance by Eugène Bareste went into three editions in Paris in its year of publication, 1840.

Before he died Nostradamus became known in England, and two of his Almanacks were translated and published in London, but it was not until 1672 that there was published *The True Prophecies or Prognostications of Michel Nostradamus . . . Translated and Commented by Theophilus de Garencières*, who was a doctor in the College of Physick, London. In 1691 another book attracted attention, *Predictions before 1558 and 1715, the first commentary*, *Prophecies of the Kings and Queens of Great Britain.* This contained only those quatrains that could be interpreted as referring to them. Then we have to wait exactly two hundred years for another English commentator in Charles A. Ward, whose *Oracles of Nostradamus* were printed in 1891.

Quatrain 74 of *Century VI* was regarded by these commentators as predicting Queen Elizabeth I's accession and her death at the age of seventy in 1603:

La déchassée au regne tournera
Ses ennemis trouvez des conjurez;
Plus que jamais son temps triomphera,
Trois et septante, la mort trop asseurez.

The rejected one will come to the throne
Her enemies will be regarded as traitors;
More than ever her reign will be triumphant,
At seventy she will assuredly die in the third year.

An important event in Elizabeth's reign was the attack by the English on Cadiz Bay in 1596, when they destroyed forty treasure-ships from South America through the Spaniards' sluggish response. This is usually regarded as foretold by:

Devant le lac ou plus cher fut getté
De sept mois et son ost desconfit,

Seront Hispans par Albannois gastez,
Par delay perte en donnant le conflit.

Before the lake where many riches were thrown
After seven months' voyage and the host discomforted,
Spaniards shall be despoiled by the Albions,
By delaying before giving battle.

(VIII, 94)

James I was the first King of England and Scotland, and it is interesting to note that in an apparent allusion to him Nostradamus uses the term Britain instead of, as usually, England.

Le jeune nay au regne Britannique,
Qu'aura le père mourant recommandé,
Iceluy mort, Lonole donra topique
Et à son fils le regne demandé.

The youth born to reign over Britain
Whom his dying father shall recommend
After his death, Lonole will make speeches
And will demand the government from his son.

(X, 40)

Commentators have been puzzled by 'Lonole' in the penultimate line. Ward suggested that it is an anagram of 'Ole Nol', which could be as close as a foreigner might get to 'Old Noll', Cromwell's nickname. Nostradamus had a habit of using anagrams, like 'Rapis' for 'Paris', and he also occasionally made puns in Latin and Greek, which was common practice with writers and scholars in the Renaissance period.

James Laver in his study of Nostradamus had an ingenious explanation for 'Lonole'. He pointed out that in experiments with telepathy 'sometimes half a word is transmitted, and then itself gives rise to a new chain of associations which may or may not have some reference to the original idea'. He suggested that if the power of prophecy is in some way related to the receptive mood which renders telepathy possible—and there are grounds for supposing that it is—then something of the kind may have occurred in this instance. Perhaps Nostradamus picked up only the first syllable of Oliver Cromwell's sobriquet and his conscious mind changed it into Olleon, influenced by his acquaintance with the Greek verb 'to destroy', of which it is the present participle.

But, if Nostradamus had used an indeterminate noun instead of committing himself specifically with 'Lonole', the stanza would still be noteworthy, for it could apply only to James I and his son, Charles I. The latter's execution is actually prophesied in another quatrain, which states, 'The Senate of London shall put their King to death' (IX, 49).

Two remarkable predictions meriting mention were those of the Great Plague and Fire of London which, as a convinced believer in the Divine Right of Kings, Nostradamus regarded as fit punishment for the execution of Charles I. The 'dame' in the first clearly means St Paul's, as this was a metaphor the prophet used for a cathedral, while 'the feigning saints' in the second is an apt description of the Puritan Roundheads.

Le sang du juste à Londres fera faulte,
Bruslés par fouldres de vingt trois les six,
La dame antique cherra de place haute,
De mesme secte plusieurs seront occis.

The blood of the just shall be demanded of London,
Burnt by fire in thrice twenty and six,
The old cathedral shall fall from her high place,
And many [edifices] of the same sect shall be destroyed.
(II, 51)

La grande peste de cité maritime,
Ne cessera que mort ne soit vengée
Du juste sang par pris damné sans crime
De la grande dame par feincte n'outragée.

The great plague of the maritime city,
Shall not cease until the death is avenged
Of the just one's blood taken and condemned without
crime
And the great cathedral outraged by feigning saints.
(II, 53)

Quatrain 52, between the two quoted, is more vaguely worded, telling of a sea-war between two evenly matched combatants, and has been interpreted as signifying the war of 1665–7 between England and the United Provinces of the Netherlands.

Coming to this century, some commentators claim that quatrain 22 of *Century X* foresaw the abdication of King Edward VIII and the succession of George VI, whose shy, retiring character made kingship a burden for him:

Pour ne vouloir consentir au divorce,
Qui puis après sera cogneu indigne,
Le Roy des Isles sera chassé par force
Mis à son lieu que de Roy n'aura signe.

For being unwilling to consent to divorce
Which later shall be recognised as unworthy
The King of the Isles shall be expelled by force
And replaced by one whose nature will not be that of
King.

All commentators have been puzzled by quatrain 66 of *Century X*:

Le chef de Londres par regne l'Americh
L'Isle d'Ecosse tempiera par gelée
Roy Reb auront un si faux Antechrist
Que les mettra très tous la meslée.

There will be a head of London from the government of
America
He will tempt the Island of Scotland by a trick
They will have Reb for King, a very false Antichrist
Who will put them all in confusion.

This is the place where Nostradamus mentions America, which had been discovered only comparatively recently in his time. It would seem to refer to some event that has not yet occurred. 'Reb' can hardly be an anagram, so may stand for the initials or the nickname of this mysterious American. Some commentators have suggested that the 'head of London' might be Sir Winston Churchill, whose mother was of course American, but it is hard to see how the rest of the verse could possibly refer to him.

There are those with misgivings about the eventual outcome of the North Sea gas and oil exploration and who wonder if it will cause subsidence. Should such a disaster take place the seer's prophecy might be fulfilled:

> Great Britain including the whole of England
> Shall suffer severely from an inundation of waters.
> (III, 70)

Believers in Nostradamus's powers will usually quote in support of their case his verses apparently foreseeing both the French Revolution and Napoleon's rise and fall. As regards the date of the former event's outbreak, he had been forestalled by Cardinal Pierre d'Ailly, almoner and astrologer to an earlier King of France, for in his book published in 1490 the latter mentioned the year, 1789, saying, 'Should the world still remain in existence at that time, which God alone knows, then astounding upheavels and transformations will occur which will effect our laws and political structure'.

White and red were respectively the colours of Royalists and Revolutionaries. In *Century I*, quatrain 3, Nostradamus tells of a coming social upheaval and conflict between the 'Whites' and 'Reds', culminating in the setting up of a Republic; in quatrain 14 he mentions the songs and chants of the slavish mob, while Princes and aristocrats are captive in prison; and in quatrain 53 Christianity will be abolished, the Church persecuted and a new currency brought out backed by its wealth—on 19th December 1789 a decree of the National

Assembly did just this by authorizing the issue of 400 million *assignats*.

Three days later the Assembly turned the old provinces into *départements* with new names. Quatrain 14 of *Century VII* goes:

Faux exposer viendra topographie,
Seront les cruches des monument ouvertes;
Pulluler secte, sainte philosophie,
Pour blanches, noires et pour antiques vertes.

Topography will be falsified,
The urns of the monuments shall be opened,
Sects swarm, and philosophy usurp religion's place,
Black will pass for white and novelties be substituted for
old traditions.

As we know, the mob were to violate the sepulchres of the French kings at Saint-Denis, the teachings of Voltaire to prevail, and naked women impersonating the Goddess of Reason were to desecrate the altars of the churches. Quatrain 12 of *Century II* alludes to the people's eyes being blindfolded against Christianity and the wearing of priests' habits outlawed. Quatrain 44 of *Century I* adds that there will be no more monks, abbots or novices, and honey will be dearer than wax (probably because candles would no longer be required for religious purposes).

Sceptics have attempted to undermine the validity of these verses as accurate predictions by claiming that they could apply to any cataclysm when Monarchy and Church are overturned. But one cannot explain away Nostradamus's prophecies when he mentions the town by name where one of the most significant events of the French Revolution took place, Varennes. Here is the often-quoted verse:

De nuict viendra par le forest de Reines,
Deux pars, vaultorte, Herne la pierre blanche,
Le moyne noir en gris dedans Varennes
Esleu Cap: cause tempeste, feu, sang tranche.

By night shall come through the forest of Reines
A married couple by a tortuous route, Herne the white stone,
The monk in grey into Varennes
Elected Cap: thereafter tempest, fire, blood, slice.
(IX, 20)

Dr Theophilus de Garencières in his English commentary of 1672 wrote:

> Rennes is the chief Town of little Britanny, the second verse being made of barbarous words is impossible to be understood. The third and fourth Verse signified that when a black Monk in that town of Varennes shall put on a grey suit, he shall be elected Captain, and cause a great tempest of broils by fire and blood.

But, of course, he wrote nearly 120 years before the event. Now, with our knowledge of what actually occurred, it is easier to interpret the quatrain more exactly, and to see in it a description of the flight of Louis XVI and his Queen from Paris and their recapture in Varennes. Garencières mistook Reines for the town of Rennes. Modern commentators have been unable to locate any such forest in maps of France, but a writer who lived during the period in question, Jean-Théodore-Claude Bouys, discussing this quatrain in his *Nouvelles considérations puisées dans la clairvoyance*, published in 1806, states that a Fôret des Reines then existed, and that the road to Varennes passed through it.

'Cap.' is used elsewhere by Nostradamus as an abbreviation for Capet, the surname Louis was given when brought to trial. He can be regarded as elected because he was the first King of France to surrender his powers and be reappointed King of the French by the vote of the Constituent Assembly, and as a monk in so far as he was undersexed and, in the early days of his marriage, impotent. He was usually dressed in grey, and Marie Antoinette in white. Those who saw her after the return to Paris state in their memoirs that her hair had turned white.

The 'white stone' may also refer to the famous diamond necklace. The 'slice' clearly indicates execution by the new form of execution, the guillotine.

Quatrain 34 of *Century IX* reads:

Le part solus mari sera mitré
Retour: conflit passera sur le thuille
Par cinq cens: un trahyr sera titré
Narbon: et Saulce par coutaux avons d'huile.

The husband alone will be mitred
On return: attack will pass over the tiles
By five hundred: one traitor will be titled
Narbonne: and Saulce will have oil by [handing him] over
to the soldiers.

When Nostradamus wrote the site of the Tuileries, to which Louis was taken after Varennes, was occupied by tile-kilns, after which the palace was named. There he was later forced to don a red cap of Liberty by the five hundred Marseillais who invaded it. This was called the Phrygian bonnet through its being copied from the mitre-shaped headdress of the priests of Mithras. The Count of Narbonne, Minister of War, was secretly intriguing with Louis's enemies, and Sauce, who sold oil in Varennes and was its mayor, betrayed the King and had him arrested.

It might be instructive to compare this interpretation with Garencières's of 1692:

> The first Verse signifieth, that some certain man who was married, shall be parted from his wife, and shall attain to some great Ecclesiastical Dignity. The second Verse is, that in coming back from some place or enterprise, he shall be met and fought with, and compelled to escape over the Tyles of a House. The third Verse is, that a man of great account shall be betrayed by five hundred of his men. And the last, that when these things shall come to pass, Narbon and Salces, which are two Cities of Languedoc, shall reap and make a great deal of oil.

The conclusion to be reached from this is, as I have written earlier, that it is usually only after the prophecy has been fulfilled that Nostradamus's true meaning becomes apparent.

The tragedy of Louis XVI ends with quatrain 92, *Century VI*. The 'beautiful prince' (which he was in his youth) who became King and then was deposed will be murdered in '*la cité au glaive*'—the city of the guillotine—and his body will be consumed with a powder that burns—it was thrown into a pit and covered with quicklime.

There are verses, too, that appear to refer to Marie Antoinette's end. She was tried by jury, an innovation, and unknown to France in Nostradamus's time. Yet he wrote, 'The rulers who have replaced the King will convict him. His captive lady will be condemned to death by a jury chosen by random.' (IX, 77). No other Queen in history was put to death by jurors chosen by lot. The last two lines of the same quatrain are remarkable:

> Life shall be denied to the Queen's son
> And the concubine share the fate of the consort.

The former Dauphin, Louis XVII, died in captivity and the celebrated mistress of King Louis XV, the Du Barry, was also guillotined.

The 'Theory of Probabilities' is sometimes quoted against Nostradamus. One is told it is only necessary to write a large enough number of quatrains for some of their predictions to be fulfilled, and that resourceful commentators could make them seem to apply to historical happenings. But to make this feasible he would have needed not a thousand but a million verses. Dr Max Kemmerich, in his *Prophezeungen*, published in Munich in 1924, reckoned that by the law of chance the odds were mathematically as one to infinity that he could have guessed the names of actual people and places.

Nostradamus seems to have had prevision of the whole of Napoleon's career. Here is the first reference to him:

Un Empereur naistra près d'Italie
Qui à l'Empire sera vendu bien cher.
Diront avec quels gens il se ralie
Qu'on trouvera moins prince que boucher.

An Emperor shall be born near Italy
Who shall cost the Empire dear
When it is seen with whom he allies himself
He shall be found less a prince than a butcher.

(I, 60)

Elsewhere the seer calls him 'Pau Nay Loron', which is 'Napoleon Roy' scrambled. All French kings from Louis XIII onward had worn long hair. In the following, Bonaparte is given a nickname—*teste razé*:

The man with cropped hair shall assume authority
In a maritime city held by the enemy.
He will expel the vile men who oppose him
And for fourteen years will rule with absolute power.

(VII, 13)

The English had seized Toulon, and Bonaparte recaptured it. As a result of the personal prestige thus gained he was able to overthrow the Directory, and held absolute control from 1799 to 1814.

Another quatrain translated reads:

Of a name which no King of France had before him
Never was a thunderbolt so feared.
Causing to tremble Italy, Spain and the English,
He will be greatly attentive to foreign women.

(IV, 54)

Regarding the last line, Napoleon's wives were both foreigners: Josephine, a creole from Martinique, and Marie Louise, Austrian. (And, of course, there was Marie Walewska!)

Other verses can be interpreted as describing the various

battles in his campaigns, and this one the disenchantment that spread in France as he sacrificed the blood of half the country's manhood on the battlefields of Europe:

It will have chosen badly in the cropped one
Its strength will be sapped by him,
So great will be the fury and violence that they will say
That he is butchering his countrymen with fire and sword.
(V, 60)

Following his escape from Elba, Napoleon, one of whose emblems was bees, landed in the south of France and was later defeated at Waterloo by the Allied armies of Wellington and Blücher. Though not killed in action, he was now a spent force.

The vanquished prince exiled in Italy
Escapes by sea sailing past Genoa to Marseilles,
He is then crushed by a massive concentration of foreign armies
Though he escapes the fire [from the guns] the bees will be drained to extinction.
(X, 24)

A faithful picture of what happened after Waterloo, culminating in peace treaties of 1815 to which seven nations were signatories, seems well drawn by:

From Bourg la Reine they shall not come straight to Chartres
They shall camp close to Pont Anthony:
Seven chiefs for peace, wary as martens,
Shall enter Paris cut off from its army.
(IX, 86)

Finally, the last days in St Helena are indicated by:

The general who led infinite hosts
Will end his life far from where he was born

Among five thousand people of strange customs and
language
On a chalky island in the sea.

(I, 98)

The year 1871 was a critical one for France, and one might expect to find some prediction that is apposite. Quatrain 43 of *Century VIII* forewarns:

By the fall of two bastard things,
The nephew of the blood will become Emperor,
In Lectoyre there will be a battle,
The nephew through fear will fold up his standard.

The first and second lines could be regarded as applying to the overthrow of Louis Phillipe and the Second Republic, and the advent to power of Napoleon III. Regarding 'Lectoyre', Charles A. Ward through examining old maps discovered that the meadows south of Sedan, where the French camp was pitched on that fatal 2nd September were known in the seer's day as Le Torcey—which is an anagram of 'Lectoyre'.

Another verse (X, 51) implies the loss to France of Alsace-Lorraine. The first half goes, 'Lorraine and the region to the south will be added to lower Germany'.

What of more recent times? In the nineteenth century the following quatrain was regarded as referring to a future Calvinist conference, as Geneva was the home of John Calvin, but in this century commentators have suggested it foretold the failure of the League of Nations:

From Lake Leman [Geneva] the speeches will vex
Days will drag on into weeks,
Then months, then into years when they shall fail.
The magistrates will condemn their own ineffectual laws.

(I, 47)

They have also suggested that the following predicted the Spanish Civil War and Franco's dictatorship:

One of the great ones shall fly into Spain
Which will then bleed with a long wound,
Armies will pass by the high mountains,
Destroying all, after which he will reign in peace.
(III, 54)

Franco's actual name is given in one quatrain:

De Castel Franco sortira l'assemblée
L'ambassadeur non plaisant fera scisme:
Ceux de Ribiere seront en la meslee
Et au grand goulphre desnier ont l'entrée.

From Castille Franco will bring out the assembly,
The ambassador not pleased will cause a schism:
Ribiere's supporters will be in confused fighting
And shall deny entry to the great gulf.
(IX, 16)

Of this, ingenious commentators have surmised that the personages named are the late General Franco and his predecessor, the dictator Primo de Rivera, and that the verse refers to the struggle for power between the two men. The last line, some suggest, alludes to Franco's exile in Morocco, or to his meeting on 12th February 1941 with Mussolini on the Riviera, when he refused to permit the troops of the Axis to pass through Spain and attack Gibraltar. The 'great gulf' is the Mediterranean.

The rise of Hitler appears to be foreseen by 'A leader of the greater Germany will come to give false help (IX, 90). He will extend the Reich to include 'Brabant and Flanders, Ghent, Bruges and Boulogne (V, 94). Three quatrains give the German leader's name as 'Hister' (II, 24; IV, 68; V, 29).

The new techniques of destruction employed in the Second World War need no apter description than:

There will be let loose living deadly fire,
Hidden in horrible, terrifying globes.

By night hostile forces shall shoot against the city,
The city shall be on fire, favourable to the enemy.
(V, 8)

This would suggest that Nostradamus had foreknowledge of the use of incendiaries to illuminate targets for the bombers.

The London blitz, with its inhabitants sheltering in the Underground, seems indicated by:

In the islands shall be such horrible tumult
That nothing shall be heard but a warlike surprise.
So great shall be the attack of the raiders
That everyone shall shelter himself under the great line.
(II, 100)

As we peer into the future, what help does Nostradamus offer us? His forebodings are depressing: 'In the year 1999 and seven months there will come from the skies the great King of Terror' (X, 72). He foresees three Antichrists. If Napoleon and Hitler were the first, then this personage will be the third and his war of blood and 'red hail' will last twenty-seven years (VIII, 77).

The Pope, we are told, will have to leave Rome, and by the power of three temporal rulers be transferred to another place 'where the substance of the Incarnate Spirit shall be restored and admitted as the true seat' of St Peter (VIII, 99).

At the end of the twentieth century, according to Nostradamus, Europe will be invaded from the East:

The Oriental shall leave his homeland,
Through the Apennine mountains he will press into France.
He shall go through the sky, the waters and snow
And shall attack all with his scourge.
(II, 29)

Although Nostradamus wrote that his last prophecy was for

the year A.D. 3797, he gave a much later date for the actual end of the world:

> Twenty years after the reign of the moon passes
> Seven thousand years another will hold his monarchy.
> When the sun shall resume his days past
> Then is my prophecy accomplished and ended.
>
> (I, 48)

First there will be a terrible drought, leading to fires and burning stones falling from the sky, turning the whole world into desert. This will be followed by a second flood, leaving hardly any dry land anywhere.

It is said that Nostradamus's son, César, tried to follow in his father's footsteps as a prophet, but had no success. In despair he announced that the town of Pouzin (Vivarais), which was being besieged by the King's troops, would be destroyed by fire and to ensure that this time the prediction would be fulfilled, he set fire to it himself, but was caught and killed.

1

2

3 Dr Dee

Dr John Dee, mystic and astrologer, was in many ways one of the most remarkable men of the sixteenth century, an age rich in genius, but on account of his preoccupation with the occult he has often been dismissed as a quack—one seventeenth century writer calls him 'an old imposturing juggler'. Shakespeare is reputed to have based Prospero on him, while Butler pilloried him in *Hudibras*.

He was born in London on 13th July 1527, of Celtic descent and the son of one of Henry VIII's gentlemen servers. When only fifteen he was sent to St John's College, Cambridge, where from November 1542 to 1545, he was, to quote his own words,

> so vehemently bent to studie, that for those years I did inviolably keep this order: only to sleep four hours every night; to allow to meat and drink (and some refreshing after) two houres every day, and of the other eighteen houres all (except the tyme of going to and being at divine service) was spent in my studies and learning.

In 1546, having graduated B.A., this indefatigable scholar was appointed Under-Reader in Greek at Trinity College, which had just been founded, and of which he was also elected a Fellow. Soon Dee caused the first sensation of his bizarre career when he directed a production of Aristophanes' comedy, *Peace*. By the ingenious use of mirrors, he staged an optical illusion, the apparent flight of Trygaeus, seated on a huge scarab-beetle, from the ground up to Jupiter's palace in

---

1 Dr Dee. *British Library*

2 Edward Kelly, Dee's scryer, after digging up a newly buried malefactor's corpse in order to question him 'or an evil spirit speaking through his organs respecting the future of a noble young gentleman then a minor'. *British Library*

the sky above. Through this he gained notoriety as a conjurer, and even among the credulous as a magician. (Dee himself noted, 'whereat was great wondring, and many vain reports spread abroad of the means how that was effected'.)

The subjects that interested him most were mathematics, optics and practical astronomy, and to further his studies in May 1547 he went to the Low Countries, where he formed a close friendship with Gerard Mercator, the Flemish cartographer, who gave him two of his globes, which the young man brought back to England and presented to Trinity together with newly devised astronomical instruments.

The following year Dee left Cambridge and went to continue his studies at the University of Louvain, the greatest centre of the New Learning in Europe, and soon so distinguished himself for erudition that the Duke of Mantua and other eminent persons came to him to be taught logic, rhetoric, arithmetic and astrology, and even the Emperor Charles V came to visit him.

Louvain had been the home and refuge of the alchemist Cornelius Agrippa, who in his celebrated work *Occulta philosophia* had upheld the practice of magic as a legitimate method whereby man could acquire 'greater knowledge of God and Nature'. As a result of reading this Dee became fascinated by alchemy and astrology.

In 1550 he left Louvain for Paris, where he gave a course of lectures on Euclid, the first time this had ever been done at a university. He spoke so brilliantly that many climbed the walls outside and listened at the windows when they could not gain admittance to the crowded hall. He was offered a professorship, but refused and returned home.

Although Dee had never taken his doctorate, he had acquired such a reputation for learning that people assumed he must have been awarded the degree and addressed him accordingly. At Cambridge Sir John Cheke, now the young King Edward VI's tutor, had befriended him, and thanks to this connection he was granted a yearly pension. This provided financial security, and enabled him to devote his time to writing treatises on the cause of tides and on the stars.

In 1552 Geronimo Cardano (1501–76), esteemed physician from Padua, who in medicine and physical science anticipated modern thought, was summoned to England to examine the sickly young King and advise on suitable treatment. He lodged with Sir John Cheke, whose protégé John Dee was introduced to him. Cardano had also made a deep study of the occult, and could, he claimed, practise astral projection and have prophetic dreams. He believed himself to be guided in all he did by a spirit like Socrates' daemon. His *De subtilitate rerum*, published in 1551, contained the best physical learning of the period, and later, in *De varietate rerum*, he was to claim that the inorganic side of nature was no less animated than the organic, and that it should be possible to change baser metals into gold.

Before leaving England Cardano cast Edward VI's horoscope and predicted that he would have his most critical illness at the age of 55 years 3 months and 17 days. When the King died soon after at the age of sixteen Cardano tried to explain his failure by advancing an 'environmental' theory that when people were constitutionally weak it signified that they had not been adequately marked by the stars, and that in such cases the horoscopes of all immediate associates ought to be cast as well. This was ridiculed at the time.

Dee's conversations with Cardano while the astrologer-physician was in England inspired in him two ambitions, to have angel guides himself and to discover the philosopher's stone. His own love of learning also made him a collector of rare books, and to obtain the money for purchasing these he started casting horoscopes for courtiers, with such success that he not only eventually assembled a library of more than four thousand volumes but was commissioned by Queen Mary I on her accession to do the same for her.

Dee's cousin, Blanche Parry, who was a maid-of-honour to the next heir to the English crown, Princess Elizabeth (then in semi-imprisonment) heard of this, and it was arranged for him to visit the Princess at Woodstock and prepare her chart. He let her examine that of her step-sister, comparing its planetary aspects with her own, and revealing that, according to Mary's nativity, she would die childless. Unfortunately, a spy among Elizabeth's attendants sent a report to London, alleging that Dee had predicted a splendid future for her, while offering to take away the Queen's life through magic. As a result, Dee was arrested and tried in the Star Chamber, but was acquitted in August 1555.

His next act was one which should endear his memory to all bibliophiles. Books and manuscripts to him were even more precious than gold. During the previous two reigns monasteries had been dissolved and their priceless libraries dispersed, often burned and buried. In a praiseworthy petition to Queen Mary, he suggested the formation of a national library. First a commission ought to be appointed to discover what important manuscripts still existed. If present owners refused to part with any permanently, then they should be borrowed and fair copies made. This required immediate action, lest those affected hide away their literary treasures. One national library, centrally situated, should house originals and replicas.

Dee also offered to devote the rest of his life to copying unique manuscript volumes in the great libraries abroad. The only expense the State would have to bear was the cost of transcription and transportation to England. Nothing, unfortunately, came of his inspired idea, and his native land had to wait over two hundred years for what he advocated to be put into being; first with the birth of the British Museum and later, at the beginning of Queen Victoria's reign, with the appointment of the Historical Manuscripts Commission.

Following Elizabeth's accession to the throne, Dee was taken into her service and became known as 'hyr astrologer'. On being brought into her presence by the Earl of Pembroke and Lord Robert Dudley, later Earl of Leicester, she declared, 'Where my brother hath given him a crown, I will give him a noble'. Dudley then commanded him to select by astrological calculation a fortunate day for her coronation. He chose 14th January 1559. The weather being unexpectedly clement on that day, the new monarch was impressed and promised him a lucrative sinecure.

While he waited for this promise to be kept he travelled extensively abroad, taking one of his own manuscripts, on which he had been working for seven years, to be printed at Antwerp. When this was completed he went to Pressburg in Hungary, where he presented a copy of this work, *Monas hieroglyphica*, to the Emperor Maximilian II, to whom he had dedicated it. He even voyaged as far as St Helena and wrote an account of the journey.

On returning to England in June 1564 he found that his *Monas*, a curious mystical treatise on alchemy and the relation of numbers to natural magic, had been criticized by university graduates on account of its abstruseness but that, as he puts it, 'Her Majestie graciously defended my credit in my absence beyond the seas'. Hardly had he reached home than Elizabeth summoned him to Greenwich and asked him to read the book with her.

> She vouchsafed to account herself my schollar in my book . . . and said whereas I had prefixed in the forefront of the book: *Qui non intelligit aut taceat, aut discat*: if I would disclose to her the secrets of the book she would *et discere et facere*.
>
> Whereupon her Majestie had a little perusion of the same with me, and then in most heroicall princely wise did comfort and encourage me in my studies philosophicall and mathematicall.

When Lord Burghley, the Queen's chief Minister, had read the *Monas* he commented that the work was 'of the utmost value for the securities of the Realme', which seemed a strange compliment to pay such a book. It has been suggested that this was because the idea occurred to the wily statesman that the codes and symbols of the language of magic described in the *Monas* could be used by Walsingham's spies to conceal the secrets they had ferreted out and sent him in their dispatches.

Richard Deacon in his biography of Dee advanced the theory that he may have become one of the early members of the English Secret Service, thus conveying to the Queen in cipher information collected during his extensive travels abroad. In fact, shortly after this he was sent by her to the Duchy of Lorraine on a confidential mission, the nature of which no one was allowed to know. Elizabeth's letters to him usually began 'My noble Intelligencer' or 'My Ubiquitous Eyes', while he cryptically signed his communications to her with two circles (representing his eyes) followed by a figure seven with its top part extending backward over the former. In numerology, seven is the number of mystery. Ian Fleming, of course, in this century was to give his character, James Bond, the same code signature of '007'.

But despite the royal approval the *Monas* gained for Dee, he still failed to receive the promised post that would ensure a steady income. In fact, the only gift the Queen sent him was a cheese. At last, in December 1564, she granted him the deanery of Gloucester, but he had enemies in the Church who viewed his growing interest in the occult with disapproval, and owing to their opposition the preferment went elsewhere. Then, in 1566, he was given the lay-rectorships of Upton-on-Severn in Worcestershire and Long Leadenham in Lincolnshire.

When in 1570 the first English translation by Sir Henry Billingsley of Euclid's *Elements of Geometry* was published a much admired preface for it was written by Dee, in which he called arithmetic next to theology, 'the most divine, most pure, most ample and generall, most profound, most subtele, most commodious and most necessary'. Referring to the refraction of light, he foresaw the invention of the telescope some forty years later and suggested that a military commander might use

> an astronomical staffe commodiously framed for carriage and use, and may wonderfully help himself by perspective glasses; in which I trust our posterity will prove more skilful and expert and to greater purpose than in these days can almost be credited to be possible.

He lists extraordinary inventions seen on his travels and says that such things are

> easily achieved by skill, will, industry and ability duly applied to proof. . . . But is any honest student, or a modest Christian philosopher, to be, for such like feats, mathematically and mechanically wrought, counted and called a conjuror? . . . He that seeketh . . . to find juste cause to glorifie the eternall and Almightie Creator by, shall that man be condemned as a companion of Hell-hounds and a caller and conjuror of wicked damned spirits?

He tells of all the time he has spent in study and enquires:

> Should I have fished with so large and costly a nett, and been so long drawing, even with the helpe of Lady Philosophie and Queen Theologie, and at length have catched but a frog, nay a Devill? . . . How great is the blindness and boldness of the multitude in things above their capacitie!

He is now alluding to rumours that had been in circulation accusing him of practising the black arts.

Dee was now living in an old rambling house belonging to his mother at Mortlake, on the river Thames, which had the advantage of easy access by water to all Elizabeth's favourite palaces. But although the Queen saw him regularly, he received no further recompense for giving her astrological advice, though when he was seriously ill in 1571 she sent two of her own physicians and 'divers rareties' from her cooks. So on 3rd October 1574 he wrote to William Cecil, Lord Burghley, pointing out how he had devoted his life to acquiring knowledge, but had not received the monetary rewards his learning deserved, and, 'in fact of money he had next to nothing'. Obviously not believing in false modesty, he asserts, 'I know most assuredly that this land never bred any man, whose account therein, can evidently be proved greater than myne'.

Certain people claimed to possess the power of divining where gold and silver lay buried. Some had allowed him to put them to the test, and had convinced him that they were capable of doing this. He asks to be granted a licence to use such diviners under royal protection 'at my own cost and charge to discover and deliver true proof of a myne, vayn, or ore of gold or silver, in some place of her Grace's kingdom, for her Grace's only use'.

In return he requests the right to retain all treasure-trove he might find, after paying an agreed proportion of its value to the Queen, and one-half to Lord Burghley for his services in the matter. If only he were certain of three hundred pounds a year, he would then feel secure and be able to concentrate his entire attention upon his researches.

The reason for his seeking official royal approval was because the statutes against sorcery rendered the recovery of hidden treasure 'by aid of magic' a penal offence that might be punished by death.

But nothing seems to have come of his request, though the Queen continued to consult him on various matters. One such occurred in 1577, when the Court was disturbed by the appearance of a comet and he was summoned to Windsor, where he spent three days making astrological calculations and discussing the matter with the Queen. Finally he told her that the comet had no significance for her or England.

This was 'the blazing star' which Kepler, the German astronomer, said foretold the advent of a prince in the north of Europe who would lay waste to all Germany and disappear in 1632. This was fulfilled, for Gustavus Adolphus, born in Stockholm in 1594, involved Central Europe in the Thirty Years' War and was killed in that year.

Shortly after this a waxen image representing the Queen, with a pin stabbed into its breast, was found in Lincoln's Inn Fields, and again he was hurriedly sent for. After examining it he assured her that as it had been fashioned by an amateur inexperienced in black magic, and being also a poor likeness, she need fear no personal ill effects.

Nevertheless, the following year Elizabeth suffered grievously with rheumatism and toothache, and when her doctors failed to give her relief Dee was summoned and sent to visit the most reputed physicians in Germany to obtain their advice. He records that the Earl of Leicester regarded the matter as so pressing that he was allowed only one hundred days for 'my very painful winter journey, about a thousand five hundred miles by sea and land'.

Dee was very friendly with the great Elizabethan navigators, Davis, Frobisher, Hawkins and the Gilberts. None of their voyages were undertaken without his being consulted to select a propitious day and time for sailing. Sir George Peckham, who sailed with Sir Humphrey Gilbert, came to consult Dee in 1583 to ascertain what were the astrological portents for his planned exploration in North America, and promised if successful to give him a share in his patent of the new lands.

Dee spent a good part of 1576 writing *General and Rare Memorials pertayning to the perfect Arte of Navigation.* In this, he urged the creation of 'a Petty Navy Royale' in addition to a 'Grand Navy Royale' to protect fisheries and merchants from pirates, 'to decipher our coasts', sound channels and harbours, and observe tides. He suggested that every natural-born son of this 'British Empire'—the first time this phrase can be traced anywhere in print—would willingly pay a tax based on a percentage of his income to meet the cost of this. The English must become 'Lords of the Seas', so that their 'wits and travayles' may be employed at home for the 'enriching of the kingdom', that their commodities may be safely exported and that peace and justice may reign. 'For we must keep our own hands and hearts from doing injury to any foreigners on sea or land.'

In 1580 Queen Elizabeth requested his help in establishing her right to foreign lands discovered by her sea captains, and he prepared with admirable accuracy and skill hydrographical and geographical descriptions of such countries on two large rolls of parchment, of which work Lord Burghley highly approved.

But if Dr Dee was popular in Court circles he was not so popular with some of his neighbours at Mortlake on account of his keeping jays, which ate their peas and fruit, and his three mechanical birds, an owl, a raven and another jay, four times life-size, fully feathered and with glaring eyes, which when wound up would screech, hoot, yell and croak. The inner machinery producing these effects had been contrived for him by a Dutch horologist, a German musical-instrument-maker accomplished in reproducing bird noises by means of tiny brazen horns, while a Frenchman fashioned the eyes. Their purpose was to scare away any would-be robbers and to amuse visitors.

On the other hand, Dee's reputation as an astrologer led to neighbours seeking his services in a variety of ways. When Goodwife Faldo lost a basket of clothes Dee saw in a dream where they were to be found; likewise when a butler was dismayed to discover that a parcel of his master's plate entrusted to his care was missing Dee said that if the servant went to the owner of the boat on which he had been travelling he would meet a man who had taken the package in error, and who would give it back to him. The plate was duly recovered in this way. Trifling prognostication, of course, but it all helped to build up the sage of Mortlake's reputation.

John Dee was first married in 1574, but there is no record of where the ceremony took place, neither is his wife's name known. All he mentions in his diaries is that a year later she died, on the day the Queen called to see the 'magic glass' he had told her he possessed. He writes that both she and her attendant courtiers were convulsed with laughter when they looked into it, which suggests that it was a concave mirror which would have distorted their reflections.

Dee's second wife, Jane Fromond, was one of Elizabeth's ladies-in-waiting, and from the time of their marriage he became interested in dreams, and there are references in his diaries to hers and to his own. Some appear to have been foretelling ones. He records hearing strange rappings and knockings in his house, twice a mysterious fire broke out at night in a room where the women servants slept. The knocking was accompanied by an indistinct voice repeating something ten times—'like the screech of an owl, but more longly drawn and more softly, as it were in my chamber'.

Dr Dee was becoming obsessed with the occult, but does not appear to have succeeded in developing psychic powers to any extent on his own, although he acquired a crystal and in his diary for 25th May 1581 is the entry 'I had sight in Chrystallo offered me and I saw'. Crystal-gazing was then known as scrying (or skrying), this term being a North English dialect word from 'to descry'. It is one of the oldest forms of divination, and a possible explanation for the phenomena thereby experienced is that the percipient, by staring fixedly at a point of light in the centre of the sphere, falls into a hypnoidal state, causing hallucinations which can be categorized as either (i) memories drawn from the subconscious of the scryer, or telepathically received from that of the consultant; (ii) objectivation of ideas or images from either mind; or (iii) visions, motivated through the reception of information by supernormal means.

Dr Dee found that he was not very successful as a scryer, so thought he might achieve better results with a medium. He believed he had discovered one with genuine gifts in a preacher, Barnabas Saul, who came to live with him.

The first séance he records as taking place on 22nd December 1581. The 'great crystalline globe' was used, and Saul stared into its depths and gave Dee a message that was supposed to come from Anael, the angel who in Talmudic tradition reveals God's secrets to man. This said that many things should be divulged to Dee, not by the present worker 'but by him that is assigned to the stone'.

After New Year's tide, on any day except the Sabbath, the crystal was to be set in the sun, the brighter the day the better, and sight should be given. The sitters might 'deal both kneeling and sitting'. When one allows for the fact of how unquestioningly the devout then believed in their guardian angels ever present to protect them against evil spirits, there seems nothing at all extraordinary in Dee's conviction that other angels might also be allowed to make themselves apparent and respond to his longing for cosmic wisdom.

Some two months later Saul was charged with some offence and brought to trial in Westminster Hall, but owing to his lawyer's clever defence he was acquitted. This resulted in his giving up crystallomancy, however, for Dee sadly states, 'He confessed he neyther herd or saw any spirituall creature any more'. If he had been accused of witchcraft he was sensible to risk no further indictments.

The post of scryer to the sage of Mortlake was now vacant. When an applicant appeared he was to transform the pattern of Dee's life. It was a perverse twist of fate that brought Edward Kelly to Mortlake at this time, and it was typical of him that he arrived under an assumed name.

On 8th March 1582, two days after Saul conveniently confessed he was no longer clairvoyant, Dee wrote in his diary that Mr Clarkson, a friend of his, had brought a Mr Talbot to his house. It is obvious that this twenty-seven-year-old stranger had heard of Saul's departure and hoped to take his place, and also from what Dee went on to record that the fellow was trying to curry favour by disparaging Barnabas Saul, who, he alleged, had 'cosened' both Clarkson and Dee. This Talbot professed to have been told by 'a spirituall creature'.

Talbot—or Kelly (sometimes spelt 'Kelley'), which he later told his new patron was his real name—is said to have been born at Worcester and after being employed as an apothecary's apprentice, to have taken up the law. For falsifying deeds and counterfeiting coins he was tried at Lancaster, and lost his ears on conviction. To conceal this disfigurement he wore a black skull-cap. His past makes one inclined to dismiss Kelly at once as a plausible, unscrupulous charlatan, taking advantage of a man of great intellect with an *idée fixe* that rendered him easily gulled in all matters concerning it; and yet it is a familiar pattern that one encounters so often in the history of mediumship—the existence of genuine supernormal powers in persons of low character ready, whenever those powers fail, to resort to any kind of trickery.

On 10th March Dee put his would-be scryer to the test. He

recorded in his *Book of Mysteries* that Kelly

> settled himself to the Action, and on his knees at my desk, setting the stone before him, fell to prayer and entreaty. In the mean space, I in my Oratory did pray and make motion to God and his good creatures for the furthering of this Action. And within one quarter of an hour (or less) he had sight of one in the stone.

This was Uriel, the Spirit of Light.

It seems that Dee was favourably impressed by this, so despite protests from his wife Jane, whose feminine intuition told her that no good would come of it, the stranger joined the household as resident scryer, receiving a salary of £20 a year.

On 14th March Kelly had a vision of the angel Michael in the crystal. Elaborate instructions were now received from the two angels for a 'table of practice' to be made of sweet wood about six feet high with four legs, and marked in various places with mystical signs. On the centre of the table was fixed a seal of wax, nine inches in diameter, twenty-seven inches in circumference and an inch and an eighth thick, and on the upper side of which a table of forty-nine squares was drawn containing the seven names of God, which were 'not known to the angels, neither can they be spoken or read of man. These names bring forth seven angels, the governors of the heavens next unto us. Every letter of the angels' names bringeth forth a son. Every son hath his son.' This 'was not to be looked upon without great reverence and devotion'.

Each table leg was placed upon a waxen seal similar to the upper one (two of these, incidentally, are in the British Museum, together with one of Dee's 'shew-stones'). A red cover of shot silk, adorned with tassels, was laid over the table, and the crystal globe in its frame placed in the centre. The scryer would then sit in a green chair, while his employer arranged himself by his desk, ready to write down all that transpired in a great folio book.

Kelly would first see a golden curtain in the crystal. According to Dee, the spirits normally appeared in the globe, but at times they would emerge into a blinding beam of light shining from it and move about the room. Occasionally he carried on a conversation with the apparition, while at other times Kelly solely caught what was said and repeated it to him. Now and then only a voice would be heard. The sittings were always accompanied by prayer, for Dee was a deeply religious man.

He did try to puzzle out an explanation for the phenomena, stating that one day he told an angel:

> I do think you have no organs or Instruments apt for voyce, but are meere spirituall and nothing corporall, but have the power and property from God to insinuate your message or meaning to ear or eye so that man's imagination shall be that they hear and see you sensibly.

The angels, through the mediumship of Kelly, taught the two men a strange language supposed to have been first spoken by the prophet Enoch, which they were to use in invocations when they wished to summon them before scrying. Here is a sentence of it: '*Madariatza das perifa Lil cabisa micaolazoda saanire caosago of fifa balzodizodarasa iada*'. This in English meant 'Oh, you heavenly denizens of the first air, you are mighty in the parts of the earth, and execute the judgment of the highest'.

Dee was by no means as easily deceived as his detractors have alleged. He must have learnt something of Kelly's past. A few months after the latter's arrival Dee mentions in his diary the scryer's 'abominable lyes' and adds, 'Of this K., I doubt yet'.

Edward was half his age, moody and temperamental. Sometimes becoming bored with the crystal-gazing routine, he would burst into a violent fit of temper and threaten to leave. Then his placid, gentle employer would calm him down and persuade him to stay.

After one reconciliation Dee says that on 21st November 1582 a child angel appeared in the rays of the setting sun and presented him with a crystal 'as big as an egg: most bryght, clere, and glorious'. St Michael told Dee that he and Kelly must continue their work as master and man with the new 'shew-stone'. This Dee was to call in the future his 'Angelicall Stone' and to carry with him wherever he went.

Most of the time Kelly was conveying to his patron communications from angels, which were reproduced by Dee in his voluminous *Book of Mysteries*, together with detailed accounts of every happening. Written in a sermon-like style, they made mostly tedious reading, but here and there are beautifully phrased passages, and suddenly Dee's descriptive powers take wing and an episode comes to life with considerable dramatic effect. The visitants too, the 'spirituall creatures', become astonishingly real, as they must have been to Dee.

For example:

> They that now come in are jolly fellows, all trymmed after the manner of Nobilitie now-a-dayes with gylt rapiers and curled haire, and they bragged up and downe. Bobogel standeth in a black velvet coat, and his hose, close round hose of velvet upper-stocks, over layd with gold lace. He hath a velvet hat cap with a black feather in it, with a cape on one of his shoulders; his purse hanging at his neck, and so put under his girdell. His beard long . . . Seven others are apparelled like Bobogel, sagely and gravely.

Dee also records predictions that were later fulfilled. In the margin of his diary, one night four years before Mary, Queen of Scots, was executed, he drew an axe against an entry describing how Kelly had observed in the crystal a woman whom Uriel, his spirit guide, told them was the Queen. She was kneeling down, and a tall man clad in black was about to behead her. On another occasion the scryer saw 'the sea full of ships' and Uriel revealed that a foreign Power was preparing a vast fleet 'against the welfare of England'. As a result Dee warned Elizabeth against an invasion from Spain.

In 1583 an impoverished prince from Bohemia, Albert Laski, visited the English Court. He hoped to find a solution to his financial troubles by discovering the philosopher's stone, and was seeking an alchemist who might have found it or be on the verge of doing so. Having heard about Dee from the Earl of Leicester, he asked to meet him.

Elizabeth's favourite introduced the foreigner to the Doctor, saying that he would bring him to dine at Mortlake. Dee replied that he could not afford the cost of suitable entertainment. This was reported to the Queen, who for a jest showed generosity at last. She knew, she said, that Dee had many Angels in his house, but as it appeared they could not provide him with money she was sending him forty of her own golden Angels to provide the feast.

Dee soon became very intimate with the prince. Séances were held. In his *Book of Mysteries* he describes how a child angel appeared.

> There seemed to come out of my Oratory a Spirituall creature, like a pretty girl of 7 or 9 years of age . . . with her hair rolled up before, and hanging down very long behind, attired in a gown of Sey, changeable green and red, with a Train . . . She seemed to play up and down . . . to go in and out behind my books, lying on heaps, the biggest . . . .

When Dee asked her name she said it was Madimi. 'I am the last but one of my mother's children, I have little Baby-children at home.' She became a regular visitor at these séances and, according to him, grew into a woman by the time they eventually ended. She foretold that Laski would be elected King of Poland and that his family should become the bulwark of Christendom against the Mohammedans. Neither prediction was fulfilled, and one suspects that Kelly was trying to ingratiate himself with the Pole.

During one séance Tanfield, an attendant to the Prince, arrived from Richmond Palace and burst into the room while the spirit of an angel named Jubanladee was speaking and telling the visitor to 'look to the steps of his youth, measure the length of his body, live better and see himself inwardly'.

The angel, it appears, was annoyed at the interruption and prophesied that Tanfield would within five months be 'devoured by fishes'. Presumably this happened, for he was before that time-limit drowned at sea.

Jubanladee went on to say that Cecil hated Laski and 'desired he was gone because the Queen loveth him faithfully'. He should return home together with Dee, who would help him to establish his kingdom. Then, according to Dee, the familiar spirit sank through the table 'like a spark of fire'.

This led to the three men leaving for the continent. It seems that Kelly had told Dee that during his wanderings in Wales he had stayed at a remote inn, mine host of which had shown him an ancient parchment which, with two small ivory bottles containing a red and a white powder, had been discovered in the ruins of Glastonbury Abbey when looters in search of hidden treasure had broken open the tomb of St Dunstan, once Abbot there and later Archbishop of Canterbury. He was also a smith and worked in all kinds of metals in his cell, and as a result became the patron saint of goldsmiths and jewellers. The thieves had later given their find to the taverner in payment for food and drink.

On examining the manuscript Kelly claimed that he had discovered it to be a treatise on transmutation containing a puzzling formula. He had deduced that the powders were to be used in the preparation of a tincture that could turn inferior metals into gold.

Dee was always short of money, as he spent all he acquired from casting horoscopes on additions to his library and open-handed hospitality to all visitors. He therefore allowed Kelly to have a small laboratory in the house, where he conducted alchemical experiments with the mysterious powders in the hope of one day making gold. When Laski, already impressed by the séances, learned this he became convinced that the two Englishmen could be instrumental in securing for him both the Polish Crown and all the precious metal he coveted.

As for Kelly, he was weary of his constrained existence and

longed for change and luxury abroad, while Dee, who had been a great traveller, was attracted by the prospect of seeing new foreign parts, and also felt that he was doing God's will in following the advice of an angel. He was not to return to England for nearly six years.

In September 1583 Laski and his attendants, Dr and Mrs Dee and their children, Edward Kelly and the wife he had wed while living at Mortlake, set out in secret for the Low Countries. As soon as it was discovered that Dee had gone abroad those jealous of his being a favourite with the Queen spread malicious rumours about him, which were easy to credit in view of Kelly's past. It was discovered that once in Wales Kelly had been suspected of digging up a newly buried malefactor's corpse for the purpose of 'questioning the dead or an evil spirit speaking through his organs respecting the future of a noble young gentleman then a minor'. He and Dr Dee, it was alleged, had been practising necromancy, with the result that their house was haunted by a legion of devils. No one in Mortlake would ever prosper again until something was done about it. Agitators raised a mob that broke into Dee's vacated home, smashed his furniture and chemical apparatus, destroyed the ear-piercing mechanical birds with all else regarded as the paraphernalia of sorcery, and finally burned many of the rare books in his library.

Kelly seems to have received telepathically news of this. Dee records that Madimi said, referring to Mortlake, 'I would not come into your study. The Queen has caused it to be sealed.' This was after the rioters had ransacked it.

On 3rd February 1584 the party reached Laski's palace near Cracow. He had heavily mortgaged his estates there, and the loan was due to be repaid by the end of April. When Kelly failed to produce any gold the Prince was obliged to find the money by raising it on property he owned elsewhere.

In August the three men went to Prague to meet the eccentric Emperor Rudolph, whose pastime was alchemy. Dee told him how for forty years he had searched in vain for true wisdom in books and men. Then God had sent him His

Light, Uriel, who for two and a half years with other spirits had taught him divine knowledge, had completed his books for him, and had brought him his priceless crystalline globe. This angel guide had given a special message for the Emperor. He was bidden to sin no more and to do the Lord's work in future. Dee was to show him the Holy Vision in the crystal.

Rudolph was no doubt wearied by this proselytizing farrago. He excused himself witnessing the vision at present owing to another engagement, Dee must tell him more on a later occasion. But they never met again, for the Emperor when approached always found reasons for not granting him an audience.

Disappointed, Dee, however, obtained an introduction through Laski to King Stephen of Poland in April 1585, who told the monarch that if he took the two men into his service they would make the philsopher's stone. Dee promised to try, if the King would pay for the cost of experiments. He could not guarantee positive results, but he hoped that his angel guides would teach him the secret of transmutation. So that the King might see the 'spirituall creatures' for himself, a séance was held in his private chamber, but it cannot have been successful, for he lost interest, and in August the two men, abandoning hope of patronage from Poland, went back to Prague.

Unfortunately, ecclesiastical disapproval of their activities had arisen, and the new Pope, Sixtus V, issued a Papal edict in May 1586, ordering Dee and Kelly to leave Prague within six days. They found a temporary asylum with a new patron, Count Rosenberg, in his castle at Tribau on the Moldau, in southern Bohemia. Here the crystal in its frame of gold, with its table and appurtenances, was set up in, as Dee puts it, 'a goodly chapel next my chamber', and the séances took place at night in the Count's presence, while during the day they went on experimenting with Kelly's powder, trying to turn base metals into gold.

A report having reached Russia that Dee had in fact succeeded, its Emperor invited him to move to Moscow, promising £2 000 a year, food from the royal kitchen, payment of all travelling and removal expenses, together with a guard of five hundred horses to convey him there. But Dee, after considering all the pros and cons, decided not to accept this enticing offer.

Shortly after receiving it, Dee states that Edward Kelly 'made projection with his powder in the proportion of one minim (upon an ounce and a quarter of mercury) and produced nearly an ounce of best gold'.

Dee was delighted. For while he himself had toiled doggedly with scientific methods to achieve this, Kelly had raced ahead and, by some process he refused to disclose, had found the key to the long-sought secret. Whether Kelly had actually accomplished this or whether (and most likely) he had staged a clever deception, it is impossible to tell for certain.

In Dee's eyes the hired scryer was now an outstanding alchemist whose momentous achievement would perpetuate his name with posterity, and he now treated him with the deference he felt due to his new stature. But far from Kelly's appreciating such a compliment, it only made him arrogant and presumptuous, and led to his making an outrageous proposal. Although Dee had been married four years, Jane, his obedient wife, had produced no offspring, for which he considered her to blame. Then one day in April 1587 Kelly informed Dee that Madimi, the girl angel, had appeared naked in the crystal and had bid them share everything in common, including their wives.

Dee was outraged. He asked Kelly to tell Madimi how distressed and astounded he was that a good angel could put forward 'so hard and unpure a doctrine'. The two men went on arguing and praying until two o'clock in the morning of 18th April 1587. Kelly claimed that a little spirit, Ben, when visiting him alone the previous day in the laboratory, had predicted the deaths that summer of Queen Elizabeth, the King of Spain, the Pope and Count Rosenberg (by poisoning) if Madimi were not obeyed. All these disasters would be accompanied by famine and bloodshed and, worst of all, Kelly's precious powder that had brought about the transmutation would lose its virtue. He now alleged that the powder was one which Ben had recently brought him.

All this Dee found too much to credit, and he retorted that he had reached the conclusion that there was so much which was unconvincing and obviously untrue in Kelly's account of what had transpired in Dee's absence that in future he would believe only what he personally could witness.

But when he retired to bed he had already begun to waver, dismayed at the thought of breaking with Edward, of whom it appears he had grown very fond. Poor Mrs Dee lay trembling, unable to sleep.

'Jane, I can see that there is no other remedy, but as hath been said of our cross-matching, so it must needs be done', Dee reports himself as saying.

His wife sobbed, implored, then flew into a fury. But after a while her loyalty to John prevailed despite her repugnance. 'I trust that though I gave myself thus to be used, that God will turn me into a stone', she cried, 'before he would suffer me in my obedience to receive any shame or inconvenience.'

Next day she insisted on speaking to Madimi herself through the crystal, but the girl spirit and Kelly's other guides proved intractable, and on 21st May the 'Angel Raphael' dictated an agreement, which all four had to sign, which threatened them with death if they did not obey his instructions or failed to keep them secret. The 'Angel' stressed that he was not advocating impurity. It was a pact that should be regarded as 'an allegory of closer spiritual union'.

This last concession on the 'Angel's' part must have made the Dees sigh with relief: so the agreement could be regarded more as an expression of mutual love. He went into the Castle's chapel, laid the document on the altar and prayed. Having gained their submission, it seems that Kelly was at least sensible enough not to attempt to put the plan into action. But the incident had completely undermined the relationship between the two men.

Now that Kelly was producing gold, it was he who stood highest in their present patron Count Rosenberg's estimation.

Dee was treated with disdain, and the scryer refused to share with him the new-found secret. His aim now became to drive the Dees away, and he did this with cunning by decrying John to the Count.

'September the 15th, the Lord Chancellor came and left on the 17th', Dee wrote. 'The rancour and dissimulation now evident to me, God deliver me! I was not sent for.' It must have been humiliating and galling for him with his widespread renown as a savant to see the ex-criminal whom he had befriended fêted and admired. He was poorer than he had ever been, while the other might well become one of the richest men in the world.

The Court installed Kelly in fine apartments on his own. Now that he no longer had to scry for Dee, he gave himself airs, and sent for his former employer to visit him as though their positions were now reversed and master had become servant. He would have dropped him completely had he not thought that there was still knowledge in the other's brilliant brain that might be of use to him. That was partly his purpose in making the 'Angel Raphael' bid them share everything with each other, though he himself was in no way inclined to share his secrets. Quarrels erupted, and eventually ended in a complete break.

Back in England, Queen Elizabeth's spies had brought details to her of the many ships Philip of Spain had mustered for England's conquest. As this fulfilled Dee's earlier prediction, she wrote and asked for further advice. 'Hyr astrologer' after consideration of the aspects replied that she should wait until the Armada reached the English Channel before ordering an attack, then all would be well for England.

The Queen heeded his message, although some of her advisers had urged that the Spaniards be attacked while still in port, and Dee sent her a letter of congratulation following the Armada's defeat and destruction. His prestige with her must now be very high, following the felicitous outcome of his second prophecy, so he told the Queen that he now intended to return home and begged for a safe conduct. She sent a magnificent coach and a guard of honour to meet him and his family in the Low Countries and bring them back to Mortlake.

On 4th January 1589 Dee says he handed over to Kelly 'the powder, the bokes, the glass and the bone for the Lord Rosenberg' and on the 16th left Tribau. The seven-year-old partnership had ended, and the two men were never to see each other again.

Kelly's own star was very much in the ascendant, and when the mad Emperor Rudolph heard of his achievement he invited him to Prague. His personal charm, plausible manner and golden miracle at first succeeded in impressing Rudolph to such an extent that he was given an estate and created a Baron of the Kingdom of Bohemia. According to all contemporary accounts, he made large quantities of gold. How he staged the deception is impossible to say for certain. Figuris assures us that in the house of the Imperial physician, Thaddeus de Huzek, he saw Kelly transmute a pound of mercury into excellent gold through adding a single drop of red oil.

Reports of all this found their way to England, and to excite Queen Elizabeth's interest Kelly dispatched to her a warming-pan and an oblong-shaped piece of gold, which fitted exactly into a hole in the former, and which he claimed to have transmuted from the baser metal. Her Lord Treasurer, Burghley, who was shrewd and sharp-witted and not easily taken in, wrote in 1591 to Edward Dyer, the Queen's agent in Germany, pressing him to do all he could to persuade Kelly 'to come over to his native country and honour Her Majesty with the fruits of such knowledge as God has given him'. Should the alchemist refuse, he asks Dyer to try to induce him to part with a little of his powder so that the Queen could witness transmutation taking place before her eyes.

Kelly would not comply, so Burghley entered into direct correspondence, pleading with him to help to make England rich with his secret formula. The old statesman was worried about ageing. Could Kelly let him have a prescription for a rejuvenating elixir? In a short reply dated 18th February 1591 the absentee promises he will 'shortly send the good thing desired for your health'. But he failed to do this, so in May Burghley beseeched him for 'something of your operation to strengthen me afore next winter against my old enemy, the gout'.

But Kelly ignored these pleas, and soon he must have regretted not returning, for he fell out of favour with the deranged Emperor and died trying to escape from the castle of Pürglitz, where he had been imprisoned. Thus was fulfilled a 'spirit' warning he had received eleven years earlier at a séance that he would die a violent death. Three centuries later Aleister Crowley was to claim he was his reincarnation.

It was not until late in 1589 that the Dees reached their house at Mortlake and John saw for himself his wrecked library. His income was a mere pittance. Nothing had been remitted to him from his rectorships since leaving England. The Queen promised a Christmas gift of £100, but only half was forthcoming. Further unredeemed promises were received from her.

At last, with destitution facing him, he petitioned the Queen on 9th November 1592, begging her to appoint a commission to investigate his affairs so that she might have proof of how near penury he stood. He wrote that for thirty-four years he had served her faithfully. It was a national reproach that a man of science like himself should be left in beggary.

This brought immediate results. Two commissioners were appointed to examine his affairs. When they arrived he greeted them in his library and read to them from a manuscript divided into fourteen chapters relating the story of his life. The shortest is the twelfth, which was headed 'The Resolution for generall, very easy, and speedy Remedy in this Rare and Lamentable Case'. The remedy he suggested was to make him either Master of St Cross, Warden of Manchester, Provost of Eton, or Master of Sherborne, one of which posts had been already promised him four times in three years.

He made a detailed statement of his financial position. His friends had lent him about £500. He owed £333. He had pawned all his plate and wife's jewellery. He had spent but £566 in three years for housekeeping. He had mortgaged his house for £400, and now would have to sell it for half its cost to pay his debts, leaving him and his family homeless vagabonds furnished only with bottles and wallets.

The immediate result of this investigation into his finances was a gift of a hundred marks from the Queen, but it was not until May 1595, after many disappointments, that he was granted the wardenship of Manchester College. Unfortunately, he went there with a reputation besmirched by rumour's brush, depicting him as a senile and credulous dabbler in the occult. His colleagues disapproved of him from the start, and went out of their way to upset him whenever possible. Lancashire was then notorious for witchcraft, and that winter he was asked to exorcise a woman and seven children suspected of being demoniacally possessed. He refused to meddle with the affair, and advised the father 'to consult with godlye preachers and appoint a private fast'. He had brought a large part of his library with him. It was well stocked with books on demonology and possession, and Lancashire justices of the peace who had to deal with cases of witchcraft visited him to consult works such as the *De praestigiis daemonum* of John Wier, whom he had met at Louvain, and who was one of the first to plead that witches be shown mercy on the grounds that 'their brains being disordered by melancholy, they merited pity, not punishment'.

In 1603 his royal patroness, Queen Elizabeth, died. Her successor, James I, saw that Parliament passed as the first Act of his reign a new and harsher one against witchcraft. He regarded Dee with the utmost suspicion and dislike.

Dee was now in very poor health, and in November 1604 he gave up his post in Manchester and returned to Mortlake, where he sought consolation from life's disappointments through séances with a new scryer, Bartholomew Hickman. Messages were received from the angel Raphael promising restoration of his health to full vigour, and advising him to go on long journeys to friends in Germany where the secrets of wisdom, the philosopher's stone and the secret the 'book of St Dunstan' contained should be revealed to him. But he never went, for, worn out by age and infirmities, his powers now swiftly declined. He passed away in December 1608, and was buried in the chancel of Mortlake Church.

John Aubrey was the grandson of Dee's cousin and neighbour, Dr William Aubrey, the Master of Requests, who helped the old man to obtain the Manchester post. Half a century later he wrote that his relative had 'a very faire cleare rosie complexion, a long beard as white as milke; he was tall and slender; a very handsome . . . mighty good man he was. . . . He wore a Gowne like an Artist's, with hanging sleeves, and a slitt'. Eighty-year-old Goodwife Faldo, who had known Dee, told Aubrey that her mother had nursed him during his last illness. She added other details apart from the anecdote earlier mentioned. He kept a great many stills going and used to distil eggshells. He laid 'a mighty storme and tempest that broke out in harvest time' of which 'the country people had not known the like'.

▲1 2▲ ▼3

4 *The Brahan Seer*

Second sight or prophetic vision is a phenomenon very common in primitive countries and sparsely populated parts of the world, of which instances may be found since the earliest times. Some are only legends as unproven as the average tale of the family ghost. Others have been fulfilled with all the details given at time of vision and then recorded by reliable sources.

The Scottish Highlands have been regarded as the traditional home of *taibhsears*, or seers, and this is chiefly because more has been written about second sight occurring there than elsewhere. A cherished superstition in the Highlands is that a seventh child or the seventh child of a seventh is born with the Sight. This, of course, has its origin in the reported magical power of the number 7. The gift was common to persons of either sex, and it could happen at any time or place, in or out of doors, and it did not matter what the percipient might be doing.

A Scottish writer, Dr Beattie, held that the sight was caused by the effects of the wild and weird scenery and the light and shadow passing across it have upon the imagination. Others were convinced that all such visions were optical illusions.

But such theories cannot explain how Mary Queen of Scots's execution was foreseen by several Highland seers and described by them in remarkable minuteness. King James I refers to this in his *Demonology*, and it was brought as a charge against certain Shetland witches during his reign. Neither can they, for example, explain the fulfilment of the visions of several inhabitants of the Isle of Harris in which they frequently saw

---

1 Kenneth, third Earl of Seaforth. *Reproduced by courtesy of Fortrose Town Council*

2 Isabella Mackenzie, third Countess of Seaforth. *Reproduced by courtesy of Fortrose Town Council*

3 Chanonry Point, where the Brahan Seer was burnt alive

a certain landlord with an arrow in his thigh. This gave rise to a belief that he would be shot there before he died. However, he passed away through natural causes, but on the day of the funeral another hearse arrived at the kirk at the same time as his. The two bands of mourners began arguing as to which burial should take place first, and as neither would give way a fight began. One of them seized his bow and fired several arrows. When the minister had stopped the unseemly brawl it was discovered that an arrow had pierced the dead landlord's thigh, thus fulfilling the strange prevision.

Dr Samuel Johnson toured the Western Isles in 1773, mainly for the purpose of investigating the phenomenon. Sceptical by nature, he did not allow his personal inclinations to make him over-credulous. In the account he wrote of the journey he stated:

> The Second Sight is an impression made either by the mind upon the eye or the eye upon the mind, by which things distant or future are perceived and seen as if they were present. A man on a journey far from home falls from his horse; the Seer sees him lying injured on the ground, commonly with a landscape of the place where the accident has befallen him.

Of his experiences in Skye, Johnson says, 'To talk with any of these seers is not easy. There is one living in Skye with whom we would gladly have conversed; but he was very gross and ignorant and knew no English.' The Doctor discovered that the islanders of all ranks regarded the existence of second sight as proven beyond argument. The only dissentients were the ministers of the kirk, who no doubt blamed the demon drink or the Pope for such fantasies. At the end of his account Johnson admits that he could not reach any definite conclusion. 'I never could advance my curiosity to conviction, but came away at last only willing to believe.'

Investigators have written that those with Second Sight are often unhappy possessors of such a gift and would prefer not to have it, for so much of what they foresee tells of disaster and death. One researcher claims that the seers he encountered were all of very melancholy dispositions, with poor eyesight. Others who have been present when a seer has had the Sight describe his speech as sounding as though he is highly excited, even delirious, and that the vision of events to come is accompanied by a 'nerve storm', ending in complete prostration, which reminds one of descriptions of how the prophesying process affected the Pythias at Delphi. As another observer puts it, second sight is like a waking nightmare.

The phenomenon would appear to be caused by a dormant power of mind in man hardly ever used when he is no longer in close contact with Nature. Apart from the explanations already mentioned, it has been suggested by another investigator, Mr Evans Wentz, that there is some indefinable psychic element in the earth's atmosphere upon which all human and physical actions are photographed or impressed. He wrote:

> Under certain inexplicable conditions, normal persons who are not seers may observe Nature's mental records like pictures cast upon a screen—often like moving pictures. Seers can always see them if they wish, and uncritical seers frequently mistake these phantom records or pictures existing on the psychical envelope of the planet for actual events now occurring and for actual beings.

Mr Wentz thought that his theory would explain how Miss Moberly and Miss Jourdain saw in 1901 the gardens of Versailles peopled and laid out as they were in the latter part of the eighteenth century, the subject of their famous and controversial book, *An Adventure*. This was, of course, an instance of second sight operating backward, of post-cognition.

About the beginning of the seventeenth century there was born in the Island of Lewis at Baile-na-Cille in the parish of Uig, Kenneth Mackenzie, better known as Coinneach Odhar Fiosaiche, Warlock of the Glen, and better still as the Brahan Seer, foreteller of the trivial and the terrible. He is the most celebrated of the Highland Seers, and popular faith in his prophecies has always been strong; among others, Sir Walter Scott, his son-in-law and biographer J. G. Lockhart and Sir Humphry Davy firmly believed in them, while the situation in Scotland and the North Sea today bring added interest to the Seer's strangely apposite predictions.

There is a charming legend about the way in which he is supposed to have gained his gift. It was said that one evening when his mother was tending her cattle in a summer shieling on the side of a ridge overlooking the burying-ground she saw towards midnight the tombstones swing back as if on hinges, and folk, old and young, step out and hurry away in all directions. Within an hour they had all returned beneath ground save one. Being a brave woman, Mrs Mackenzie determined to discover the reason for this, so she laid her distaff across the open grave's mouth, which she knew according to popular belief would prevent a wandering spirit's regaining its resting-place.

Shortly afterwards she noticed a lady with long fair hair come rushing through the air from the north towards the churchyard. On arrival the wraith was distressed to see what the other had done and cried, 'Lift your distaff from off my grave, and let me enter my dwelling of the dead'.

'I shall do so', replied Kenneth's mother, 'when you explain to me what detained you so long after your neighbours.'

'That you shall soon hear,' responded the fair lady. 'My journey was much farther than theirs. I had to go all the way to Norway. I am a daughter of its King, and was drowned while bathing. My body was carried out to sea and eventually swept on to the shore not far from here, where it was found and interred in that grave. Now please remove your distaff so that I may once more take my rest.'

When Mrs Mackenzie had complied with this request the Princess said, 'In remembrance of me, and as a small reward of your courage, I shall tell you where you will find something of rare value. If you will search in that loch over there you will come across a small round blue stone. Give it to your son,

Kenneth, who by it shall see into the future.'

There is another version of this tale where the stone's colour is given as white, and where the Seer came by it in an entirely different way through employment by a farmer, whose wife proved such a hard task-mistress that he rebelliously played her up, and eventually so angered her with his sarcastic humour that she decided to kill him.

One day the farmer sent young Mackenzie to a remote heath to cut peat. It was too far off for him to come back for a meal, so the woman, seizing the occasion as a suitable opportunity for ridding herself of the youth who plagued her, brought him for his repast sowans and milk mixed with noxious herbs. She found him asleep on a conical fairy hillock and, her courage failing her, instead of rousing him she set the food down by his side and went home.

When Kenneth awoke he would have begun to eat had he not felt something cold press heavily against his heart. On investigation he discovered it to be a beautiful small stone with a pearly white sheen, which had apparently been dropped there while he slumbered. Then, as he gazed admiringly at it, he suddenly had a vision which revealed the murderous plan of the farmer's wife. To test the truth of this he gave the dinner intended for himself to his collie, which soon after died in agony.

Such stories invariably become embroidered as they circulate from mouth to mouth, and in a later variation the woman was even more fiendish and sent Kenneth's own wife to take the poisoned food to him. Tiring of cutting peat, he lay down, resting his head on a little knoll, and fell asleep. On awaking he felt something hard pressing against the back of his neck and discovered the cause to be a small round stone with a hole through the centre. He picked it up and, looking through it, had a vision of the farmer's wife poisoning his food and then handing it to his wife. The shock, however, blinded him in the eye he had applied to the stone, and he never recovered the sight in it.

In this respect Kenneth Mackenzie is peculiar among

Highland Seers. He was a scryer, for the employment of which method of seeing into the future any bright object that focuses the attention will serve, be it a crystal, stone, polished lump of coal, mirror, oil, water or ink in the palm of one's hand or on a fingernail, or even a bright leaf.

No sooner had Coinneach Odhar Fiosaiche, as he preferred to call himself, realized that he had the gift of divination than he started to put it into practice. The tales about how he came to own his divining-stone were probably invented by himself. He found it helped to lend colour to his fortune-telling. It was a 'gimmick' which made him unique among those claiming to have second sight. He continued to earn his living as a farm-hand, while telling fortunes to the island folk in his spare time. Apparently he was so successful that his fame spread to the mainland itself, and he was soon receiving large sums there with predictions for the gentry and those who could afford them. Now people began to call him the Brahan Seer.

Those who knew him considered that he was very shrewd and clear-headed, always ready with a riposte, and if anyone tried to ridicule him he usually managed to turn the tables on his detractors.

He no doubt predicted many things which the sceptic may ascribe to his perspicacity. For example, some hundred and fifty years before the Caledonian Canal was built, he forecast that ships would one day sail round the back of Tomnahurich Hill. A resident of Inverness, interested in recording folklore for posterity, took down several of his prophecies, but when he heard this one he thought it so far-fetched he destroyed what he had already written and refused to see Coinneach again.

Fortunately, someone else was more amenable and noted the offending prediction, which read, 'Strange as it may seem to you this day, time will come, and it is not far off, when full-rigged ships will be seen sailing eastward and westward by the back of Tomnahurich, near Inverness'. It is quite possible that a man of discernment might, from the appearance of the country with its chain of great island lakes, predict the future Caledonian Canal.

Among other prophecies which might safely be made without the aid of any supernormal gift are 'that the day will come when the hills of Ross-shire will be strewed with ribbons, and a bridge on every stream'. The 'ribbons', of course, are roads. Older people often take a jaundiced view of youth and coming generations, and any of Coinneach's age, without any claim to second sight, might have written, 'The people will degenerate as their country improves, and the clans will become so effeminate as to flee from their native country before an army of sheep'.

But there are many more of the Brahan Seer's predictions that cannot be so easily explained away, especially when actual names and personal characteristics are given. For example, a chieftain in the Isle of Skye, who was rash enough to ask him what the future held in store for his race, was told that the MacGilles would be beggared through a spendthrift descendant born when there was 'a fair-haired Lochiel, a red-headed Lovat, a squint-eyed, fair-haired Chisholm, a big, deaf Mackenzie, and a bow-crook-legged MacGille-chailum, who shall be the great-grandson of John (or little) Beg of Ruiga. He shall be the worst MacGille-chailum that ever came or ever will come. I shall not be in existence in his day, and I have no desire that I should.'

This prediction came about. The Seer was proved correct concerning all these lairds' hair and blemishes, and MacGille-chailum in particular was the black sheep of his family, and had to sell all its lands to pay his debts.

To the Mackenzies of Lochalsh, who had offended him, Coinneach foretold that they would have to dispose of their estates to an Englishman 'who shall be distinguished by great liberality to his people and lavish expenditure of money'. He would have one son and two daughters, and after his death the property would revert to the Mathesons, the original owners, who would build a castle on Drum-a-Dubh at Balmacarra.

Some hundred and fifty or so years later this occurred when a Mr Lullingstone purchased it. He became extremely well liked on account of the qualities mentioned, and though he had been married for seventeen childless years, it was not long before his wife gave birth to a son and later two daughters. Following Lullingstone's death, Lochalsh was sold to the then M.P. for Ross and Cromarty, Alexander Matheson.

Coinneach appears to have been particularly prejudiced against any branch of his own clan. The Mackenzies of Rosehaugh bore a deer and its horns on their coat-of-arms. He predicted that there in the place of the seed of the deer would be the seed of the goat. In this century the Fletchers were lairds at Rosenaugh, and their heraldic device was the goat.

Of another family of Mackenzies, those of Fairburn (now Conha), the Brahan Seer gloomily prophesied that they would lose their entire possessions, disappear almost to a man from the face of the earth, that their castle would become uninhabited and that 'a cow shall give birth to a calf in the uppermost chamber in Fairburn Tower'. Coinneach told this apparently to a large crowd at a time when the castle was occupied by a rich and powerful chieftain, and he was ridiculed for saying what he did.

But in the 1870s misfortune struck the family, the tower was left uninhabited and fell into disrepair, and 'the uppermost chamber' was used for storing straw by a tenant-farmer. Then one day a cow of his, finding the door open, went in and noticed a trail of straw on the stone steps where a hand had dropped some while carrying a load upstairs. The animal began picking up the straw as she climbed upward. On reaching the top shc was unable to descend, being heavy in calf. When discovered there she was allowed to remain until she gave birth to a fine calf. Remembering the prophecy, many local people went to see them and the event was reported in Scottish newspapers at the time.

Coinneach's harshest prediction regarding his clan is surely this one:

The day will come when a bloody and destructive battle will

> be fought on the Muir of Ord and when the ravens will drink their full of the blood of the Mackenzies for three successive days from the top of the Clach an t-Seasaidh, and they will be so reduced in numbers that they will be all taken in an open fishing boat [*scuta dubh*] back to Ireland from whence they originally came. A squint-eyed [*cam*], pox-pitted tailor will start the battle, for men will become so scarce in those days that each of seven women will strive hard for the squint-eyed tailor's heart and hand, and out of this strife the conflict will originate.

It is possible that such a battle did occur, for in the middle of last century several writers mention that near the Muir of Ord there then was an angular stone, sharp at the top, which at one time stood upright and was of considerable height, but which then was partly broken and lying on the ground.

In the Rev. Donald Macleod's life of his father, Dr Norman Macleod, published in 1876, some autobiographical reminiscences are given which were dictated to the son in old age. In the summer of 1799 he visited Dunvegan Castle, the stronghold of the Macleods in the Isle of Skye, and he refers to a prophecy of the Brahan Seer, couched in Gaelic verse, regarding his family, and which he was certain had been widely known in the Highlands at least a hundred years previously.

It was foretold that when Norman, the 'Third Norman', son of the 'hard-boned English lady', would perish by an accidental death—when the 'Maidens' of Macleod (certain well-known rocks on the coast of Macleod country) became the property of a Campbell—when a fox had young ones in one of the turrets of the Castle—and particuarly when the Fairy's enchanted banner should be for the last time exhibited, then the glory of the Macleod family would depart, most of the estate would be sold to others, so that a small currach would carry all gentlemen of the name of Macleod across Loch Dunvegan; but that in times far distant another member of the family would arise, who would redeem those estates, and raise the power and honour of the house to higher pitch than ever. Such, in general terms, was the prophecy.

Now as to the curious fulfilment. Dr Norman Macleod wrote:

> There was, at that time, at Dunvegan, an English smith, with whom I became a favourite, and who told me, in solemn secrecy that the iron chest which contained the 'fairy flag' was to be forced open next morning; that he had arranged with Mr. Hector Macdonald Buchanan to be there with his tools for that purpose.
>
> I was most anxious to be present, and I asked permission to that effect of Mr. Buchanan (Macleod's man of business), who granted me leave on condition that I should not inform anyone of the name of Macleod that such was intended, and should keep it a profound secret from the chief. This I promised. Next morning, we proceeded to the chamber in the East Turret, where was the iron chest that contained the famous flag, about which there is an interesting tradition.
>
> With great violence, the smith tore open the lid of this iron chest; but, in doing so, a key was found under part of the covering, which would have opened the chest, had it been found in time. There was an inner case, in which was found the flag, enclosed in a wooden box of strongly-scented wood. The flag consisted of a square piece of very rich silk, with crosses wrought with gold thread, and several elf-spots stitched with great care on different parts of it.

Dr Macleod goes on to say that shortly afterwards 'the melancholy news of the death of the young and promising heir of Macleod reached the castle. Norman, the third Norman, was a lieutenant of H.M.S. *Queen Charlotte*, which was blown up at sea, and he and the rest perished. At the same time the rocks called Macleod's Maidens were sold, in the course of that very week, to Angus Campbell of Ensay, and they are still in possession of his grandson.

'A fox in the possession of Lieutenant Maclean, residing in the West Turret of the Castle had young ones.' Macleod ends.

The Brahan Seer's prophecies mentioned so far have concerned the futures of great families. He also made many affecting the people in general. He wrote some two hundred years before the event that 'a chariot without horse or bridle' will go through the Muir of Ord 'when there shall be two churches in the Parish of Ferrintosh, and there is a man with two thumbs on each hand in the Black Isle, and a man with two navels at Duneen'. There is reliable evidence that these last three portents happened when the Muir of Ord railway was built. He also said, 'Long strings of carriages without horses will run between Dingwall and Inverness', and that 'the day will come when fire and water shall run in streams through all the streets and lanes of Inverness'—a prediction the fulfilment of which was quite incomprehensible until piped gas and water was laid.

Another prediction was that the bridge spanning the Ness would be destroyed by flood-waters when crowded with travellers while a man riding a white horse and a pregnant woman were crossing it. In 1849 this partially occurred when a certain Matthew Campbell and a woman were walking over it. The arches collapsed one by one at their heels as they ran across, but they succeeded in gaining the western shore just as the last arch was crumbling. Campbell, however, was not riding a horse, and there is no record to show whether or not the woman was with child.

It has been argued that some prophecies come true through people deliberately setting out to accomplish what has been foretold. This might be so in the case of the Seer's assertion in 1663 that the eight-ton Stone of Petty, on the border between Moray and Culloden, would be discovered 'as far in the sea as it is now away from it and that no one will see it moved or be able to account for its transportation'. During the night of 20th February 1799 the Stone was taken away, and was found the following morning an eighth of a mile offshore. A hurricane was blowing from the sea that night, and it was supposed that this was responsible, together with the action of ice.

Culloden, of course, is a place with grim associations for Scots, and it was the scene of one of the Brahan Seer's most memorable prophecies. When crossing the ground where the battle was to take place, he suddenly started to sob and cried,

'Oh, Drummossie, thy black moor shall, before many generations have passed away, be stained with the best blood in the Highlands. Glad am I that I will not see that day, for it will be a fearful period, heads will be lopped off by the score, and no mercy will be shown or quarter given on either side.' This extraordinary forecast appears in records printed many years before the 1745 rebellion.

Strathpeffer did not become established as a spa until the early nineteenth century. Pointing at the mineral wells, Coinneach Odhar is recorded as having said, in Gaelic, 'Uninviting and disagreeable as it now is, with its thick crusted surface and unpleasant smell, the day will come when it shall be under lock and key, and crowds of pleasure and health seekers shall be seen thronging its portals, in their eagerness to get a draught of its waters'.

The Seer accurately foresaw a large exodus of the population from the Highlands. 'Ancient proprietors of the soil will give way to strange merchant proprietors. The whole Highlands will become one vast deer forest . . . people will emigrate to islands yet unknown which will be discovered in the boundless ocean.'

In view of the current impetus given to commerce in Scotland by North Sea discoveries, Coinneach's further prediction looks like being fulfilled: 'Whisky and dram shops will be so plentiful that one may be met with almost at the head of every plough furrow. . . . Travelling merchants will be so plentiful that a man can scarcely walk a mile on the public highway without meeting one of them.'

Up until recent times people were puzzled by Coinneach's warning that 'a dun hornless cow' would appear in the Minch, off Carr Point in Gairloch, and make a bellow causing the six chimneys of Tigh Dige (the house of the ditch) to fall off. The manor in the Seer's time had no chimneys, but the present one has. Then 'the whole country will become so utterly desolated and depopulated that the crow of a cock shall not be heard', and following this ominous decline 'deer and other wild animals shall be exterminated by horrid black rain'.

However, fortunately that will not be the end of the Highlands, for he goes on, 'The people will then return and take undisturbed possession of the land of their ancestors'.

The atomic submarines now based on the Holy Loch a short distance away enabled one to identify the 'dun hornless cow' as the Brahan Seer's colourful description of something that did not exist when he glimpsed into the future, the 'bellow' as a violent explosion and the 'horrid black rain' as radiation fall-out.

Coinneach also foretold that there would be a great revolution in Scotland, which would occur when the waters of the Beauly had thrice ceased to run, and that on one of these occasions a sturgeon would be caught in the river. It was dried up twice, the second time in 1826, and in 1946 a sturgeon was caught in the estuary. One wonders, in view of Scottish nationalism's growth in strength, and 'Tartan Army' sabotage, what will happen when the Beauly dries up a third time.

If such a revolution should take place, then the following prophecy of the Seer might also come to pass: 'However unlikely it may now appear, the Island of Lewis will be laid waste by a destructive war, which will continue till the contending armies, slaughtering each other as they proceed, shall reach Tarbert in Harris.'

The Brahan Seer's pearl among prophecies was the 'Doom of the Seaforths'. It also proved a boomerang, as it led to his own doom.

Kenneth, the third Earl of Seaforth, paid a visit to Paris on business after the Restoration of King Charles II. Promising to return as soon as he could, he left his wife Isabella behind at Brahan Castle, but the amusements and dissipations of the French capital proved so attractive that he prolonged his stay. The Countess meanwhile was becoming increasingly anxious, as she had received no messages from him for some months. Unable to endure such neglect any longer, she summoned Coinneach from Strathpeffer.

When he arrived at the Castle she commanded him to give her news of her truant husband. The Seer asked where the

Earl was supposed to be, and when told declared he thought he would be able to find him if he were still alive. Then he concentrated his attention on the centre of his famed stone. Suddenly a smile spread over his usually grim countenance. 'Madam,' he is reputed to have told the Countess, 'there is no need to worry concerning your husband's welfare. He is well and merry.' Lady Seaforth was curious to learn more. She asked where exactly he was, and what was he doing.

Coinneach replied that it would be best if he kept silent. She should be content with the knowledge that her lord was thoroughly enjoying himself. But this did not satisfy her. 'Where is he?' she repeated. 'With whom is he, and is he making any preparations for returning home?'

To try to placate her, the other revealed that the Earl was in a magnificent room, in very fine company, and far too agreeably engaged to consider leaving Paris. This response, however, only hurt the Countess's pride and roused her jealousy. How could Kenneth amuse himself and be so happy away from her! She detected almost a sneer in the Seer's expression which disturbed her. This made her determined to discover what precisely Coinneach Odhar had seen in his stone. So she entreated, offered bribes, then cried that if he did not obey her he would suffer punishment.

Irritated by such threats, the Seer became irascible. If she insisted on knowing what would make her miserable, he would tell her the truth. In his vision he had glimpsed the Earl, very elegantly dressed, kneeling before a fair lady with his arm round her waist and her hand pressed to his lips.

The Countess gasped, then flew into a rage. All the wrath with which she would have attacked her husband had he been present was hurled in his absence at Coinneach. Instead of making these disclosures to her in private, he had somewhat maliciously (for he had a spiteful nature) revealed her lord's infidelity before the family and all the principal retainers. To be shamed in public, she regarded as unpardonable. She denounced him as a vile slanderer. For sullying her lord's good name in the hall of his ancestors, and ravaging her feelings, she would close his evil mouth for ever. He must die, and on that very day. She had another reason for desiring this—being secretly wanton, she feared Coinneach might discover that and expose her, too.

When the outraged Seer found that no mercy was to be expected from the vindictive Countess he is said to have once more concentrated his attention on his stone to induce the prophetic mood and then to have predicted, 'I see into the far future and I read the doom of the race of my oppressor. The long-descended line of Seaforth will, ere many generations have passed, end in extinction and in sorrow.

'I see a chief, the last of his house, both deaf and dumb. He will be the father of four sons, all of whom he will follow to the tomb. He will live careworn and die mourning, knowing that the honours of his line are to be extinguished for ever, and that no future chief of the Mackenzies shall bear rule at Brahan or in Kintail.

'After lamenting over the last and most promising of his sons, he himself shall sink into the grave, and the remnant of his possessions shall be inherited by a white-coifed [a white-hooded] lassie from the East, and she is to kill her sister.

'And as a sign by which it may be known that these things are coming to pass, there shall be four great lairds in the days of the last deaf and dumb Seaforth—Gairloch, Chisholm, Grant and Ramsay—of whom one shall be buck-toothed, another hare-lipped, another half-witted and the fourth a stammerer.

'Chiefs distinguished by these personal marks shall be the allies and neighbours of the last Seaforth; and when he looks around him and sees them, he may know that his sons are doomed to death, that his broad lands shall pass away to the stranger, and that his race shall come to an end.' Then the Seer is said to have hurled his stone into Loch Ussie, declaring that whoever should find it would be similarly gifted.

Lashed into vengeful fury by these words, Lady Seaforth ordered Coinneach to be charged before the Presbytery of Chanonry with trafficking with the Devil, and he was sentenced to be burnt alive at Chanonry Point. As he was being led to the stake, fast bound with cords, she declared that, for having had so much unhallowed intercourse, he would never go to Heaven. To which the Brahan Seer gravely retorted, 'I will go to Heaven, but you never shall. After my death, a raven and a dove, flying in opposite directions, will meet and for a second hover over my ashes, on which they will instantly alight. If the raven is foremost, you have spoken truly; but, if the dove, then my hope is well-founded.'

While he spoke the maddened Countess gave the signal for him to be thrown, head foremost, into a barrel of burning tar, the inside of which was studded with sharp spikes driven in from the outside.

Then, tradition alleges, a dove, swiftly followed by a raven, darted down and was first to alight on all that remained of the Brahan Seer.

It is said that on the very day Coinneach was taken away to his cruel fate the Earl himself returned home and learned what was about to take place. Not waiting for food or refreshment, he ran to the stables and rode off at full speed to try to prevent a barbarous murder. Unfortunately, he arrived too late.

A large stone slab, now covered by the sand, lies a few yards east from the road leading from Fortrose to Fort George Ferry, and about two hundred and fifty yards north-west from the lighthouse. It marks the spot where this inhuman tragedy supposedly took place under ecclesiastical supervision.

The Seaforth prophecy was fulfilled with the last Earl, Francis Humberston Mackenzie, born in 1794. When he was twelve years old scarlet fever broke out in the school at which he was boarding. He and some other infected boys were kept isolated in a dormitory. One evening the nurse in charge, who had left it for a few minutes, was alarmed by a cry and hurried back, to find young Francis extraordinarily excited.

After the boy had calmed down he told her that soon after her departure the door opposite to his bed opened to admit a hideous old woman, who stole from bed to bed. Some she passed, but in other cases she crept up to the head and, taking a mallet and peg from the wallet hanging round her neck, she would drive a peg into that boy's forehead.

When she reached young Francis he felt he could not resist or even cry out, and he never could forget in after years the agony felt in the dream when he saw her hand feeling his ears in turn before driving in two nails.

At last she shuffled off and disappeared noiselessly through the same doorway by which she had entered.

The nurse laughed at the boy's tale and told him to go to sleep. When later, noticing how feverish and upset he was, the doctor questioned the nurse, she told him the cause. Concerned, he made the lad repeat the details of his dream and took them down in writing. Later it transpired that all those Francis had described as having pegs driven into their foreheads died, while he himself became stone deaf.

Accounts of this macabre occurrence were related to so many people at the time that it cannot be dismissed as merely an old wives' tale. Towards the end of his life the last Earl's speech became more and more halting, until in his last months he was unable to articulate. Knowledge of the Brahan Seer's prediction made him increasingly apprehensive as to what would happen to his four sons, especially when he discovered that four contemporary Highland lairds as the Seer had said were buck-toothed, hare-lipped, half-witted and a stammerer.

On 11th January 1815 Lord Seaforth died, the last of his race, all his sons having predeceased him. The Seer had foretold that what remained of his estates would be inherited by a white-coifed or white-hooded lassie from the East. The Earl's eldest daughter was married to Admiral Sir Samuel Hood, who died while serving in Indian waters, so that she returned to Scotland in the traditional white clothes of mourning—and a Hood by name.

After some years of widowhood Lady Hood married a Mr Stewart, who assumed the name of Mackenzie and settled on his wife's estates. Thus the lands of the Seaforth passed away from the male line, and later a large portion of them were sold out of the family.

It had also been predicted by Coinneach that the white-hooded lassie would kill her sister. One day when the former Lady Hood was driving her younger sister in a carriage through the woods near Brahan Castle the ponies took fright and bolted. This caused an accident, as a result of which the Hon. Caroline Mackenzie died.

In 1921 James Stewart-Mackenzie was created Baron Seaforth of Brahan, but he died without issue in March 1923, and once more the title became extinct.

1
2
3

5 Cagliostro

To comprehend Cagliostro one must study first the age in which he lived, its disenchantment with conventional religion, its search for something to fill the void. Though European society had lost its faith and become sceptical of the old beliefs, yet it displayed an ingenuous willingness to accept new cults at their face-value. This was particularly true in France, where the aristocracy would acclaim anyone who would distract their attention as they drifted on to the rocks of Revolution. As Charles Kingsley once wrote, 'And so it befell that this 18th century, which is usually held to be the most "materialistic" of epochs, was in fact a most "spiritualistic" one'. Cagliostro could not have appeared on the scene at a more favourable moment when a new *dernier cri* to succeed Mesmerism was being sought.

It was due to Thomas Carlyle's diatribe against him that he was for so long regarded as a complete charlatan. The Sage of Chelsea's essay, first published in *Fraser's Magazine* in 1833, was based entirely on second-hand information about a man who had died the year he was born. He denounced him as a 'King of Liars' and a 'Prince of Scoundrels', with 'a fat, snub, abominable face; dew-lapped, flat-nosed, greasy, full of greediness, sensuality, ox-like obstinacy; the most perfect quack-face produced by the eighteenth century'. But since Carlyle had never met Cagliostro he cannot be regarded as an authority, and such a description hardly corresponds with the impression given by Houdón's bust.

Cagliostro's confessions to the Inquisition near the end of his life were later reproduced by them in the form of a bio-

---

1 Count Cagliostro. *British Library*

2 Cagliostro's wife

3 Madame Du Barry, Louis XV's mistress, in the character of a vestal virgin. In her memoirs the Du Barry recorded how she fainted on staring into Cagliostro's mirror. Did she foresee her coming execution? *The Mansell Collection*

graphy. According to this, his early days were spent as follows. He was born Giuseppe Balsamo at Palermo on 8th June 1743, the son of a small tradesman of Jewish extraction, who died bankrupt shortly after his son's birth. At the age of thirteen the boy was enrolled as a novice with the Brothers of the Misericordia. They discovered his interest in herbs and set him to work assisting the monk-apothecary, who taught him the first principles of chemistry and medicine, and aroused his lifelong interest in alchemy and the search for the philosopher's stone.

But he was soon in trouble, for he had a perverse nature, and, told to read aloud during dinner in the refectory from an edifying martyrology, he substituted for the saints' names those of local courtesans. As a punishment he was confined in a cell, but escaped and made his way to the home of a fond uncle who decided that as he had a gift for drawing he should be given lessons, so as to enable him to earn a living that way.

Freed from monastic restraint, he now spent his nights wenching and gambling. Fond of the theatre, he misused his talents as a calligraphist to forge tickets for himself and for sale to his friends: then he did the same with a will for a loose-living Marquis, so that the latter inherited a fortune. By now he had left his uncle's home for the freedom of lodgings.

Nowhere in southern Europe was there greater interest in the occult than in Sicily, and to amuse himself young Giuseppe began to pose as a seer, and aided by a persuasive manner, plausible patter and a cultivated hypnotic stare, he had success telling fortunes to impressionable girls.

An avaricious and superstitious goldsmith named Marano lived in Palermo. Giuseppe arranged for stories of his having been seen evoking spirits to be passed on to the credulous man, who soon longed to be introduced to him.

When this occurred Marano knelt before the youth begging the loan of his occult powers to help him search for hidden treasure. After obtaining a pledge of secrecy, Balsamo declared that he knew of a cave where such treasure was buried: but it was supposed to be guarded by demons, so it would be necessary to pay a priest to exorcise them. If Marano brought him sixty ounces of gold to cover both this expense and his own recompense he would take him to the place and help dig up the rich hoard.

Some nights later, after parting with the gold, Marano was conducted to the cave where the 'priest' performed the ceremony of exorcism. Then Giuseppe's hirelings, terrifyingly made up to resemble demons, emerged from where they had been concealed to the accompaniment of deafening noises, clouds of sulphur and blue flames. The goldsmith had an apoplectic fit, and Balsamo after paying his accomplices decamped with the remaining ounces of gold.

Realizing that once Marano had recovered he would denounce him to the police, Giuseppe went to Messina, hoping to stay with an old aunt, but found she had died leaving her all to the Church. He went to lodge for the night at an inn. Next day he encountered near the harbour a weirdly dressed Armenian named Althotas, with whom he fell into conversation. He learned that the other was about to board a ship for Egypt, which he described as not only the cradle of scientific knowledge but also a land of mystery where were taught the arts of predicting the future.

His interest roused, Balsamo asked Althotas if he might join him. Although he had defrauded Marano through faked magic, his own small success in fortune-telling had made him realize that there might be some who really possessed strong occult powers. Perhaps in Egypt he could learn how to develop his own, and, most attractive prospect of all, how to transmute baser metals into gold.

But Giuseppe was not to find the philosopher's stone in Althotas's company. Opinions are divided regarding the latter. Was he merely a pedlar quack who tutored the young Sicilian in the concoction of nostrums, mystical patter, legerdemain and ventriloquism, and with whom for four years he wandered through the Near East, hawking universal remedies and charms and telling fortunes, or was he a genuine mystic and magician? Possibly the truth is much of the former and a little of the latter.

When Althotas died Balsamo went to Rome, where he found employment as a calligrapher and in 1768 married Lorenza, the daughter of a copper-smelter. As Giuseppe's income was small, he and his bride started married life in her parents' home. He discovered that Lorenza's angelic appearance rendered her attractive to elderly roués, and so he urged her to earn money from her delicate appeal to jaded appetites. At first she took exception to his suggestion. In time, however, through persistent pleading and wheedling, he managed to wear down her scruples until she followed his precepts, much to the scandalized indignation of her parents, who in the end bundled them out of the house; whereupon Lorenza in despair disregarded her moral misgivings and did as her husband bid her.

The next two years were spent in vagrancy. Disguising themselves as pilgrims, the young couple lived on such alms as Giuseppe's tales of misfortune, assisted by his wife's lachrymose loveliness, could draw from the soft-hearted. They travelled northward to Genoa, then through the south of France to Barcelona and Lisbon, and hence by ship to London, which they reached in the summer of 1771, where a Sir Edward Hales engaged him to decorate the ceilings of his country house. But his employer's daughter, a plain spinster, developed a passion for the Sicilian, with the result that Sir Edward turned him out, so the Balsamos made for Dover and France after a year in England.

On the boat to Calais they encountered a M. Duplessis de la Radotte, agent of the Marquise de Prie. Captivated by Lorenza's charms, he invited them to stay with him in his employer's town house in Paris, where she was soon paying for their keep in kind.

Giuseppe now styled himself the Marquis de Balsamo and, making use of the cachet his fashionable address gave him, bought everything he happened to fancy on credit. When the shopkeepers came clamouring for payment Duplessis seized the opportunity thus provided to evict his charmer's husband, while retaining the unreluctant lady.

Balsamo retaliated by issuing a writ demanding restitution of his conjugal rights and accusing the other of trying to poison him. The court's verdict went in his favour, and Lorenza was imprisoned. They were reconciled, however, and she was released.

We now have a mysterious gap in the story. The couple travelled to Brussels, then went on to Germany, where they disappear from view. In 1776 a Marchese Pellegrini arrived in London with his wife Seraphina. That they were the Balsamos in new plumage is most likely, and the main evidence for such an assumption is the confession later extracted from Cagliostro by the Inquisition, used by them in the biography already mentioned published in Italian under the auspices of the Apostolic Chamber, Rome, in 1791, and also in French at Paris and Strasbourg that year under the title *Vie de Joseph Balsamo, connu sous le nom de comte Cagliostro*.

A fascinating attempt was made in 1910 in a biography by Mr W. R. H. Trowbridge to prove that Cagliostro was not Giuseppe Balsamo, but the case he makes out is not really convincing, neither was the Count's own account of his early life, given in court in 1786 at the time of the Diamond Necklace trial before he was imprisoned by the Inquisition. He then maintained that he spent his childhood in Medina in Arabia, where he was brought up under the name of Acharat with his own apartment in the palace of the Mufti Salahaym, chief of the Mahometan religion, that his governor, the 'noble Althotas', told him his parents were Christian nobles. He had been born in Malta and left an orphan when only about three months old.

Althotas according to this version treated him with all the care and attention of a father, teaching him the sciences and most Eastern languages, and at the age of twelve took him to Mecca for three years. Then he spent a further three in the principal countries of Africa and Asia, and in 1766 visited Malta, where he first wore European dress and was given the title of Count di Cagliostro by the Grand Master, Don Manuele Pinto d'Alfonsea, whom he suspected had known his parents and birthplace. Here Althotas died. He then begged leave of the Grand Master to leave the island in order to travel all over Europe, although Pinto promised him every preferment if he joined the Knights of Malta. In Rome, through a letter of introduction from the Grand Master, Cardinal Orsini became his patron. There in 1770 he met and married Seraphina Feliciani, 'a young lady of quality'.

From here onward Cagliostro became very vague about his activities. Avoiding mention of where he went after Rome, he next described his work in Strasbourg.

This account of his parentage, childhood and youth sounded so incredibly fantastic that the public treated it with derision. Nevertheless, there were those who coloured his story still further by suggesting that he was the Grand Master's illegitimate son by a Turkish lady who had been made captive by a Maltese galley, while others pretended that they knew from an authentic source that he was the only son of the Prince of Trebizond. His father having been murdered by his seditious subjects, he was conveyed by a trusty friend to Medina, where the cherif was broadminded enough to have him educated in the faith of his Christian parents.

The Pellegrinis rented a furnished apartment in the then fashionable Whitcomb Street, where the Marchese spent much of his time studying chemistry and mathematics and assiduously experimenting in a room he set up as a laboratory.

Soon their talkative landlady was spreading intriguing stories about her tenant, who had now decided he preferred to be known under what he claimed to be another of his titles, that of Count Cagliostro. According to her gossip, he had discovered the secret of transmutation and owned an ancient manuscript that provided an infallible key to winning numbers in lotteries and the like. Lotteries were then being regularly held in London, and an adventurer masquerading as Lord Scott, and a Miss Fry who pretended to be his wife, persuaded the landlady to introduce them to the Count.

Cagliostro later, in his *Letter to the English people*, gives his version of what then happened.

I had in my possession a manuscript which contained very curious secrets, and among others different Kabalistic operations by the aid of which the author claimed to be able to test the lottery with invariable success. To submit chance to calculation appeared to me to be an absolutely unlikely thing; however, as I had long since contracted the habit of not pronouncing judgment upon matters not known to me, I was willing to try if, according to the rules indicated in my manuscript, I could succeed in divining some of the numbers which were to emerge from the Wheel of Fortune.

The drawing of the English lottery commenced on the 14th November: I jokingly suggested the first number. None of my acquaintances wished to play on it, but chance decreed that the number actually turned up. I suggested for the 16th, No.20: Scott risked a little, and won. I suggested for the 17th, No.25: No.25 turned up, and Scott won a hundred pounds. I suggested for the 18th, Nos.55 and 57, both of which turned up . . . .

One can judge of my astonishment on seeing chance so instantly follow calculations which I had thought chimerical. Whatever might be the cause of this extraordinary fact, I considered I ought from delicacy of feeling to refrain from giving any number in future. Scott and the woman he said was his wife pestered me in vain; I resisted all their importunities . . . .

Then apparently the woman called when Cagliostro was out and told Seraphina that 'Lord' Scott was an impostor to whom she was not even married, her real name being Miss Fry, and that he had decamped with all the lottery winnings, leaving her with their three children. When Seraphina repeated this to Cagliostro he sent Miss Fry a guinea and suggested No.8 for 7th December. She then sold and pawned everything remaining to her and put all the money on that number, winning nine hundred pounds. He discovered later that she had passed on the tip to Scott, who won seven hundred guineas.

But Miss Fry's greed was not satisfied. She busied herself with efforts to obtain new numbers. First she tried to gain Seraphina's support by giving her a gold box containing herbal snuff for a complaint from which the Countess suffered. The box proved to be double-bottomed, and also contained a diamond necklace, which she found only after the woman had left.

Cagliostro wrote that when his wife told him of her discovery he would have sent the box back to Miss Fry the same instant, if he had not 'feared to afflict and humiliate her'.

The Cagliostros moved in January 1777 to the first floor of a house in Suffolk Street. When Miss Fry heard this she hastened to rent the second floor. Now it was almost impossible for the Count to avoid seeing her. She cajoled and she wept and invented one hard-luck tale after another to try to make him give her winning numbers.

According to Cagliostro, his assistant, Vitelli, often saw Miss Fry and 'Lord' Scott in secret.

> He had had the indiscretion to speak to them of the chemical experiments which I had let him witness; and as he was naturally presumptuous, he had assured them that if he could lay hands on a certain powder which I used in my experiments, he could in a very short time make his fortune and that of his friends. As to the lottery numbers, he likewise claimed that if he had in his hands the manuscript I possessed, he could predict them quite as well as myself. 'Lord' Scott and Miss Fry had enough command over Vitelli to persuade him to point out to them the cupboard where I had shut up the golden box that contained the powder and the manuscript. From that moment the couple planned to rob me of everything and compel me to communicate to them the knowledge with which they credited me. For this purpose they associated themselves with a Mr. Raynold, an attorney, who has since undergone the infamous punishment of the pillory for swindling and perjury.

A writ was taken out against Cagliostro, accusing him of owing Miss Fry £190 he had borrowed from her. He was arrested and forced to spend the night in the sheriff's house. Meanwhile the conspirators had broken into the cupboard and had stolen the gold box containing the powder and the Kabalistic manuscript. However, they could not understand the latter or discover how to use the powder, so Raynold, acting for Miss Fry, procured a warrant and had the Cagliostros arrested on a charge of practising witchcraft.

The legal battle that ensued, with Miss Fry making one false accusation after another, is too complicated a story to tell briefly. Suffice it to say that when the Cagliostros left for Brussels the Count had no more than fifty pounds in cash and some jewels. The money, he says, took him to Brussels 'where Providence awaited me, to rebuild the edifice of my fortune'. He later claimed that during his eighteen months in London he had lost through various frauds about three thousand guineas.

While in London he had made contact with Masonic circles. The particular Order he wished to join was that of Strict Observance, which was Continental in its origin and whose members consisted of French and Italian tradesmen, valets and other servants living in Soho. He was admitted into the Espérance Lodge in April 1777, and the ceremony took place in the King's Head in Gerrard Street. The candidate described himself as 'Joseph Cagliostro, Colonel of the 3rd Regiment of Brandenburg'. The Christian name he gave is, of course, the Anglicized form of Giuseppe, and it is significant that after this he changed it to that of Alessandro.

Two other clues suggest that he and Balsamo were the same person. The surname of Balsamo's maternal great-uncle was Cagliostro, and that of his maternal great-grandfather was Martello. The 'Count' was to boast of descent from Charles Martel, and it seems obvious why he chose a great man with such a name.

The Espérance Lodge proceedings upset him. He was harnessed to a rope and hoisted to the ceiling, then without warning allowed to fall onto the floor. Next a bandage was tied round his eyes, a loaded pistol placed in his hands, and the order was given, 'Blow out your brains!'

His hesitation brought derisory cries of 'Coward!' To encourage him the Master now required him to take the oath. An unloaded pistol was put into his hand. He pulled the trigger. As he did so another pistol was fired close behind him and he was hit on the head. The bandage was then removed and he was told that he was now a Freemason.

According to his Inquisition biographer, Cagliostro by chance bought an unpublished manuscript about Egyptian Masonry which he came across among some odds and ends in an old shop. Its magical practices and mystical aspirations fascinated him, kindling his imagination and giving him a new ambition that spurred him into evolving his own system with it as model.

This, of course, he kept secret, professing that this form of Masonry was that of the prophets Enoch and Elias, and that he had acquired his knowledge of its ancient traditions during his travels in Egypt. With the passage of time it had been forgotten, and he had resolved to revive it with all its original impressive ceremonial.

From England Cagliostro went to The Hague, where he addressed the local Lodge of Strict Observance and took the opportunity to preach for the first time the gospel of his Egyptian rite to its members. It seems that they were most impressed. He assured them that through its principles and practice they could regain the pristine innocence man had possessed before original sin. There were other benefits, too, of physical rejuvenation, long life and wealth. Remembering his experience in London, he claimed that common Masonry had degenerated into mere buffoonery. It was wrong that women should still be excluded from its mysteries. The time had now arrived to restore the glory of Masonry and allow its benefits to be enjoyed by both sexes.

People of all religions could be admitted to membership of the Order providing they believed in the immortality of the soul and were already Freemasons. There were three grades: apprentice, companion and master Egyptian—the latter were given the names of the Hebrew prophets.

To himself he had assigned the title of Grand Cophta,

which he said was that of Enoch, the first Grand Master of Egyptian Masonry. In this capacity he was empowered to bestow upon those who attained the highest grade the secret of angelic evocation. When anyone was admitted into this class, a boy or girl in a state of virgin innocence acted as a medium. This *pupille* (pupil) or *colombe* (dove) was given power over the spirits governing the seven planets and surrounding the throne of the Eternal, Anael, Michael, Raphaël, Gabriel, Uriel, Zobiachel and Anachiel.

This use of children as mediums goes back to the earliest times. Roger Bacon wrote that God allowed 'daemons to exhibit themselves by reflections in polished bodies, so that boys looking into a mirror can see the spectral appearances of things stolen, the persons who took them, and the places whither they have been carried'.

Camerarius mentions a man living in Nuremberg who owned a crystal from which he could learn what he wished by employing as his seer a boy or girl who had not reached the age of puberty. He wrote that not only did this stone 'reveal events, but it solved all the doubts and perplexities of learned men'. It was smashed by Camerarius, who feared that his friend would imperil his soul.

In Cagliostro's Egyptian rite the *pupille* or *colombe*, dressed in a long white robe, adorned with blue ribbons and a red scarf, would be rendered clairvoyant through his breathing in the young medium's face from brow to chin while he or she and the other members prayed. Then the child would sit in a tabernacle hung with white and lit within by three tapers. This had a window in its door, through which responses were given as to whether the planetary spirits and Moses had agreed to the elevation of the candidate to the rank of master Egyptian.

Women on joining became Sibyls. Their Grand Mistress was called the Queen of Sheba, and she could promote suitable ones to the advanced degree of *Maîtresse Agissante*. The Queen of Sheba was, of course, Cagliostro's wife, Seraphina. She, like the Grand Cophta, initiated neophytes by breathing upon them and performing a form of exorcism that prepared them for moral regeneration. This was followed by a short exhortation ending with the phrase 'In the names of Helios, Mene and Tetragrammaton'—words signifying the Sun, the Moon and the four letters by which God is designated in Hebrew.

As a result of the interest aroused by Cagliostro's discourse, a lodge of Egyptian Masonry was founded at The Hague, open to both sexes, and of which the Countess was appointed Grand Mistress of the women's section. Her husband now dreamed of a far-flung network of such Lodges with himself as its high priest, and this seems to have brought home to him the need to maintain appropriate standards. Certainly from now on he seems to have refrained from perpetrating petty frauds.

Next he visited the Freemasons of Nuremberg, then of Leipzig, where a banquet was held in his honour, after which he lectured brilliantly on Egyptian Masonry, stressing how superior were its ideals and rites compared with those of the Lodge whose guest he was, and finally pointed dramatically at its Grand Master, a man named Scieffort, and warned, 'If you do not adopt the Egyptian rite, you will feel the weight of God's hand before the month ends'.

Scieffort's suicide shortly following this prophecy caused consternation, and made Leipzig buzz with talk of the mysterious stranger with the piercing eyes and the prophetic tongue. He was now certain to be received with awe and respect by the Lodges of the Order of Strict Observance wherever he went. The Freemasons of Danzig and Königsberg in particular tried hard to persuade him to remain permanently with them. As the Lodges there were entirely dedicated to the practice and study of occult phenomena, he must no doubt have provided them with convincing displays of supernormal powers.

In this manner, lauded from Lodge to Lodge, he came in March 1779 to Mittau, the capital of the Duchy of Courland, where the most important family, the von Medems, gave him an approving welcome. Marshal von Medem was the head of the town's Masonic Lodge, and he and his brother had spent their whole lives studying magic and alchemy.

Some days after his arrival Cagliostro told them that he was a Freemason sent by his superiors to the North on important business.

The Countess Elsa von der Recke, the Marshal's daughter, wrote in her memoirs that she found their visitor 'the most wonderful man' she had ever met.

> He and his wife inspired my aunt, my cousin and myself, with high conceptions of a Lodge of Adoption. He also expressed himself as wanting to found this Lodge here out of friendship for us because he believed we could be worthy companions in this secret society, which strives for the moral regeneration of mankind. This idea pleased us and we decided to become the foundresses of this society in our fatherland under his leadership. We made one condition that only those who were Freemasons should be members.

The Marshal, however, and Elsa's uncle were unco-operative, so the three women reluctantly told him he must abandon the project.

> Then he made some chemical experiments in my father's house before him, my uncle and Herr von Howen, and assured them that he would impart some of these secrets to the newly established Lodge, and as a proof that he possessed the higher powers, he would make a magical experiment in their presence with a six-year-old lad.

The day came and, according to the Countess, Cagliostro employed the son of her dead brother as a *pupille*. Having anointed the head and left hand of the boy with the 'oil of wisdom', he wrote some mystical characters on both, and told him to sit at a table on which stood a bowl of water, surrounded by six candles, and to stare into it. Cagliostro then drew a magic circle and made passes with a naked sword, followed by incantations.

He had earlier asked the Marshal in private what kind of vision he would wish his grandson to have. Von Medem thought it should be one that could not frighten the child, and suggested that it be of his mother and sister who had remained behind in their house some distance away.

About ten minutes after the conjuration the boy called out that he saw his mother and sister. Then Cagliostro asked, 'What is your sister doing?' and the other answered, 'She is pressing her hands to her heart as if in pain'.

After a while the child cried out, 'Now my sister is kissing my brother, who has come home.' This astonished von Medem, for the elder grandson was absent on a visit to friends seven miles away and not expected back for some days.

Cagliostro ended the séance and suggested that the Marshal should visit his daughter-in-law and find out the truth for himself. It was as seen in the vision. Just before her brother's unexpected return, the girl had such strong palpitations of the heart that it made her feel quite ill.

The three men were so impressed that they changed their minds and became strong supporters of their strange visitor, with the result that a Lodge of Egyptian Masonry was founded. Now he gave them daily lectures on magic, instructing them never to mention what he told them after his departure 'except on Lodge-days and only in the inner circle of the initiated'.

The Countess told him that she had lost interest in worldly things following her favourite brother's death, and had spent many a night in prayer in the churchyard in order to become worthy to see her brother's apparition, but in vain. Could Cagliostro help her to attain her wish?

He replied that he had no power over the dead, but only 'over the intermediate spirits of creation, which, as the Scriptures say, are sent for the service of man and are subject to him'. Through these, he enjoyed instructive intercourse with higher spirits, but he had not the power to procure visions for grown persons. Besides, he dared never summon spirits merely as a pastime. If he made his evocations only to satisfy the curiosity of others, as from personal pride, then evil spirits would soon creep in among the helpful ones.

The Path of Magic which she was thinking of treading, and

to which she was now initiated as a member of the Lodge, was extremely dangerous. 'If anything else than the wish to do good attracts you to Mysticism, go no further', he warned. 'Otherwise temporal as well as eternal misery will be your portion.'

She assured him that nothing but a longing for self-perfection and the wish, where possible, to be able to work for the good of thousands, led her to this Path.

'Excellent', he commented. 'I am not at this moment quite convinced of the purity and sincerity of your intentions, but I shall know in a few hours through my Master, how you think.'

Next day Cagliostro told her that his Master had assured him her intention to devote herself to magic was a noble one. In order to lead her more quickly to the Sacred Mysteries he would if possible that night by means of a magic dream try to procure instruction for her through her dead brother's spirit. When she went to sleep she must firmly resolve to speak with him about magic when he appeared.

'I will deliver a sealed paper to your father in which there will be a question to which I want to obtain an answer through your dream. So remember as much as ever you can of the conversation you will have with your brother.'

That evening before they parted Cagliostro took the Countess by the left hand and her father by the right hand to establish rapport with them, then gave the Marshal a sealed triangular paper and told him to promise not to break the seal until she had dreamt of her brother.

But that night the Countess never slept at all, neither could she the following one. This somewhat nettled Cagliostro, who possibly had hoped that through suggestion she would in her state of mental excitement dream of her brother. He said, she recorded, that he had supposed she had greater aptitude for Mysticism than she in reality had, that she might no longer count on having the dream, and asked for the return of the sealed paper.

The Grand Cophta needed to make some spectacular revelation if he were to maintain his position. Inspired no doubt by his youthful imposture with the goldsmith in the cave, he asserted at the next meeting of the Egyptian Lodge that Anachiel had revealed to him the whereabouts of the spot where centuries previously a most puissant wizard had buried his magical instruments and manuscripts, together with gold and silver. This was now being sought by evil necromancers, one of whom had already been for some time in Courland, but he had not yet been able to discover from his subject-spirits where the great magician had buried these things which were so important for humanity's welfare.

If the 'Great Architect of the Universe' so willed it, Cagliostro hoped he would have the good fortune of unearthing and keeping these important treasures.

> This would be a most dangerous undertaking, for all the evil spirits were in an uproar and were attacking him with the object of converting him into a necromancer, and by this means to let the Evil Principle get the upper hand. For should the magical treasures fall into the hands of the black magicians, the most grievous consequences for the world would ensue and centuries would pass before our earth would recover from the plagues with which these disturbances were connected.
>
> So we ought to join our prayers with his and entreat the eternal source of all Good for strength for him to withstand the evil spirits and to abide true in faith. After he had made this disclosure to us, he pointed out to us on a chart the neighbourhood where these things lay buried, and described to us in exact terms the place in the forest, this without his having been in Wilzen. My uncle was not a little astonished that Cagliostro knew a place so exactly, which his eyes had never seen and his feet had never trod.

Then Cagliostro told them that earlier, he had by the strength of his spirit translated himself to Wilzen, taken everything in at a glance, and what he had just confided to them he had learned from the spirit who there watched over the treasure and magical things. He assured her uncle that the treasure which he would unearth there should be his, but the magical things were for himself or, rather, for his Master.

Some days later they set out to Wilzen. 'When we were not far from Wilzen he spoke, and prayed to himself quietly in a foreign language,' wrote Elsa,

> read something out of a little red book, and when we saw a wood, he said, with fiery enthusiasm: 'There, there lie the writings buried! Thou, Great Architect of the world, help me to complete the work!' After a time, he added: 'These magical writings and treasures are watched by the strongest spirits and only spirits can take them away. Whether I am to be the fortunate one, only He knows who sent me. But I will bind the spirits who guard the treasures in such a way that any followers and helpers can undertake nothing without my knowledge, even if I should be three hundred miles away.'

The Countess continues that immediately after his arrival in Wilzen Cagliostro went with her father, uncle and von Holzen into the forest, and when they came to a broken tree he announced that this was the spot where everything lay buried. 'There he made an evocation for himself and bound one of his spirits to the place.'

Next morning they returned and he held 'another magic experiment' with Elsa's nephew behind a screen and attended by all the members of the Lodge. He bid the *pupille* make the spirits show him the treasure. The boy saw the earth open, revealing a staircase and a long passage.

Cagliostro ordered, 'Go down. Count the steps aloud and then tell me what you see.'

Elsa goes on that the child hidden behind the screen now counted the steps and they could hear his footfalls. Then he said, 'Here are many gold rods—gold and silver coins—all kinds of iron things—written papers—and red powder.'

The Grand Cophta then ordered the vision to disappear, made another conjuration, and the *pupille* then saw 'seven very beautiful men, all in long white robes'. One had a red heart on his breast and the others red crosses and something written on their foreheads, but he could not read what it was.

These men were then bidden by Cagliostro to guard the treasure, after which he told the boy to embrace all seven and let himself be kissed by them all. They heard fourteen kisses. The apparitions were dismissed and a great iron nail, following consecration by Cagliostro, was fastened above where the magic documents were supposed to be lying.

Apart from these open-air séances Cagliostro also gave lectures to the Lodge of Adoption. Elsa comments, 'Sometimes he said sublime things, on other occasions there would be so much nonsense mixed up with his talk that we were all confused.' Then one day he declared that angels sometimes fell in love with holy women, and that not only the demigods of Greece and Christ but he himself was conceived in this way. Shocked by such presumption, the Countess, who was very religious, became convinced that he had become possessed by an evil spirit. She told her father she would not attend any more séances, but he persuaded her to change her mind. However, when Cagliostro, unaware of her defection, opened the meeting with a talk on love potions Elsa von der Recke felt confirmed in her suspicions, and left.

Now aware of the position, he thought it wise to move on while he was still held in high regard by most of Courland's aristocracy, and especially because the spirits had not allowed the treasure to be excavated and the Lodge was becoming restive about this.

So he told them that he had been ordered by his Master to go to St Petersburg. The Countess writes:

> Before his departure he revealed to us that he was neither a Spaniard nor was he 'Count Cagliostro' but that at the bidding of his Masters he had had to take this name and title. He said that he had served them for some time under the name of Frederick Gualdo; he was still obliged to conceal from us his proper rank and name, but perhaps he might show himself in St. Petersburg in his real greatness. . . . Also, he could not now state the time when the magic documents and treasures of Wilzen should be raised. Yet he was

glad that he had anticipated the agent of the Evil Principle, and had so removed the magic treasures that these things could never come into the hands of necromancers.

Armed with letters of introduction from Marshal von Medem to some of the most important people in Russia, he went away to St Petersburg, where he made an unfortunate début. He had trouble in finding the right sort of child to act as medium, so, impatient to make a start, he resorted to trickery.

Staying in the same lodgings as the Cagliostros was a forward little girl, an actress's niece, who, he decided, was sharp enough to co-operate with him in another way, though she had no clairvoyant gift. He began with his customary elaborate ritual. Behind a screen decorated with cabalistic symbols sat the *colombe* gazing into a jug of water. She amazed the distinguished gathering with her descriptions of the spirits and places she saw. But after the séance was over, while the Grand Cophta in all his fantastic finery was lecturing on the merits of Egyptian Masonry, a suspicious sceptic led the girl into an anteroom and frightened her into admitting that she had seen nothing in the water, and that Cagliostro had taught her beforehand what to say.

After this exposure no one was interested in supporting his plan to found an Egyptian Lodge in the capital, so he turned his attention to medicine and tried to build up a reputation as a healer. If one is to believe the Empress Catherine's Scottish physician, his clients were few and his cures fewer. 'A bald major entrusted his head to his care, but he could not make a single hair grow. A blind gentleman who consulted him remained blind; while a deaf Italian, into whose ears he dropped some liquid, became still more deaf.'

As within a short while he was to establish himself at Strasbourg as a healer with almost miraculous powers, it is likely that malice prompted such an account and that the Scot, scenting a rival, did all he could to discredit him. Certainly it was due to the man's attacks that the Cagliostros departed for

Warsaw, where thanks to the von Medems' recommendation they were befriended by an eager occultist, Prince Poninski, with whom they stayed and who took them to Court, where Seraphina's blonde beauty enchanted the men and where Alessandro became a great favourite with King Stanislas Augustus, who never wearied of discussing divination and the search for the philosopher's stone with him. This, as might be expected, bred jealousy and enmity among the royal entourage. An incident occurred as a result, the outcome of which enhanced Cagliostro's reputation.

The Marquis de Laborde, the French Fermier-Général, who was in Warsaw at the time, wrote in his published correspondence that one day in the King's presence a Court lady declared she believed Cagliostro to be an impostor, and was so certain of it that she defied him to tell her of events in her past of which only she knew.

The King passed on this challenge to the Grand Cophta, who replied that if she would meet him he would cause her 'the greatest surprise in her life'. Laborde goes on:

> The proposal was accepted, and the Count told the lady all that she thought it impossible for him to know. The surprise this occasioned filled her with a burning desire to know what was to happen to her in the future.
>
> At first he refused to tell her, but yielding to her entreaty, and perhaps to gratify the curiosity of the King, he said: 'You will soon make a long journey, in the course of which your carriage will meet with an accident, and, whilst you are waiting for the repairs to be made, the manner in which you are dressed will excite such merriment in the crowd that you will be pelted with apples. You will go from there to some famous watering-place, where you will meet a man of high birth, to whom you will shortly afterwards be wedded. There will be an attempt to prevent your marriage, which will cause you to be foolish enough to make over to him your fortune. You will be married in a city in which I shall be, and, in spite of your efforts to see me, you will not succeed. You are threatened with great misfortunes, but here is a

talisman by which you may avoid them, so long as you keep it.'

The Marquis ends that these predictions were all fulfilled. 'I have this on the authority of several persons, as well as the lady herself.'

Cagliostro, however, despite this successful fortune-telling, did not remain long in the King's good books. He had made a promising start by converting Poninski and his friends to Egyptian Masonry and founding a Lodge within a month of his arrival. They had, however, no interest in his mystical ideals. They wanted instead visible demonstrations of his occult powers. If he possessed, as he claimed, the secret of the philosopher's stone, then let him prove it by making some gold in their presence.

The Grand Cophta agreed to do this. Madame Böhmer in her memoirs records what then happened. 'A day was set for the operation, and a suspicious courtier, knowing that he had as an assistant a young girl, bribed her. . . . "Keep your eye", she told the courtier, "on his thumb, which he holds in the hollow of his hand to conceal the piece of gold he will slip into the crucible".' Cagliostro as a result was caught in the act and flung out of the King's palace.

On 26th June 1780 Alessandro and Seraphina once more fled, to appear next in Strasbourg on 19th September. In the interim, it seems, he had gone to Frankfort-on-Main, where overtures were made to him by Knigge, one of the leaders of a revolutionary society—who was also a fellow-member of the Order of Strict Observance—that he should join the *Illuminées* as a secret agent. Cagliostro agreed, and in a grotto near Frankfort he was initiated into that underground revolutionary fraternity, whose main purpose was the overthrow of all monarchies and the Papacy. He received a large sum of money for propaganda purposes and was told to proceed to Strasbourg, where his arrival caused a sensation, for he entered the city like royalty, in a magnificent carriage, startlingly dressed in a gold-braided and gem-encrusted blue coat, with his multipigtailed hair in a net, while Seraphina, radiant with diamonds, sat beside him looking the personification of angelic innocence. Whenever he saw a beggar or a cripple he waved and threw him or her a handful of coins.

Having failed to become the favourite of Empress or King, he was now courting the common people, and endeared himself to them from the day of arrival by going to live in a tobacconist's shop in one of the most squalid quarters, and later lodging with a canon's caretaker, where, the Baroness d'Oberkirch wrote, 'He slept in an armchair and lived on cheese'. At any time of day or night, he was accessible to the needy and the unfortunate. Their welfare he put first and his convenience last. No one went away empty-handed, and he gave them as well comfort and hope.

A contemporary account of a séance he held in Strasbourg records that, having announced he was ready to answer any question put to him, a lady asked the age of her husband. To this the *colombe* made no reply, and the sitters were enormously impressed when the inquirer admitted that she was unmarried. Another demanded an answer to a question within a sealed letter she held in her hand. The girl medium at once read in the water of a carafe the words 'You shall not obtain it'. The letter was opened and the question found to be whether the commission in the army she had solicited for her son would be accorded her. As the reply was at least indicative of the question, it was received with applause.

One suspects that Cagliostro to enhance his efforts was also practising ventriloquism, for this account continues that a judge who suspected Cagliostro's answers were the result of some trick secretly sent his son to his house to find out what his wife was doing at the time. When he had departed the father put his question to the Grand Cophta. The medium read nothing in the carafe, but a voice answered that the lady was playing cards with two of her neighbours. 'This mysterious voice, which was produced by no visible organ, terrified the company; and when the son of the judge returned and confirmed the response of the oracle, several ladies were so frightened that they withdrew.'

A possible explanation is that the *colombe*'s clairvoyance having failed in this instance, Cagliostro then had one of his flashes of second sight, and for effect conveyed the revelation by throwing his voice.

The memoirs of the period are full of stories of his accurate fortune-telling while in Strasbourg, but he scored his most remarkable success there as a healer of the sick. As he always saw his patient in private, it is not possible to explain for certain how he achieved his cures. He is known to have spent a great deal of time in alchemical studies, so it is likely that his magic balsams and powders were made up from the ingredients prescribed in old books. The Marquise de Créquy had a potion he gave her analysed by a chemist, who stated that it consisted of a mixture of 'aromatic herbs and potable gold'.

The most likely explanation, however, is that he cured not by means of drugs but through convincing patients, with confident voice and hypnotic gaze, that they were to recover, and through the reputation he had already gained as a worker of miracles. Occasionally his claims verged on the incredible, such as when he boasted that in Turkey he had restored to health eleven million people afflicted with plague within three months.

A service that he rendered to a wealthy banker from Basle, Sarrasin, was to prove very useful to him later in adversity. This was to make the old man a father after many years of childless marriage.

Much information on Cagliostro's life in Strasbourg is contained in a letter dated 7th June 1781, written by Laurent Blessig to the Countess Elsa von der Recke in Courland. He says the Count had stated that on being admitted into a Brotherhood he had taken an oath to wander through the world for the betterment of humanity, and to give to all in need without fee or reward the benefit of the secrets he had himself been taught.

On arrival he had not at first announced himself as a physician.

Nobody expected that of a Count, which title, as he quite plainly gave everyone to understand, was founded not on birth but on his secret knowledge. Suddenly people learnt that there was a foreign philanthropist in their midst, who devoted himself specially to the sick, and provided not only medicines, but often money as well as other aid. Now gradually, one after another, poor people timidly came to him. But he received them affectionately; gave them essences, elixirs and other medicines; relieved many of fevers and other complaints; and even personally visited the very sick in their homes. His fame increased, and soon not only his rooms, but also the stairs and the passages of the house were besieged by those seeking help. He was somewhat easy and sanguine in promises of cure and this gave the sick all the more encouragement. . . . When arriving at a diagnosis, he examined pulse, complexion, gait, look of the eyes and every movement of the body. He paid much attention to the equinox, and at that season prepared most of his medicines.

Certainly among the vast number treated many have not turned out well, especially with regard to deafness and blindness; however, good fortune in many instances, the strangeness, the peculiarity of the matter, his refusal to take money, all made him the subject of every conversation, and with many the object of the greatest wonder.

At this time a secretary of our Commandant, the Marquis de la Salle, became sick with gangrene, and was given only twenty-four hours to live by his physician. On the request of the Commandant himself, Cagliostro took his case in hand and to everybody's astonishment as good as entirely set him on his feet again. Now his most brilliant period began. All those of general's rank, all who are foremost or who set themselves up to be prominent, daily visited him. The ladies did the same. Cagliostro was taken everywhere. It was the fashion to talk of him, to need him, and to praise him. An incredible number of foreigners came to him here from all parts. Some begged him to allow himself to be taken into consultation with our best physicians, but this he always refused, as indeed he had no other names for all doctors except those borrowed from the animal kingdom. If, on the other hand, the physicians are justified in their criticisms, I cannot now decide. . . . He is, for example, very free in prescribing Extract of Saturn and that indeed in very large doses (as in general with many of his remedies). It has been shown that this Sugar of Lead has an instantaneous effect with wounds and other complaints where prompt aid is necessary, but that it also leaves a certain stiffness as a rule, and not seldom brings on the unfortunate Colic of Poitou.

In various news sheets and placards in our neighbourhood satires have been published against him. His vogue has now declined; at the present time he receives only three times a week and this only at stated hours. He has left in the middle of their treatment several foreigners who came here to consult him and others he has refused to treat.

He is a very spirited man, very attractive, cheerful, frugal, energetic, conscious of himself and therefore speaks of Princes and with Princes like a man who can do them good, not they him. He speaks good Italian, and broken French; he would not, however, speak Arabic with Professor Norberg of Upsala who comes from Constantinople. One would suppose that the man has a far-reaching plan for which Strasbourg is altogether too small a theatre. Strasbourg lies on the road to France; perhaps he wants his fame to precede him and expects the King to call him of his own initiative. He speaks much of his acquaintance with Louis XV and of the Russian Empress. People have observed that he has received no money from anyone here by way of exchange or in cash, and that he always pays exactly, generously, and in advance; some suppose that he is an emissary of the ex-Jesuits.

The latter had been officially suppressed by the Pope for political intriguing.

This account is of particular interest for two things: the obvious invention about Cagliostro's having known King Louis XV, who had died in 1774, six years before the Count appeared in Strasbourg, and the fact that he avoided conversing in Arabic with the Professor, which suggests that the story of his having been brought up in Medina was another fabrication.

So far as his own personal advancement was concerned, the highlight of Cagliostro's stay in Strasbourg was his meeting with Cardinal Louis de Rohan, Grand Almoner of France and Prince of the Holy Roman Empire, whose interest was always roused by anything to do with magic. When reports of the activities of the larger-than-life character who had arrived in Strasbourg reached the Cardinal he invited Cagliostro to visit him, but with supreme aplomb the Grand Cophta replied, 'If His Eminence is ill, let him come to me and I will cure him, but if he is well, he has no need of me nor I of him'. It was a reply that proved the Count to be a clever psychologist. If the Cardinal were arrogantly self-centred and likely to be a nuisance it would offend him, and that would end the matter. But if he were a true student of the occult, and the sort of person likely to be easily influenced, Cagliostro felt that his curiosity would only be stimulated by this response. He was proved right, for the Cardinal pretended to be ill, which gained him a call from the mysterious healer. A close but ill-omened friendship developed as a result. Soon de Rohan, who longed to discover the philosopher's stone, had installed Alessandro in a laboratory at the top of his château. Here they worked together, for the Count had declared that the Cardinal's soul was worthy of his, and that he would confide to him all his secrets.

What particularly impressed the Cardinal at the beginning of their association was how Cagliostro saved the life of his cousin, the Prince de Soubise, whose doctors had pronounced him incurable. What he did when alone for an hour with the patient is not recorded. He then sent for de Rohan and said, 'If my prescription is followed, in two days the Prince will leave his bed. Within a week he will be able to take a drive, and within three go to Court.' He returned later that same day with a phial, and himself dispensed ten drops of the liquid it contained into the sick man's mouth. As he left he told the Cardinal, 'Tomorrow I will give your cousin five drops, the day after two, and you will see that he will sit up the same evening'.

The Baroness d'Oberkirch describes in her memoirs how she and her husband were visiting the Cardinal de Rohan in his château of Savorne when a footman announced, 'His Excellency the Count Cagliostro'. She gives this impression of him:

> He was not exactly handsome, yet never was a more remarkable face presented for my observation. He had in particular a look of almost supernatural depth; I cannot describe his eyes; it was like fire and ice together; he was both attractive and repellent; he inspired both dread and invincible curiosity. One could draw two different portraits of him and both would be like him, yet they would be as dissimilar as possible.
>
> On his shirt, his watch-chain, his fingers, he wore diamonds of magnificent size and purity; if they were not paste, they must have been worth a king's ransom. He pretended to have made them himself. All this frippery stank of charlatanism a mile away.

The Cardinal hurried towards Cagliostro and greeted him effusively.

> The couple then approached us. I had stood up with the bishop, but I quickly sat down again, not wishing to let the adventurer imagine that I was paying any attention to him. Soon, however, I was compelled to take notice of him. . . .
>
> After five minutes, and a little resistance from me and Monsieur d'Oberkirch, His Eminence managed to bring us directly into conversation with each other; he was tactful enough not to mention my name. . . . Cagliostro looked at me steadily; my husband signalled to me to leave, but I did not notice it, I was only conscious of that look boring into my bosom like a drill—I cannot express it otherwise. Suddenly he interrupted Monsieur de Rohan, who incidentally was overflowing with delight, and said abruptly to me: 'Madame, you have no mother, you hardly ever knew your mother, but you have a daughter. You are the only daughter of your family, and you will have no children beyond the one you already have.'

The Baroness, offended at his audacity, did not answer him and rose to leave, and so did the bishop and her husband. But the Cardinal approached the latter and said amiably, 'Monsieur de Cagliostro is a savant who must not be treated as if he were a nobody. Remain a few moments, my dear Baron, and allow Madame d'Oberkirch to answer. . . . Baroness, tell us if Monsieur de Cagliostro is wrong, tell us, I beg of you.'

She wrote:

> 'He is certainly not wrong about the past,' I replied reluctantly. 'And I am not wrong about the future either', he announced in a voice so metallic that it vibrated like a trumpet muted with crape.
>
> I must admit that at that moment I had an irresistible desire to consult this man; what withheld me was the fear of annoying my husband. . . . That day will remain irrevocably engraved upon my memory. I found it difficult to tear myself away from a fascination which today, though I cannot deny it, I can hardly understand. I have not done with Cagliostro, and what I have now to say is at least as singular and ever more inexplicable. He predicted the death of the Empress Maria Theresa in a particular manner, and at the very hour at which she gave up the ghost. Monsieur de Rohan told me so the same evening, and the news did not arrive until five days later.

Later, at a dinner party, the Cardinal told the Baroness she was too sceptical about Cagliostro, and said that to change her opinion he would confide to her a great secret. He showed her a large diamond that he wore on his little finger, and on which the Rohan arms were engraved. She thought that it must be worth at least twenty thousand francs.

'It is a beautiful ring, monseigneur,' she replied. 'I have been admiring it.'

'Well, it is he who made it, made it out of nothing,' returned the Cardinal. 'I was present during the whole operation—my eyes fixed on the crucible. Is not science wonderful, Baroness?

People cannot say that he is wheedling or deceiving me. The jeweller and the engraver have valued this ring at 25 000 livres. You will admit that he would be a strange kind of cheat who would make such presents.' I acknowledge that I was stunned. M. de Rohan perceived it and continued, believing himself now sure of victory.

'This is not all—he can make gold! And has made in my presence five or six thousand livres in this palace. I shall have more; I shall have a great deal; he will make me the richest prince in Europe! These are not dreams, madam; they are positive facts. All his prophecies that have been realized! All the miraculous cures that he has effected! I repeat that he is a most extraordinary—a most sublime man, whose knowledge is only equalled by his goodness. What alms he gives! What good he does! That exceeds all power of imagination.'

The Baroness says she returned, 'What, monseigneur, has not your Eminence given him anything for that—no promise in writing that may compromise you?'

He assured her that Cagliostro had never asked or received anything from him.

But the Baroness was unconvinced. 'Oh, monseigneur,' she claims to have cried. 'This man must hope to induce you to make extraordinary sacrifices when he purchases your confidence at so high a price. In your place, I would be on my guard!'

The Baroness ends her impressions of him:

> It would be impossible to give an idea of the passion, the madness with which people pursued this man. It would appear incredible to anyone who had not seen it. He was surrounded, he was beset; happy was the person esteemed upon whom his glance fell. Nor was it alone in our province that this infatuation prevailed, the furore was not a whit less intense at Paris . . . a dozen women of rank, as well as two actresses followed Cagliostro there that under his direction they might continue the prescribed regimen.

What intrigues one most about Cagliostro's experiments in

the Cardinal's laboratory is how, if achieved through trickery, he could have produced diamonds and such large quantities of gold—unless, of course, he had obtained it all through being financed by the *Illuminées*.

Eye-witnesses described how he had added rose-coloured powder to lead in a crucible before inserting it in the furnace. They had waited and watched until half an hour later he had opened the door and had taken out not lead but molten gold.

If a deception, it may have been engineered through the furnace being in two sections, each with identical crucibles. He might then have placed lead in one and have closed the door. Doing this might have made contact with a lever which pushed aside that section of the furnace and replaced it with the other in which he had earlier on planted a crucible containing gold. But it is hard to see how he could have managed all this while working in the Cardinal's own laboratory.

After having spent nearly four years in Strasbourg, Cagliostro must have decided that the time had come for him to attempt the conquest of Paris. As he had already failed in two other capitals, St Petersburg and Warsaw, he began his campaign in the French provinces. Scottish Masonry, which he considered an inferior, degenerate form, was predominant there. First he went to Bordeaux, calling himself Count Phoenix, then to Lyons, where in 1784 he converted hundreds to Egyptian Masonry and founded a parent Lodge of Triumphant Wisdom. When later he was arrested in Rome there was found among his papers a letter from an adept of this Lodge, in which the writer describes a séance when Moses, 'the first philosopher of the New Testament appeared without being called, and gave the entire assembly, prostrate before the blue cloud in which he was seen, his blessing. Moreover, two great prophets and the legislator of Israel have given us similar convincing signs of their goodwill'.

If we decline to believe that Moses and company actually materialized, we are left with a choice of two explanations—either that Cagliostro hypnotized those present into certainty that they saw them, or that impersonations took place.

Even if at the outset Cagliostro was aware that Egyptian Masonry was largely the product of his own imagination, his enthusiasm for its precepts and objectives grew in time so strong that he himself in the end came to believe that he had been divinely inspired. In France, where he gathered the most followers, the representatives of the French Lodges after listening to him stated in their report with what conviction and sincerity he had addressed them, and how they had found in him 'a promise of truth which none of the great masters had so completely developed before'.

The purpose of his mission, the betterment of humanity and its closer contact with God and the invisible world, did him credit. Where he laid himself open to charges of charlatanism was by employing sleight-of-hand and other impostures to impress people when his supernormal powers failed, by his pretentious ritual and own garish costume.

All this while Cagliostro and the Cardinal had been in regular correspondence with each other, and when de Rohan went to stay in Paris at the beginning of 1785 he sent one of his secretaries to Lyons to beg the Grand Cophta to join him there, which he did on 30th January 1785. At first he stayed in his patron's palace while the latter selected and furnished a house, complete with laboratory, where once Cagliostro had settled in he would call four times a week, coming for dinner and usually remaining until the early hours.

A blasé aristocracy craving novel distractions greeted the Grand Cophta with delight. Mesmer had become *vieux jeu*; worshipped and scoffed at in turn, he had ended his reign with a fortune of 340 000 livres. No sooner had the news spread of where Cagliostro was living than his house was besieged by the sick and the lame, both rich and poor.

Most memoirs of the period mention how his appearance startled people when they first saw him. Count Beugnot, later one of Louis XVIII's Ministers, wrote that he wore an iron-grey coat adorned with gold lace, a scarlet waistcoat trimmed with broad Spanish lace, red breeches, his sword looped to the skirt of his coat, and a laced hat with a white feather—'the latter a decoration still required of mountebanks, tooth-drawers, and other medical practitioners who proclaimed and retailed their drugs in the open air'. His hair was dressed in a way new to France, 'being divided into several small tresses that united behind the head, and were twisted into what was then called a club'.

Another writer, who met him taking the air one day with gaping urchins at his heels, says that he was wearing a blue silk coat and that his hair 'in powdered knots was gathered up in a net'. His shoes were fastened with jewelled buckles and his stockings ornamented with gold buttons. Rubies and diamonds sparkled on his fingers and on the frill of his shirt. From his watch-chain hung a diamond drop, a gold key adorned with diamonds and an agate seal—'all of which, in conjunction with his flowered waistcoat and musketeer hat with a white plume, produced an instantaneous effect'.

Seraphina's beauty helped to win over those somewhat put off by her husband's flamboyance. She had a slender, graceful figure, soft unpowdered blonde hair, enormously appealing gentle blue eyes, an exquisitely shaped little nose, besides the snowy skin and rosebud mouth that sent poets into raptures. A fine horsewoman, she knew how to dress to advantage, and wore dazzling diamonds that were the envy of every woman in Paris. The fact that she could neither read nor write betrayed her humble origin, but, through moving in aristocratic circles, she had acquired the veneer of a lady. Mentally she had not grown up, but to sophisticated society her artless small talk was a refreshing change from *bons mots*, and they regarded her lack of knowledge as an endearing affectation.

'The admiration she excited was most ardent among those who had never seen her', stated one writer. 'There were duels over her, duels proposed and accepted as to the colour of her eyes, which neither of the adversaries knew, or as to whether a dimple was on her right cheek or on her left.'

Again one finds a clue suggesting that she and Lorenza Balsamo were the same person in the persistent gossip that she was sexually promiscuous and received encouragement from

Alessandro, although he undoubtedly loved her. It was rumoured that she was the Cardinal's mistress for a time, but there is no evidence for this.

'What is singular about Cagliostro', commented the Baron de Besenval, 'is that in spite of possessing the characteristics of a charlatan, he never behaved as such all the time he was at Strasbourg or Paris. On the contrary, he never took a sou from a person, lived honourably, always paid with the greatest exactitude, and was very charitable.'

Gossip exaggerated his success as a healer, and to say one had been cured by him gave one a fashionable cachet. It was said that he had given a bottle of the elixir of youth to an elderly lady, with strict instructions to take the draught a spoonful at a time. Her middle-aged maid, during the night, abstracted the bottle and drank half of it. When she entered her mistress's bedroom the next morning the lady asked her sharply who she was and what she wanted. The maid, on looking into the mirror, found herself transformed into a young girl.

Equally apocryphal are some of the stories about his ability as an occultist. For example, it was alleged that at a dinner party at Chaillot, where ladies preponderated and longed to dance, his hostess half jokingly, half seriously begged him to use his magical powers to summon some officers from the École Militaire.

'Yes,' he is supposed to have replied, going to a window from which this military academy could be glimpsed in the distance, 'all that is needed is an invisible bridge between them and us'.

Incredulous laughter came from the ladies when they heard this, which annoyed the Grand Cophta, who raised his arm with stiff, outstretched compelling fingers towards the Hôtel des Invalides, also in view from the window. A few minutes later eighteen army veterans with cork legs arrived at the house.

More fantastic was the tale that six stately lords, arriving for dinner with Cagliostro, found thirteen places laid, and were asked by him what dead celebrities they would like to sit beside them. The Abbé de Voisinon, the Duc de Choiseul, d'Alembert, Diderot, Montesquieu and Voltaire were chosen and then materialized on the vacant chairs. The Marquis de Luchet relates this in his largely fictional *Mémoires authentiques du Comte de Cagliostro*, and includes some of the conversation which purported to have taken place, and which were it genuine would have suggested these distinguished apparitions had turned into cretins.

Notwithstanding, the credulous were convinced that this 'Banquet of the Dead' had taken place. Parisians chattered about it for weeks, and reminiscences of the period reveal that even in royal circles out at Versailles it was momentarily mentioned.

It was at a masonic gathering held in the house of the orientalist Court de Gébelin that Cagliostro is supposed to have made his most extraordinary predictions. He told them that according to the science of the Kabbalah known as Gematria all letters of the alphabet have a numerical value, and that a person's future could be foretold from the total of the digits every letter in his or her name represented. Using the system of the sixteenth-century mystic Cornelius Agrippa, he demonstrated how by converting the names and titles of Catherine de' Medici and her sons into numbers the significant dates in their lives could be ascertained, and the accuracy of such readings be verified against what history had recorded as having happened.

He then turned to the present, and applied the same method to King Louis XVI and his Queen. For the King he forecast a violent death towards the thirty-ninth year of his life, while the Queen's would end later. She would become prematurely wrinkled through sorrow, languish in prison, then her head would fall on the scaffold.

As for Marie Antoinette's close companion, the Princesse de Lamballe, she would be imprisoned, released, then she would be murdered. 'Is there a street named the rue des Ballets in Paris ?' Cagliostro is said to have asked. When told there was he went on that she would meet with a terrible end at the corner of that street—a prophecy that was fulfilled.

Next, he is alleged to have predicted that a Corsican would end the Revolution. His name would be Napoleon Bonaparte. A victorious general at first, he would end his days 'pacing the circle of a melancholy island'.

All this sounds so incredible that one suspects it is part of the Cagliostro legend fabricated after his death. Yet one finds serious writers like Colin Wilson in *The Occult* mentioning this episode, and apparently willing to believe that such prophecies were made before the event.

In the Paris of 1785 the cult of Cagliostro certainly became the mode for many, and they called him 'the august master' or 'our revered father', and believed that proximity to his person purified them. Some fanatics vowed that 'he could tell Atheists and Blasphemers by their smell which threw him into epileptic fits'.

Women fluttered fans and men pinched snuff from boxes on which his likeness was painted. Jean-Antoine Houdon, the celebrated sculptor, known for the truth to life of his marble busts, carved Cagliostro's. It depicts him as having a rather fleshy face with the beginnings of a double chin, a broad turned-up nose and an impressive dome of a forehead. Large clear eyes on a level with the cheeks under boldly marked brows gaze heavenward, and his pleasant mouth seems about to break into a smile.

Prints of his portrait sold rapidly everywhere. They bore this inscription:

De l'Ami des Humains reconnaissez les trait
Tous ses jours sont marqués par de nouveaux bienfaits
Il prolonge la vie, il secourt l'indigence
Le plaisir d'être util est seul sa recompense.

(Recognize the features of Humanity's Friend
Every day he performs more good deeds
He prolongs life and helps the needy
The pleasure of being useful is his only reward)

He apparently resumed his foretelling of lucky numbers. According to Marcel Boll in *L'Occultisme devant la Science*, the State lottery employed ninety numbers and Cagliostro prepared charts in which, for example, if you dreamed of a priest you were certain to win with number 7, of bathing with 31, of lions with 76, and of rain with 89.

What mystified everybody was from whence came his wealth. It was the showy façade he presented to the world that led people to believe he was immensely rich, but he had lost the financial backing of the *Illuminées* as a result of their being suppressed in 1784, and the Cardinal, deep in debt, had little money to spare. When questioned in court regarding his finances during the Diamond Necklace affair Cagliostro at first refused to give any information, then added:

> Nevertheless I will condescend to tell you that which I have never revealed to anyone before. The principal resource I have to boast of is that as soon as I set foot in any country I find there a banker who supplies me with everything I want. For instance, Monsieur Sarrasin of Basle would give me his whole fortune were I to ask it. So would Monsieur Sancotar at Lyons.

These two men were the bankers for Egyptian Masonry, the subscriptions from whose rapidly growing membership gave him a steady income.

If one is to credit the memoirs of his contemporaries Cagliostro strengthened by his own behaviour the convictions of those easily influenced that he was well over a thousand years old, thus promoting the sales of his rejuvenating 'Wine of Egypt' and 'refreshing powder', of which the ingredients were supposed to consist of the seeds of pearls and precious stones, mixed with the scrapings from a stag's heart.

He was said to have paused before Jouvenet's picture in the Louvre depicting the descent from the Cross, and to have wept. Then when he had wiped away his tears he explained, 'I shed tears because of the death of this great moralist, this holy man with whom I often conversed. Indeed, I dined with Him at the house of Pontius Pilate.'

'Of whom do you speak?' asked the Duc de Richelieu.

'Of Jesus Christ,' returned the Count. 'I knew Him well.'

In a satirical pamphlet issued as a hoax in Cagliostro's name, and which many took seriously, he was made to invite those seeking permanent youth to undergo every fifty years a course of treatment that began with living for forty days on a diet of laxative and sanative herbs, drinking only distilled water or rain that had fallen during the month. On the seventeenth day, after having been let blood, six drops of a secret white elixir were to be taken at night and six in the morning, increasing them two a day in progression. Three days later a small quantity of blood was again to be let from the arm before sunrise, and the patient had to retire to bed until the operation was completed. Then a grain had to be taken of a panacea 'the same as that of which God created man when He first made him immortal'. When this was swallowed the patient lost his speech and his reflection for three whole days, and would be subject to 'frequent convulsions, struggles, and perspirations'.

Having recovered from this state, in which we are assured he experienced no pain whatever, then on the thirty-sixth day he took the third and last grain of the panacea, which caused him to fall into a deep and peaceful sleep. Then he would lose his hair, his skin and his teeth, but these would be all reproduced in a few hours and, having become a new man, on the morning of the fortieth day he left his room, completely rejuvenated.

Cagliostro made use of the excitement he had caused in Paris to win adherents to Egyptian Masonry. The spurious pamphlet's contents were probably based on the Grand Cophta's prescription for moral regeneration. One had to go into retreat for forty days, spending out of every twenty-four hours six in meditation, three in prayer, nine in the 'holy operations of Egyptian Masonry', while the rest of the time was for repose. After thirty-three days a visible communication was to take place between the patient and the seven primitive spirits, and on the morning of the fortieth day his soul would 'be inspired with divine knowledge and his body be as pure as that of a new-born infant'.

Three months after arriving in the capital Cagliostro was invited by the Grand Council of the Freemasons of Paris to attend a meeting in their own Temple on the evening of 10th May 1785, when he spoke to them on Egyptian Masonry, and again he made such an impression that shortly afterwards a new Lodge of his Order was started at the residence of a leading Mason.

The room in which his séances took place had black velvet curtains draped over the window and hieroglyphics on the walls, and was lit by wax candles grouped in mystic triangles. A table covered with a long black cloth, embroidered in red with Rosicrucian symbols, served as an altar on which at set distances were placed statuettes of Isis, Osiris, Anubis and the ox Apis, antique phials of lustral water, a crux ansata, or Egyptian symbol of life, and a glass globe full of clear water. The guests would be asked to sit in a circle about the altar and hold their neighbours' hands, thus making a chain. Two attendants attired like ancient Egyptian slaves acted as servers in the rites, while the Grand Cophta himself was the centre of attraction in his black silk robes adorned with red symbols. On his head glistened a cloth of gold turban studded with jewels, while a chain of emeralds, heavy with amulets and scarabs, sparkled imposingly upon his chest.

Count Beugnot gives a vivid description of how he met Cagliostro at a supper party in the Comtesse de la Motte's house, and later attended one of his séances. Also present, he writes, was a certain Chevalier de Montbruel, 'a veteran of the greenroom ever prepared to confirm anything, who always chanced to be wherever Cagliostro was, bore witness to the miracles he had worked, and offered himself as an example of—I do not know how many maladies, with names enough to frighten me'.

Cagliostro, he goes on to say, conversed half in French and half in Italian, and 'made many quotations which might be

Arabic, but which he did not trouble himself to translate'. He alone spoke, and had time 'to run over twenty subjects, for he only allowed them to be discussed as far as he liked. He never failed to ask now and then if he were understood, and the company bowed all round to assure him that he was.'

When he began any subject he seemed carried away with it and expatiated impressively in a ringing, sonorous voice, pausing every now and then to pay his hostess extravagant compliments, calling her 'his hind, his gazelle, his swan, his dove, borrowing his appellations from the most amiable of the animal kingdom'. He switched themes all the time, ranging from the stars, the Great Secret of Memphis, the high-priest in Egypt who taught him transcendental chemistry, giants and monstrous beasts he had seen in his African travels, and the city ten times as large as Paris in the middle of that continent where he had correspondents. 'If gibberish can be sublime, Cagliostro was sublime.'

After supper Cagliostro asked Beugnot a number of questions in rapid succession. 'I answered them all by the most respectful avowals of my ignorance, and afterwards learnt from Madame de la Motte that he conceived a most favourable idea of my appearance and learning.'

All Paris talked, says Beugnot, of how Cagliostro was able to describe an event occurring at that moment in Vienna, London or Pekin, or which would take place in 'six days, six months, six years, or twenty years' time'.

At the séance, which Comte Beugnot attended, Mademoiselle de la Tour, niece of the Comtesse de la Motte, was chosen to act as *colombe*, because Cagliostro found her angelically pure and born under the right constellation. The invocation commenced with the young girl kneeling with eyes fixed on the globe filled with water.

Cagliostro, he says, writing in satirical vein,

> summoned the genii by a concurrence of emblems and cabalistic words, requiring them to enter into the globe and there to represent unknown past or future events. It seems

that this game is not at all amusing to the spirits, and among them are some obstinate individuals who do not care to insert themselves into a glass globe full of water, and place themselves under a magician's orders, and even some are so violent as to contend with him vigorously.

Sometimes the performer has to use the most violent exertion for whole hours together to overcome the spirits' resistance and even then never achieve his object. In this case the affair is put off to another day. If on the other hand the spirits are conquered, they crowd into the great globe, the water in it is agitated and clouded, the clairvoyante falls into convulsions, cries out that she sees and is going to see, and begs loudly for help. The exorciser holds her up before the globe, and orders her in the name of the Great Being to declare what she sees.

It seems that in her turn she has more or less suffering; but the orders are repeated always in the same Name. They become more and more pressing, and proceed to menaces. The poor clairvoyante falls to the ground and rolls. She is raised up and supported before the globe. Trembling and agitated, she declares that there appear before her eyes, still in a state of confusion and uncertainty, the persons and things that compose the scene on which information is desired. The performer does not let her off so easily. She is obliged to recognize the persons, to make sure of their dress and their actions, and to repeat the words they made use of. This is only obtained by the exercise of great patience, through contortions, grinding of teeth, and such severe convulsions that at the end of the ceremony the clairvoyante is carried to bed half-dead.

He goes on to comment that he found it remarkable that such ruses could attract persons of consequence in the Court and in the city of Paris. The Comte d'Estaing had been led away by 'such follies' and become their champion. The Cardinal de Rohan was delighted, thinking of the advantage the new divination would give him over his enemies, and it was reported that the Duc de Chartres (later Duc d'Orléans and Philippe-Egalité) who had decided no longer to believe in God, was quite inclined to believe in Cagliostro. M. de Malesherbes had told him that even Voltaire went home out of humour when he heard a raven croak on his left.

Although the Comte Beugnot describes all this in a cynical manner, he admits that later on he had personal experience of the future being accurately foretold. As a result of the Revolution he was imprisoned in the Conciergerie, and was one of a group of prisoners allowed to meet in a room to play whist before being locked up for the night in their respective cells.

The aide-de-camp of the Comte d'Estaing said that he believed Cagliostro could see into the future. General La Marlière commented that he would like to witness before his death a convincing display of clairvoyance.

The young officer replied he would try to arrange this. The gaolers were bribed to find a suitable boy, who was placed in front of a great globe of water and the aide conducted the séance. He asked, 'General, mention any fact in the past or future you would like to know'.

'The result of the trial I am expecting', the other returned.

Beugnot writes that after half an hour of rather hard exercise the aide and the boy were in a violent perspiration, and the spectators had grown weary of the proceedings and of the convulsions so close to them, and felt an insurmountable oppression.

> At last every one could see that the water was disturbed, and the lad cried out that he saw two men fighting.
>
> 'Who are they ?'
>
> 'A national guard and an officer in a laced hat.'
>
> 'Who is the strongest ?'
>
> 'The national guard lays the officer down on the ground and cuts off his head.'

The boy then fell back unconscious.

They were all badly shaken by what he had said. The general, an unbeliever a moment before, visibly trembled. Some days later he was tried, condemned to death and executed the same day by an executioner dressed as a grenadier of the national guard.

Beugnot comments, 'If anyone had described to me this act of necromancy, I should not have believed it; so my readers may be forgiven if they do not believe it.'

Madame du Barry, former favourite of King Louis XV, in her memoirs published before the Revolution, records how through Cagliostro she must have had foreknowledge of her terrible end. She wrote that on the Cardinal de Rohan's recommendation she asked the Count to visit her at her Château de Louveciennes and tell her fortune. Like others, she mentions how fascinated she was by his glittering, probing eyes. Taking out from his breast pocket a leather case, he told her that it contained a magic mirror wherein she might read the events of the past and the future. 'If the vision be not to your liking,' he warned, handing it to her, 'do not blame me. You use the mirror at your own risk.'

Inside the case she found a metal mirror in an ebony frame, ornamented with mysterious symbols in gold and silver. Cagliostro muttered a magical chant and told her to stare into the glass. She obeyed, then suddenly she shrieked and fainted.

Madame du Barry does not mention what she saw in the mirror that caused her such terror, but she does say that never again would she consent to meet Cagliostro. In view of her subsequent fate, it seems likely that she must have had a prevision of the guillotine.

It was now that the scandal of the Diamond Necklace was to involve the Queen, the Cardinal and Cagliostro disastrously in a sensational lawsuit over a fraud of which they were guiltless and completely ignorant.

Mention has been made of the Grand Cophta's friendship with the Comtesse de la Motte, whom, according to Count Beugnot, he called his 'hind', his 'gazelle', and so on. He was to live to regret that he had ever met her. Married to an impecunious army officer and descended illegitimately from Henri II, the king whose death in a tournament Nostradamus had predicted, she was an unscrupulous adventuress who had become Cardinal Rohan's mistress and had learnt of his ambition to become a second Richelieu or Mazarin. This had been thwarted through Marie Antoinette's detestation of him, on account of his having once ridiculed her mother.

The Queen had bought so much jewellery from the firm of Böhmer and Bassenge that she was forced to ask her husband to settle an outstanding debt of half a million francs, and as a result stopped buying more. The jewellers had hoped to sell her a vulgarly ostentatious diamond necklace assembled years earlier in the hope that Louis XV would buy it for Madame du Barry. When he failed to do so they had visited every likely European Court trying in vain to dispose of it. Learning of this, Jeanne de la Motte told them that in return for a commission she would undertake the task of selling it to the Queen, with whom she was very friendly. She then embarked on a cunning and daring confidence trick, telling the Cardinal that Marie Antoinette had never longed for anything so much as those six hundred and forty-seven flawless stones (worth nearly two million pounds sterling in today's values). Here was his chance to regain her friendship by acting as her agent, bargaining with the jewellers and buying at the lowest possbile price—but secretly, so that the King would not learn of the transaction till it was too late to prevent the Queen from acquiring the necklace.

Before speaking thus to Louis de Rohan, the Comtesse de la Motte had told him she had persuaded Marie Antoinette to forgive him, and in proof of this there would be a private reconciliation at night in the Grove of Venus at Versailles. A prostitute closely resembling her was hired to play the part. All she had to say was, 'You know what this means', and hand the Cardinal a rose. At the meeting he was so overcome that all he could do was to kiss the hem of the impostor's dress. Later he received a letter which Jeanne had forged in the Queen's writing on notepaper stamped with the fleur de lys, which read, 'The hour is not yet propitious for your elevation to the high position you deserve, but there is a confidential matter of great importance to me that I shall entrust to you alone. The

Comtesse de la Motte will explain everything for me to you.'

Highly delighted by all this, Rohan longed to know if he would indeed attain the 'high position' mentioned, so he consulted Cagliostro, who held a séance with Mademoiselle de la Tour, the Comtesse's 'angelically pure' niece, acting as *colombe*. No doubt on this occasion she had been primed by her aunt as to what to say, for the Grand Cophta advised the Cardinal to do as the Queen asked. It would bring him honour, and hasten the day when France would benefit from his rare gifts. He should buy the necklace and thus gain his Queen's undying love. 'Make this your stepping-stone to destiny!' the occultist ended. 'Then your name shall be on all men's lips in France and throughout the civilized world.' The last part of the prophecy was to be fulfilled, but not in the way Rohan hoped.

The jewellers agreed to sell for 1 600 000 francs, which was less than cost, and the Cardinal gave them his personal signature as a guarantee on the contract. The plot was exposed when he failed to pay over the first instalment in full and Böhmer applied directly to the Queen for the money. Meanwhile Rohan had ingenuously entrusted the necklace to an accomplice of Jeanne's disguised in Court livery who was supposed to take it to his royal employer. Instead the stones were hacked from their settings on a kitchen table and then sold in London.

Such an affair called for discretion, but the King rashly allowed the Cardinal's bitter enemy, the Baron de Breteuil, Keeper of the Crown Jewels, to arrest him as well as the Comtesse de la Motte. The latter, whose husband had fled to England, pretended she was innocent, and accused the Cagliostros of having stolen the diamonds. When the Grand Cophta arrived at the Bastille he declared that the only wrongful act he had committed during the several thousand years spent by him on earth was when he had been involved in Pompey's assassination, though on that occasion he had only carried out the Pharaoh's command.

The dramatic trial that followed in the Palais de Justice

before the Parliament of Paris led to Jeanne de la Motte's being branded on both shoulders with a 'V' for *voleuse* and taken to the Salpêtrière Prison for life imprisonment. A year later she escaped to London, where she wrote and published her vitriolic and luridly fictional autobiography in which she alleged that she had been victimized by the Cardinal, the Cagliostros and the Queen (whom she said was a lesbian, and that was how she herself had gained royal friendship).

After nine months in the Bastille Rohan and the Grand Cophta were acquitted on 31st May 1786. Most people approved of the verdict, and on the latter's release he was accompanied by cheering crowds to his house, and had to appear time and time again on the balcony before they dispersed. Louis XVI, prompted by Marie Antoinette, now made the blunder of revealing his annoyance at the acquittal by ordering the Cagliostros to leave the country.

No sooner had Cagliostro reached London than he issued his stirring *Letter to the French People*, which was printed as a pamphlet and distributed throughout France. It had a deeply disturbing effect on account of its revolutionary nature. Some have claimed he predicted that within a short time the States-General would be convened and the Bastille destroyed. But what in fact he wrote was:

> Someone asked me whether I should return to France if the order banishing me were withdrawn. Most certainly, was my reply, providing that the Bastille becomes a public promenade. God will it so! . . . I was for six months fifteen feet from my wife and I did not know it. Others have been buried there for thirty years, reported dead, unfortunate in not being so. . . . Now that I am free, I repeat—there is no crime which could not be expiated by six months in the Bastille.

He calls on the French to deserve liberty 'through reason' and to work towards 'a happy revolution'. But the latter must be 'peaceful'.

This spirited letter infuriated the Baron de Breteuil, now Minister of Police, and an attempt was made to kidnap Cagliostro, and when this misfired he paid a resident spy in London, Théveneau de Morande, to attack him in his scurrilous *Courrier de l'Europe*. This journalist, according to Brissot in his memoirs, 'regarded calumny as a trade and moral assassination as a sport' and in the *Courrier* 'tore to pieces the most estimable people, spied on all the French, who lived in or visited London and manufactured or caused to be manufactured articles to ruin anyone he feared'.

An industrious and suspicious police inspector in Paris happened to read through an old file of 1772 when Giuseppe Balsamo had taken legal proceedings against the Marquise de Prie's agent over his wife. The police had then investigated Balsamo's antecedents and had unearthed the misdemeanours of his early days in Sicily. The inspector became convinced that Giuseppe and Cagliostro were the same person, and informed the Baron de Breteuil, who ordered the facts to be passed on to de Morande in London, with instructions to use them to destroy Cagliostro's reputation.

The journalist began his campaign on 1st September 1786, and for three months denounced and derided the Grand Cophta in a series of articles, suggesting that he was a forger and a pimp who had spent most of his life behind bars and that the 'Countess' was a demi-mondaine and a blackmailer.

Cagliostro counter-attacked with a *Lettre au Peuple Anglais*, in which he denied that he and his wife were the Balsamos, and exposed his persecutor's own disreputable past. He repeated the version of his early life that he had given during the Diamond Necklace trial, but it read even less convincingly in print than it had by word of mouth in court. The public which had been so ready to credit almost anything regarding his occult powers refused to believe the fanciful tale of his childhood and youth. Even the Freemasons, who had greeted him on return as a martyr to despotic misrule, now ignored him.

Defeated and dejected, in May 1787 he slipped away unnoticed to Bienne, Switzerland, where he was joined later by

Seraphina. Here they stayed for some months, living on the small pension allowed him by his friend Sarrasin, the Basle banker.

Soon, however, he grew restless and had visions of regaining his lost *aura popularis*. He would set out on a new campaign. He would bring back all those lost sheep into his fold, convert crowds with his hypnotic powers, found everywhere Lodges of Egyptian Masonry. Seraphina would have back all those diamonds she had been forced to pawn, and more beside. They would have once again their own splendid carriage.

But they were to be disappointed. The aspects were unpropitious. The magnet now repelled. People vanished, doors slammed at the Grand Cophta's approach. The police were harassing shadows, hunting for reasons to turn him out of town.

The hoped-for triumphant progress proved a chimera. Still, adversity found the Cagliostros more united than before. Seraphina made no attempt to leave him. For a year and a half they trudged from place to place, leading a hand-to-mouth existence from what he earned selling nostrums and telling fortunes.

Wearying at last, Seraphina suggested that they should go and live in Rome, where her parents were. If he gave up his Egyptian Masonry there would be no risk of persecution from the Inquisition. He could earn a living from teaching drawing. But when he arrived there he failed to find any pupils. He tried curing the sick, and was dismayed to find his old powers had waned. All the jewels with which he had enjoyed adorning himself had gone, and Seraphina's family treated him with contempt.

To be a Freemason was a capital offence in the Papal States. Only one Lodge, the Vrais Amis, meeting infrequently in secret, had escaped suppression. The ecclesiastical authorities, it seemed, knew of its existence, but had turned a tolerant blind eye to such a minor evil. This encouraged Cagliostro. If he formed a Lodge of the Egyptian rite the subscriptions would provide him with an income. He managed to interest some

Roman aristocrats who were fascinated by the esoteric, and a meeting was organized at 2 a.m. on 14th September 1789, in the Villa Malta.

Father Luca Beneditti has left a vivid description of the proceedings. After giving the password to a liveried servant, he was ushered into a large, magnificently illuminated hall on the walls of which were painted Masonic symbols. There were also statuettes of 'Egyptian, Assyrian and Chinese idols', and inscribed on one of the walls in huge letters was 'I am all that was and that shall be'. The place was crowded with a distinguished company, and he was surprised to find present Cardinal de Bernis, who was the French Ambassador, Princess Cosi, Princess Rizzonico, Princess Santacroce, Countess Soderini, the Marquis Massimi, the Abbé Visconti, the Marquis Vivaldi and a Capuchin priest.

At one end a kind of altar had been erected 'heaped with skulls, embalmed monkeys, live serpents, owls rolling their phosphorescent eyes, ancient parchments, crucibles, phials, amulets and other magical paraphernalia'. The Grand Cophta, arrayed in his usual vestments, sat on a three-legged stool resembling the Pythia's tripod. When all invited had arrived the doors were locked and he addressed them. Nothing was hidden from him. He knew everything. He was born before the Flood. He was immortal. Nothing was impossible to him. He persuaded several of his audience to taste a jug's contents and agree it was water, before filling an enormous crystal chalice to which he then added some drops from a phial. 'The water turned to a golden colour and became a sparkling wine, rather like Orvieto white.' Cagliostro announced that it was now the Falernian of ancient Rome. Many connoisseurs of the vine sipped the fluid finding it excellent.

The Count went on to offer some of his elixir of life to the most aged of the notabilities, promising immediate results. Father Beneditti wrote, 'And certainly their cheeks became reddened and their faces animated, but I believe the same effect would have been produced by a glass of good wine'.

Alessandro next declared that he would demonstrate to

them yet another of his powers, that of increasing the size of diamonds, and asked the Cardinal de Bernis for the solitaire he wore on a finger. This was put into a crucible, and liquids poured over it, together with powders, including a red one. All the while the experimenter recited what sounded to Beneditti like gibberish. Then the prelate was returned his ring, which now contained a stone twice the size of the original. He exclaimed in delight that it was a miracle. 'My own belief is that he was cleverly tricked . . . and that the new stone was a piece of rock crystal' was Beneditti's own opinion.

The Grand Cophta then had a girl brought into the room to act as a *colombe*, gazing into a bowl of water. She saw crowds of savage-looking women and men armed with scythes, sticks and pikes running along a road leading out of a great city to another place. They were shouting, 'Down with the King!'

Cagliostro asked the girl if she knew the name of the place, and she answered that the mob were yelling, 'To Versailles!' Then the *colombe* added that among them was a Duke. This seems to have been a genuine instance of prevision which, embittered by the miseries he had endured since the Diamond Necklace affair, Alessandro now used to strike back at his former persecutors. 'She had foretold the future!' he told his aristocratic spectators. 'Very soon Louis XVI will be attacked by the people in his palace at Versailles. They will be led by a Duke—the monarchy will be abolished!'

This astonishing prophecy began to be fulfilled three weeks later when on 5th October nearly seven thousand market women, fish-wives, street-walkers and male agitators in female disguise, incited by Philippe-Egalité, Duc d'Orléans, stormed out of Paris and marched on Versailles. Cagliostro spoke in the heat of the moment, and his rashness resulted in his own ruin. The Cardinal de Bernis was outraged. How could the other dare to say such things about the King whose Ambassador he was? 'I am sorry, my Lord Cardinal,' came the unrepentant reply, 'but the prophecy will be realized.'

The Grand Cophta's words caused a sensation. 'Some called him an impostor, others a prophet and a sage,' wrote Father

Beneditti. 'The Abbé Visconti rose and asked of what his science consisted.' The cryptic answer was '*In verbis, herbis et lapidus*'—'In words, herbs and stones', which meant that Cagliostro's elixirs, balms and other healing and rejuvenating preparations were made from herbs and minerals, and that his cures were aided by the suggestive power of what he said.

Then he began to speak of Freemasonry and its aims, and the Capuchin and the Marquis Vivaldi asked to be initiated, which he proceeded to do. 'Some of his experiments impressed me, but in his actions I was aware of much trickery,' Beneditti concluded. 'My own prediction is that he will end up on trial before the Holy Office.' The latter was in fact given a full report of the meeting next day by the Cardinal de Bernis, who demanded of the Pope, Pius VI, that the magician suffer capital punishment for his maledictions against the French King and Queen.

From now on the Inquisition had Cagliostro under constant watch. His parents-in-law had so poisoned relations between him and Seraphina that she tried to kill him by putting soap on the stairs. When this trap failed she denounced him to a priest in the confessional as an agent of the Freemasons plotting to overthrow the Papacy. Soon after this two men approached Alessandro and expressed a longing to learn the Egyptian mysteries. He was tricked into believing that they were wealthy, and with the customary ceremonial passed them with one wave of his sword through the three Masonic degrees of apprentice, companion and master forthwith. But when he asked them to pay him fifty crowns in subscription fees they dashed out.

A few days later he learned they were spies of the Inquisition when, on the evening of 27th December 1789, he and his wife were arrested by the Papal police and confined in the Castle of St Angelo. Then later, after forty-three interrogations dragged out over eleven months, he was brought to trial in 1791 and condemned to death as a Freemason, a heretic and a sorcerer, but the Pope commuted his sentence to life imprisonment. His manuscript of the Egyptian rite was declared to be 'superstitious, blasphemous, wicked, and heretical' and burned by the common hangman.

Cagliostro was incarcerated in a dungeon of the Castle of St Angelo from which, according to Prince Bernard of Saxe-Weimar, he made one attempt to escape.

> Manifesting deep contrition he demanded penance for his sins and a confessor, a Capuchin, was sent him. After his confession, Cagliostro entreated the priest to give him the 'discipline' with the cord he wore as a belt, to which the latter willingly consented. But scarcely had he received the first blow, when he seized the cord, flung himself on the Capuchin and did his best to strangle him. His intention was to escape in the priest's cloak. But Cagliostro was lean and wasted from long imprisonment and the Capuchin was strong and muscular. In the struggle with his penitent, he had time to call for help.

As a punishment the prisoner was transferred to the grim Castle of San Leo. The galleries hewn out of the solid rock had been divided into cells, and old dried-up cisterns turned into dungeons for the most intractable offenders. It was in one of these that he was interred in April 1791. The only time he ever saw another human being was when his gaolers lifted the trap to throw down food to him. Here the arch-enchanter wasted for three years until his plight aroused the pity of the Governor, who had him moved to a cell on the ground floor, where he died on 26th August 1795, following a violent attack of apoplexy. He was aged fifty-two, and had outlived his wife by one year. She had been confined in the Convent of St Appolonia, a penitentiary for women.

Had he lived for another two years Cagliostro would have been liberated by the French when they conquered the Papal States. The first thing they did when they broke into the prison was to ask if he were still alive. According to one story, they opened his grave, took away his skull, filled it with wine and drank a toast to the Goddess of Liberty.

1 ◄

2 ►

Je suis très inquiette, j'ai besoin de
vous voir Mlle Aubert m'a dit que
vous craigniez d'être arretée.(*) eh!
pourquoi le seriez vous? je parlerai
à Dubois. J'ai rêvé l'une de ces nuits
de serpents, ils m'enlaçaient au point
de m'oter la respiration. Que veut
dire ceci? je vous recevrai jeudi soir
à huit heures a l'Elysée, j'aurai toujour
un grand plaisir a vous prouver que
je vous accorde ma confiance. Depuis
longtemps vous avez su la meriter.

(*) L'Impératrice ignorait absolument que
j'étais menacée depuis plusieurs mois par
Mr Peyrat au nom de Mr le Préfet
de Police, d'être exilée de Paris, si je
continuais à refuser de trahir la confiance
qu'elle m'avait accordée.

Le Normand

6 *Mlle Lenormand*

Marie-Anne-Adélaide Lenormand, Queen of Fortune-tellers, who claimed to be the Empress Josephine's confidante, was born in Alençon on 27th May 1772. Her father had married a Mlle Guibert, whose beauty attracted Louis XV's attention when they were spending a holiday in the country near Versailles. He was taking the usual steps to add her to his collection of mistresses when a courtier warned the husband, who immediately sped his spouse back to the safety of Alençon, where they raised two daughters and a son.

M. Lenormand died young. His widow soon remarried, but did not long survive him. The second husband followed his late wife's example and wed again within a few months, with the result that the three orphans found themselves with both a stepfather and a stepmother. A lively child, always up to mischief, Marie was packed off as a boarder to a Benedictine convent at the age of seven. There she precociously displayed a gift for telling both the other girls and the nuns teaching her what was going to happen to them. For this the disapproving Abbess as a punishment, and a possible cure, committed her to a diet of bread and water. Shortly afterwards she herself was removed from office for sexual misconduct. The youthful sibyl disconcerted the supporters of the rival candidates for the vacant post by successfully forecasting that all their plotting would be in vain, as the King would appoint a certain religious from another establishment.

Marie worked hard at her lessons and made such rapid progress that the nuns, realizing they had a child prodigy with them, arranged for her to be moved for more advanced

1 Mlle Lenormand in prison in Brussels. *British Library*

2 Message to Mlle Lenormand from Josephine, dated 16th November 1809, a month before Napoleon divorced her. In this note, which was reproduced in *Mémoires historiques et secrets de l'impératrice Joséphine*, she says she is worried about a dream of serpents, and needs to consult the fortune-teller, and is also concerned to learn that the latter fears arrest. Lenormand has added her comments that the Empress did not know the sibyl had been threatened by the police with banishment from Paris should she go on refusing to betray the trust Josephine had shown in her (by becoming a police informer). *British Library*

education to another convent. Here again her appetite for knowledge proved so insatiable that she was sent in turn to three other seminaries of increasing academic importance. But when she started showing signs of being an embryo mystic by going into trances her stepmother thought it time to bring her down to earth, and apprenticed her to a dressmaker.

Then her girlhood friend, Jacques-René Hébert, later one of the most violent of Revolutionaries and leader of the Commune, went off to Paris after being harried out of the small town for writing defamatory lampoons. In his letters to her from the capital he pretended that he was making a fortune in the theatre. This roused her own ambitions, so she followed him there with but a five-franc piece in her pocket—only to be disillusioned, for Hébert was in reality making a fortune for others by selling tickets in a box-office.

For a time Marie slaved for a pittance as a clerk in a business house. She became interested in numerology, chose a lottery ticket with what she considered to be a lucky number for her—and won 1 200 francs. This, she says in her memoirs, she spent on visiting London, where she was tempted into a phrenologist's parlour, who after examining her bumps declared that she possessed tremendous psychic power and helped to set her up as a fortune-teller. Unfortunately, by then the French Revolution had broken out, and she thought it her duty to return home.

Back in Paris she tried in vain to exercise a moderating influence on Hébert. In 1790 she obtained employment as companion and reader to an old aristocrat, M. d'Amerval de la Saussotte, and helped him to prepare Royalist pamphlets and distribute them in secret throughout the capital. Later she was to relate a fantastic story of how, disguised as a fruit-seller, she visited Marie Antoinette in prison and tried to persuade her to exchange clothes, and thus escape.

In due course d'Amerval was arrested and imprisoned, but escaped the guillotine, and after eleven months was released. In the meantime Mlle Lenormand went to live in a lodging-house where she met a Mme Gilbert, a fortune-teller, and a

M. Flammermont, a journeyman baker. The former taught her palmistry, and how to interpret the Tarot cards, and the latter provided her with bread while stringent rationing was in force. They were soon working closely together, the two women telling fortunes while Flammermont circulated leaflets advertising their soothsaying when he went on his rounds.

Before long the trio were arrested and brought before the Tribunal de Police Correctionnelle and ordered to give up such necromancy. Their packs of cards and leaflets were burnt, and they were threatened with harsher penalties were they to offend a second time.

Mlle Lenormand on being released moved to No 153 rue de Tournon, and obtained a licence to sell books and run a letter-writing service there. Behind this screen of respectability she resumed her fortune-telling, with Flammermont acting as usher and bodyguard. Clients were usually heavily veiled in order to avoid being recognized. When summoned from the waiting-room to the sibyl's presence one entered through a secret panel in the wall to prevent any surprise visit by the police, and one departed through another secret panel via the back door. The small, square room was lit from above, and its walls were covered with huge bats, nailed by their wings to the ceiling, stuffed owls, cabalistic signs and a skeleton.

Mlle Lenormand's first customers were washerwomen. They in turn recommended her to their employers, and thus her practice grew. The Revolution provided the right climate and setting. In such dangerous times people were never more anxious to learn what the future had in store. She proved so accurate that soon her waiting-room was crowded all day long. The fact that she foretold death and disaster to many instead of repelling patrons perversely attracted them. It was proof of integrity, they said.

She told the Princesse de Lamballe she would have a terrible end, and Lazare Hoche that he would have a brilliant career as a general, but die before he was thirty. The painter David, the singer Garat, actors and actresses such as Talma and Mme Raucourt, politicians like Barras and Tallien, and many others—all sought certainty in an uncertain world.

According to her highly coloured *Souvenirs prophétiques*, Danton brought her Camille Desmoulins. Then, late one night in early 1793, she says, the three demagogues Marat, Saint-Just and Robespierre came together in secret to see her. 'As I read their hands, my vision clouded and I seemed to see them drowning in an avalanche of blood. "You will all three die violently within a year," I muttered, then turning to Marat, "You first." ' The latter flew into a rage and shouted that for daring to say such things he would have her guillotined. Robespierre, however, shrugged it off, saying that prophets must be allowed the same licence Horace had insisted should be given to poets. The trio, recovering and not wishing to seem afraid in front of a woman, laughed it off and left.

After Marat had been assassinated by Charlotte Corday Robespierre returned for another consultation. As he chose his cards he kept his eyes closed, to her amusement. It was only when he drew his last one that he ventured to look at it. He shivered as he stared at the Nine of Swords. 'I must have been the only person who ever made that monster show fear,' she wrote, 'he who would not lower his head before a King.'

This time, however, Maximilien did not shrug it off, but had her arrested and imprisoned in the Petite-Force as a counter-revolutionary. There she comforted the women aristocrats sharing her captivity by foretelling the end of the Reign of Terror. She saved from the guillotine Mlle Montansier, former director of the Court theatre, who was about to be transferred to the dread Conciergerie. She sent her a note: 'Stay in bed—pretend to be ill—a change of prison will lead to the guillotine—you will escape and live to a great age'.

After her release she became a journalist and started a paper entitled *Le Mot à l'oreille ou le Don Quichotte des dames*, of which she was the sole editress, and which dealt mainly with occult matters, and contained banal predictions such as 'Wine will retain its price. Flour will get slightly cheaper. The coming campaign will open under propitious auspices which assures the advance of our armies.' This lasted for two years.

In 1798 she installed herself some doors away in apartments at No. 9 rue de Tournon, then moved to superior ones on the ground floor of No. 5, where she carried on as a professional fortune-teller until the end of her days. It was here, almost two hundred years previously, that had lived the famous astrologer, Cosmo Ruggieri, favourite of Catherine de' Medici. Mlle Lenormand never married, and her chief companion was her much-liked little mongrel bitch Bichonne, which resembled a hare, and was eventually poisoned by her landlady as the result of a quarrel.

According to her, the young Napoleon Bonaparte consulted her incognito in 1793 when, despairing of advancement, he had decided to leave the country and seek service with the Turks. She claimed to have told him, 'You won't obtain a passport. You will play a great role in France. A widow will make you happy. You will attain high rank through her influence. But never be ungrateful to her. If you were, it would be bad for you both.' Then as he rose to leave she found herself quoting in French the words of Shakespeare's Third Witch, 'All hail, Macbeth, that shall be king hereafter!'

Some months later the future Empress Josephine, then married to the Vicomte Alexandre de Beauharnais and confined in the prison of the Carmelites, sent details of her birth to Mlle Lenormand, and the latter's note in reply read, 'General Beauharnais will die. His widow will marry a young officer whose star predicts a glorious future.'

Such a prediction must have heartened Josephine. The story of how as a girl she had been foretold her future eminence is a well-known one. Mme Ducrest in her *Memoirs of the Empress Josephine* wrote that the Empress was superstitious, but much less so than generally reported. She was averse to any conversation in her presence on the subject of predictions, as an unhappy end had been foretold to her.

'Nevertheless,' stated Mme Ducrest,

after the divorce she agreed to satisfy our curiosity to be

correctly informed of what had been predicted to her at Martinique, and this is what she told us. While she was yet unmarried, seeing on one of her walks several slaves collected round an old woman who was telling their fortunes, she stopped to listen. The sorceress on noticing her uttered a piercing shriek, grasped Mlle de Tascher's [Josephine's] hand, and appeared greatly agitated.

The latter laughed at her grimaces, and asked: 'Do you find anything extraordinary about my face?'

'I do.'

She enquired what was her future. The other said she would not credit it if she told her.

Josephine pressed her. 'You insist. Listen then to what I have to say. You will shortly be married. This will be an unhappy union for you. You will become a widow, and afterwards you will be Queen of France. You will enjoy many years of happiness, but you will be killed in a popular commotion.'

So saying, the woman forced a passage through the crowd surrounding her and hurried away.

Mme Ducrest continues that Josephine said she was consoled by the memory of that prophecy during the hundred and eight days she spent in prison. It was while she was there that her first husband went to the scaffold. Then one morning the gaoler entered the cell where she slept with the Duchess d'Aiguillon and two other women aristocrats, and said he had come to remove her hammock, which was to be given to another prisoner.

'You intend, of course, to provide Mme de Beauharnais with a better one?' remarked the Duchess.

'Never—she won't need one again!' the wretch returned with a grim smile. 'She's about to be taken to the Conciergerie and from there to the guillotine.'

On hearing this, my companions in misfortune burst into tears. I endeavoured to calm them as best I could. Then wearying of their increasing lamentations, I told them that their grief was quite unreasonable as not only would I escape death but should become Queen of France.

'Why don't you name at once the members of your household?' the Duchess retorted crossly.

'Well, my dear friend, I shall appoint you my lady of honour, depend upon it.'

Their tears now flowed more copiously than before, for they thought I had lost my reason, and especially when they saw how cool I remained. I can assure you, ladies, that this was no feigned courage on my part. I was fully persuaded that the prophecy would be fulfilled.

Mme d'Aiguillon grew faint, and I led her towards the window so that she might breathe the fresh air. Then I suddenly caught sight of a poor woman who was making signs to us that we could not understand. She kept grasping her gown and we were at a loss to understand what she meant. At last I cried out to her: '*Robe!*' She nodded, then picked up a stone and pressed it against her gown.

'*Pierre!*' I shouted. Her joy was unbounded when she discovered that we at last understood her, and she made quick and repeated signs of cutting her throat, and began to dance and to clap. This strange performance excited an emotion in our minds which it is impossible to describe, as we ventured to hope that it gave us the news of Robespierre's death.

Whilst we were alternating between fear and hope, we heard an uproar in the passage and the terrifying voice of the janitor who, as he kicked his dog, told it: 'Move on, or I'll slice your head off—like Robespierre.' This proved to us that we had nothing more to dread and that France was rid of the tyrant. . . .

My hammock was brought back to me and I never passed a more peaceful night. I fell asleep, after repeating these words to my friends: 'You see I have not been guillotined—I shall yet be Queen of France!'

When I became Empress, I wanted to keep my promise and have Mme de Girardin, who was the former Duchess d'Aiguillon, as my lady of honour, but the Emperor would not allow it because she had been divorced.

Such, ladies, is the exact truth respecting that famous prediction. I feel a little alarmed at the concluding part of it. I lead here at Malmaison an agreeable, retired life, and don't ever interfere in politics. I do all the good I can and, therefore, hope to die peacefully in my bed.

The one flaw in the Martinique prophecy proved to be that Josephine was not killed 'in a popular commotion' but died in bed from 'gangrened quinsy'.

Mlle Lenormand claimed in her *Oracles sibyllins* that on 2nd May 1801 she was invited to Malmaison, without knowing who had sent for her. She was greeted by 'a lady with a serene and unusual face wearing a very simple négligée' who asked, 'Tell me about my future. How long can all this last?'

Using palmistry and the Tarot cards, Mlle Lenormand says she told the other her fortune. Afterwards the stranger revealed herself to be the First Consul's wife, that she had consulted her visitor when imprisoned during the Terror and that the predictions then made had come true. She added that Bonaparte had confided to her that he had once called on a fortune-teller in the Faubourg Saint-Germain whose prevision had also proved accurate. This had intrigued her, and she was anxious to know if it were the same person of whom she had once sought advice.

Soon Bonaparte arrived. 'Who is this lady?' he asked. When his wife replied that she preferred not to reveal her guest's identity he began to stroke her little dog. Mlle Lenormand petted it too. 'Take care—it might bite you', he warned. 'I am very fond of animals, General,' she replied. The sound of her voice startled him. Their eyes met. Then he took Josephine by the arm and went out of the room with her. After a few moments she returned and said, 'I was right. You are indeed the person who predicted to the First Consul his brilliant career. But you must never tell anybody about it. Great men don't like the public to know that they have the same weaknesses as the common herd.'

The memoirs of the period, while confirming Josephine's interest in fortune-telling, depict Napoleon's own attitude as antipathetic. The Duchess d'Abrantès, in her *Histoire des Salons de Paris*, stated:

> Napoleon was at first amused and made fun of this weakness of hers, then later he objected to Mlle. Lenormand's presence. But Josephine, although she promised not to invite the seeress to visit her, went on doing so in secret, making an intimate friend of her and showering gifts upon her.

The Baron de Ménéval, the Emperor's private secretary, wrote in almost the same words in his *Mémoires pour servir à l'histoire de Napoléon Ier*.

> He disapproved of his wife's belief in fortune-telling, and even often ridiculed her. I was present on several occasions when he forbade her to consult Mlle Lenormand who he once even had arrested. The Empress kept cloaked in mystery her dealings with this fortune-teller and never did her treasurer know exactly what sums she paid the woman for her predictions.

Later, when in St Helena, Bonaparte has been recorded as saying of Josephine, 'One knows she believed in forebodings and seers'. In view of his disapproval, it is not surprising that Mlle Avrillon, her discreet chief lady-in-waiting, should have loyally maintained in her memoirs that the Empress had little to do with the sibyl. She writes that she herself went to consult Mlle Lenormand, who told her 'fairly correctly' her past, 'very accurately the present, but was much more vague about the future'.

She continues:

> Having told Her Majesty that I had been to Mlle Lenormand, she made me tell her in detail all about my visit and then asked me many questions. From what she said, it was clear to me that she had never met Mlle Lenormand. If the contrary had been the case, what motive could she have had for making a mystery of it all? Sure as she was of my discretion, if she had known her in the past she would undoubtedly have mentioned it.

As just then people were already discussing the possibility of a divorce between their Majesties, and as fear of this caused her cruel anxiety, she yielded to compulsive curiosity and decided to consult Mlle Lenormand; but she did so in a letter and through the intermediary of a palace lady who believed more in the fortune-teller's predictions than she did in the dogmas of her religion. It was this lady who took her Majesty's letter to the seeress and who brought back the reply, a secret by the way which she did not disclose to me till much later.

After the divorce, Her Majesty to my knowledge only saw Mlle Lenormand once. She summoned her to Malmaison and it was to me that she entrusted the care of bringing her there.

It may be that since then Mlle Lenormand saw the Empress, but what I can positively assert is that it was never with my knowledge. Why after having once employed me as a go-between should Her Majesty have chosen someone else and hidden the matter from me, I cannot imagine.

Mlle Lenormand herself maintained in her *Souvenirs prophétiques* that in the last years of his rule Napoleon himself again became her client, and she warned him to beware of an English general from Spain (Wellington), and that a barn owl (Louis XVIII) would take the eagle's perch.

Most of the celebrities of the First Empire called on her at some time or other. Talleyrand, the prince of cynics, sought her advice and married Mme Grand after she had urged him to do so. Even that tortuous diplomat, Metternich, condescended to visit her. She told Bernadotte when he consulted her in 1804, disguised as an artisan, that he would become King of Sweden, and he wrote her a letter that has been preserved promising 10 000 francs in the then unlikely event of her prophecy coming true. He never kept his word, but his queen did after his death.

The notorious Joseph Fouché, Duc d'Otranto, Minister of Police, was now having her watched. It arose through the wife of the captain in command of the élite company of gendarmes running into debt without her husband's knowledge by having spent over 4 000 francs in eighteen months on visits to the fortune-teller. As a result, the woman died from worry and the widower lodged a complaint.

The officer investigating this reported that Mlle Lenormand claimed to be a distant cousin of Charlotte Corday, enjoyed a great reputation and asked high fees. No complaints until then had been lodged against her, but she would be kept under surveillance. Occasionally one of Fouché's agents would slip into her waiting-room, listen to anything her clients might say and try to discover their names. Letters reaching her through the post would be opened and examined.

In 1804 Napoleon proclaimed himself Emperor, and a letter dated 28th November from Mlle Lenormand to the new Empress was intercepted and a copy made and kept in the police archives. It read:

> A French sibyl begs your Majesty to grant her a signal favour. Your natural goodness alone can protect you from the baleful oracle with which you are threatened. Consulting anew the book of destiny, that sibyl learns that she will obtain a post from the hands of your august person. What strengthens her in this belief is that in reading about the days of rejoicing that are being planned for the coronation of your august husband she says: 'There is another of my predictions coming true.'
>
> Penetrating the clouds which cover future events, permit me, madam, to prophesy that the celestial genius of Napoleon will give birth to new projects even more sublime than those so far realized and that posterity when paging through the annals of his glorious reign will say: 'France and Europe did not yet know him.' I have the honour of being, etc.

How Josephine responded to this unctuous petition for the fruits of patronage we do not know. But Mlle Lenormand did not need them, for receipts from her vaticinations went on steadily rising. As a disapproving writer put it, 'The fashionable world, the underworld and the Court continued to consult in her tawdry tabernacle this common, ugly thick-limbed Pythoness'.

For example, the police records for 5th March 1808 contain the following:

> A steady stream of visitors are always calling. M. de Metternich went there on Friday at 3 p.m. He was told things sufficiently relative to his present position, character and affairs as to astonish him. Mme Junot who accompanied him also had her fortune told. She had already been there last week with Mesdames Lallémand and Grandseigné and M. Caillé, all four came away very impressed by the close secrets concerning themselves which she had mentioned. Secretary Cavagnari also went there next day and was equally satisfied. M. Prévost, General Junot's aide-de-camp, also, etc.

The following year, on 15th December 1809, the police records read, 'The woman fortune-teller, Mlle Lenormand, has been arrested. Nearly all the court have consulted her over present events. She has read the horoscopes of the highest in the land, earning from this an annual income of over 20 000 francs.'

'Present events referred to the Emperor's divorce. In her 590-page-long *Souvenirs prophétiques d'une sibylle sur les causes secrètes de son arrestation*, published much later in 1814, Mlle Lenormand gave her version of what happened on Monday 11th December 1809, and subsequently. Towards eleven o'clock that morning some policemen made their way through the crowded waiting-room and entered her inner sanctum.

'With the best will in the world,' she claimed she told them sarcastically, 'I don't want to receive any new clients because today I am destined to be arrested.'

'You haven't made a mistake,' retorted one of the intruders, showing her his credentials. They then thoroughly searched the place and confiscated her divining rod, but left behind the scrying mirror that had once belonged to Luca Gaurico, the renowned sixteenth century astrologer, the Cabala of Zoroaster, and her collection of thirty-three hazel, ash and oak wands, which were all part of the *mise-en-scène* to impress clients.

She was taken to police headquarters in the rue de Jérusalem and locked in Cell No. 9, where she was questioned, but gave evasive replies. When asked for the names of her consultants she avoided giving them and said jokingly, 'His Excellency the Persian Ambassador honours me with his closest confidence. I am much respected in America. I have 99 000 followers in Africa. It's quite different in Asia. My marvellous Cabala serves as a guide to governments.'

'Now I must insist that you tell us where you spent the evening of Saturday, December 9,' demanded her chief interrogator.

Note 58 at the back of her book informs the reader that that night at eight o'clock she was summoned to the house of Queen Hortense of Holland, where the latter's mother, the Empress Josephine, revealed 'great things' to her. But Mlle Lenormand did not disclose this, and replied guardedly to the inspector, whose name was Veyret, 'I went to try and bring consolation to the soul of a woman who was in terrible distress as the victim of the most despicable ingratitude'. She was alluding, of course, to Napoleon's divorce of Josephine.

'What! Are you attacking the Emperor? Please explain yourself!' she quotes Veyret as exclaiming.

'It was all in his horoscope I cast years ago. Here is my copy of the last one I prepared in 1807', she says she replied, producing the chart in question, which the policemen gathered round and studied with mounting amazement. It was carefully stored in their archives, she declares, but one cannot check her statement, for it was destroyed by a fire in 1871.

Back in her cell, the prisoner busied herself practising her arts, disturbed from time to time by the appearance of the inspector, Veyret, or the gaoler, Vantour. She relates that on the sixth evening Flammermont brought her a roasted partridge for her dinner which was stuffed with three letters, one of which came from Josephine.

For a week and a half she remained in her cell. She was allowed visitors, and even to have her portrait painted. Then, after twelve days, Veyret threatened her with long imprisonment if she did not agree to become a police spy. 'I'd rather die than lose my honour', she asserts she protested indignantly, and, seizing the talisman that had just been restored to her, she uttered spontaneously the name 'Ariel'.

Immediately, she claims, the genie materialized in the shape of a tiny old man wearing a huge hat and armed with a black wand, which he used to trace a protective circle round them. The others watched in fright, but she reassured them. The genie touched them with his wand and all cried out, '*Agamus gratias!*' As a result of all this she was apparently released at once.

The whole book is written in this fashion, which makes it difficult to sift the truth from the trash. Her experience so upset her that she decided to retire to her country retreat at Mignaux, near Malmaison, where she stayed some time. The nearest inn soon became full every day of the week with clients, old and new, from Paris.

Eventually, she decided life would be easier if she went back to her old quarters in the rue de Tournon. There the police from time to time made honeyed approaches trying to persuade her to become their spy. To her credit, it must be stated that she resisted all their blandishments.

It was in late 1814, when Napoleon was forced to abdicate and was sent to Elba, that Mlle Lenormand published her *Souvenirs prophétiques*. In them she mentioned that over twenty years previously the Comte de Provence, now King Louis XVIII, had visited her before leaving France, and she had foretold that he would one day wear a crown.

Hofman, the editor of the *Journal des Débats*, wrote a lengthy, contemptuously scathing review of the book which he spread over three issues. This so annoyed the authoress that she hit back in a letter which was published in a rival paper, the *Courrier*, wherein she announced that the number of people seeking appointments had trebled since Hofman's review had appeared. It was obvious from the way he had attacked her that he was 'an obstinate, prejudiced fool who doubted the truth of things which his minnow-sized mind was incapable of understanding'.

The strictures of critics certainly had no effect on the sales of the *Souvenirs prophétiques*, which proved a best-seller, encouraging the authoress to publish the following year *La Sibylle au tombeau de Louis XVI*, a bombastic eulogy of the Bourbons. A garrulous angel appears to Mlle Lenormand at the tomb of the martyred monarch and discusses what has happened since Waterloo. He leaves her with a very vague prediction: 'The year 1816 and the one following it will be marked in France by memorable events'.

Vague she might be, but so were many of the quatrains of her great predecessor Nostradamus. The reason for her success was that she undoubtedly made accurate predictions to a large number of those who consulted her; otherwise she could not possibly have retained her position for half a century as the most successful fortune-teller of her time. Unfortunately, not satisfied with possessing a sixth, prophetic sense, she must needs embellish, invent guides and genies, angels and confiding royal ghosts, and, having a bad memory, frequently contradict what she had written earlier, even in the same book.

If one were to judge her on the contents of her own works one would dismiss her as an amusing charlatan. The memoirs of her contemporaries are the best and most reliable witnesses in her favour, with detailed accounts of predictions made first-hand to the writers.

For example, in the spring of 1830 Emilie de Pellapra, then Comtesse de Brigode and natural daughter of the Emperor Napoleon and Mlle Leroy of Lyons, lost her husband. She relates in her memoirs that for a time she was inconsolable, then her mother, seeking to distract the young widow, persuaded her to go with her to Mlle Lenormand, dressed in their maids' shabbiest clothes.

> We were soon in the presence of the sibyl who wore a hideous black velvet beret which accentuated the coarseness of her face. She began by staring at me, then shuffling her cards without paying them much attention, she said, 'You have done your best to disguise yourself—a waste of time. You are a rich woman of the world, and so young that everybody would take you for a spinster, but you are married and have a family. . . . You have suffered, but your troubles are over. You are a widow, madam, but you will marry again and before this autumn. You don't know your future husband. Don't try and find out who he might be, for the sea separates you and he will travel over two seas before he knows you.'
>
> Then in answer to my questions she added that I would meet within two months the man she had mentioned. I laughed at my good fortune; I told others that evening and forgot all about it next day.

But the Comtesse remembered the prediction when she became engaged to the son of the Princesse de Chimay, who had sailed from England to Toulon to attend the embarkation of the French fleet for Algiers, and had as a result voyaged over two seas.

In 1820 Mlle Lenormand decided to exploit her association with the late Empress Josephine to best advantage by producing two volumes of her *Mémoires historiques et secrets de l'Impératrice Joséphine*. The deceased's chief lady-in-waiting, Mlle Avrillon, registered her strong disapproval in her own reminiscences later:

> I had the courage to read these memoirs. I persevered and went on right to the end, despite my indignation which grew after every page of this tissue of lies and platitudes. I wanted to see how far this woman's audacity would take her. . . . Mlle Lenormand claims to have predicted to Mme de Beauharnais all that has since happened in her life. Believe it if you wish, but I wish that when people have the effrontery to publish as true such impertinences that they ought to have the conscience to put at the beginning—'Dedicated to

Imbeciles'. In effect, it is solely for such readers that this publication is intended.

In the prospectus which Mlle Lenormand sent to booksellers she wrote:

> These memoirs were not prepared for publication by the Empress. She contented herself in her sorrow after the divorce to read them aloud to me. All I have done is to edit them, and that very slightly. I had some time ago arranged in order the manuscripts recording her private and public life which she had entrusted to me. As readers may gather no doubt, on account of her confidence in me and the intimate nature of our relationship I was in a better position than anybody to collect information.

The seeress dedicated her book to Alexander I, Tsar of Russia, who had often consulted her, and published immediately after the title-page a letter from a Russian prince in which he conveyed the thanks of his master for the dedication and asked her to accept a diamond ring as a token of his pleasure.

The first volume tells of the childhood of Mlle Josephine Tascher de la Pagerie. The opening 165 pages were prepared from 'the notes truly taken down by me in great detail', then the scribe allows Josephine to speak for herself, which she does in the same manner as her fortune-teller extraordinary.

> Eugène, my devoted son by my first marriage, often reminded me of the predictions of my future grandeur made in Martinique. . . . I confess that I was weak enough to place a certain confidence in them and to permit myself to be persuaded to consult Mlle Lenormand who had the courage to tell the most savage of the Jacobins that they would suffer cruel ends. . . . It was she who gave me a sense of security by foretelling that I was about to meet again the man who would become the most astonishing of the century.

In Volume II, Josephine is made to say:

> Vainly I tried to calm Bonaparte. He became increasingly ironic about the faith I seemed to have in the predictions of a famous woman all Paris was consulting. 'I shall have this Lenormand arrested', he kept repeating to me. 'You're obsessed with her. Never mention her to me again.'

But she does. When Napoleon returns from the Congress of Erfurt in September 1808 Josephine is able to tell him all that has transpired, learned in advance from her seeress friend. 'She was right, that Lenormand woman,' he unwillingly admits. 'How the devil does she learn all this? Really it must stop. Let her occupy herself with her own affairs, but I won't have her meddling with mine.'

Reproduced in the second volume is a note in Josephine's handwriting, dated 16th November 1809, from her to Mlle Lenormand, and written a few weeks before the divorce:

> I am very worried. I need to see you. Mlle Aubert has told me that you fear to be arrested. Why should you? I shall speak to Dubois [a police chief]. I dreamt the other night of serpents. They were coiling round me tighter and tighter till I thought I should lose my breath. What can this mean? I shall receive you on Thursday night at eight o'clock in the Elysée. I shall always have great pleasure in proving to you that you have my confidence. For a very long while you have known that you deserved it.

Eugène de Beauharnais, Josephine's son by her first husband, in a published letter from Munich to the editor of the *Moniteur universel*, contended that there was not in Mlle Lenormand's book 'a single line which is really written by my mother, my sister or myself, not an anecdote which conforms with the truth'.

Some months later a protest from M. Deschamps appeared in the *Constitutionnel* and the *Courrier* in which he asserted that during the time he was the Empress Josephine's private secretary, from 1808 to 1814, it had never come to his knowledge 'that she had written about or had arranged for the recording of events in which she personally was involved'. The papers entrusted to his care had never been made available to Mlle Lenormand, and for a correct account of the Empress's life during the period 1804 onward reference would have to be made to such documents. He ended, 'For the reasons given I think I can assure your readers that the Princess was in no way connected with the writings published under her name'.

But Mlle Lenormand was unruffled by these denials, and when some fifteen years later, on 28th September 1835, Josephine's remains were exhumed and moved to a finer tomb the Chevalier de Pougens, the fortune-teller's representative, called on the Mayor of Rueil and requested permission to leave on the coffin a copy of the *Mémoires*, bound in vellum, but the Mayor would not allow it.

This was in fact a copy of the new edition she brought out in 1826, with an additional third volume and a foreword that read, 'Like a faithful historian I have tried to include all sides of her life. I made a start in 1820. I shall be bolder in 1826. Apart from additional historical facts, it seemed to me that my book should also be a character study with new and valuable reflexions. . . .'

There was a further inducement for purchasing this new edition. It now included *Les derniers Souvenirs de Napoléon*, 'sent secretly to me by his orders just before his death in 1821'. It seems incredible that she should have tried to persuade the public to believe this—and have succeeded with so many. She makes Napoleon write that on returning from Elba to Fontainebleau he found 'by chance' on his desk a copy of her *Souvenirs prophétiques*.

> More than once the fancy took me to talk to the authoress. . . . She had announced to me in 1793 that I would rule France and would continue to do so till the day when the ambition of a new marriage would part me from Josephine. It was this woman who dared to publish in 1814: 'If Bonaparte leaves the Island of Elba to return to France, he will

die without glory. . . .' Mdlle Lenormand, your prediction has been accomplished.

Actually what she had written in her *Souvenirs prophétiques*, published before his escape from Elba, was 'Take care to have nothing to do with those who through their intrigues and deceptive schemes seek to stir up trouble in your name and to rekindle civil dissension, otherwise you will die without glory'.

Les derniers Souvenirs de Napoléon ends, 'I leave these reminiscences in the hands of Mlle Lenormand. I intend them to be added to the "Historic and Secret Memoirs" of Josephine my first wife. The editress, Mlle Lenormand, has worthily performed her task: she has distinguished herself in my eyes and made certain of her literary glory. . . .'

On 25th February 1821 Mlle Lenormand set out for Brussels. An account of her misadventures was eventually published by her in October 1822, in her 400-page-long book, *Souvenirs de la Belgique*. She tells us that from the moment of departure she had 'the most sinister foreboding' about crossing the frontier. She did not turn back because she was determined to offer her literary works to the King and Queen of Holland.

Lodged in the Hotel Bellevue, from the moment of arrival she started seeing clients. Then on 18th April she was arrested by the police and charged with illegally telling fortunes. Various witnesses gave evidence of having consulted her at prices of either 10, 20, 40 or 60 francs, and on 7th June 1821 she was fined 23 florins and sentenced to one year's imprisonment.

'When the President pronounced his vile judgment,' alleged Mlle Lenormand,

> the people present were filled with consternation and an unanimous shudder of indignation heralded the storm about to burst against these legal evildoers. All rose to their feet expressing their horror against this violent and tyrannical measure. The magistrates withdrew, overwhelmed with reproaches, self-doomed to obscurity.

From her cell she penned her appeal, pointing out that according to their testimony all her visitors had left their money voluntarily on a table without being asked for it. When, at the end of July, the High Court reviewed the case the Attorney-General defended the sentence with vehemence, and she replied, 'Why are you astonished by the influence I have over people? I have often sold them peace of mind and my art is to sow a few flowers in life's arid field.'

The court revoked the previous judgment except for the fine. Her confinement in a damp cell had worsened the rheumatism from which she suffered, almost paralysing an arm and her left leg, so she went to Aix-la-Chapelle to take the waters. Here she had already been when Napoleon fell and the unholy alliance of kings met there to reshape Europe. On that occasion she had told fortunes in a room rented for the purpose in an hotel. The King of Prussia is said to have consulted her, disguised as a peasant, and to have introduced himself as *un paysan sans souci*. 'But you own *Sans Souci!*' she returned, referring to his famous palace.

After six weeks at the spa, she says, she was cured and returned to Paris, where she complained to her friends that the law-suit in Belgium had cost her over a hundred thousand francs. It seems that she was continually short of ready cash, and as a result some of her belongings were always in the local pawnshop. Originally she had invested her money in property. She owned a château near Poissy, a house divided into apartments in the rue de la Santé in Paris and three dilapidated cottages at Alençon, one of which she intended to renovate so as to end her days there. Then she decided to spend most of the money she acquired in fees on publishing her own books, confident that they provided the best medium for securing her fame with posterity. In 1824, she announced that the following works of hers printed in octavo would be appearing in the coming three years: *La vie privée du prince Eugène de Beauharnais* (3 volumes); *Mes souvenirs de trente ans* (12 volumes); *Wilhelmine de Prusse* (2 volumes) *Le fond du sac, ou la vérité sur Napoléon* (6 volumes); *La Tour du Temple, et le Château de*

Vincennes (4 volumes); *Maximilien de Robespierre, ou l'enfant du crime* (3 volumes); and *L'église de Rueil* (4 volumes).

The public were offered these 34 volumes for 264 francs, and for payment in advance they would also obtain free in due course an unpublished treatise on celebrated dreams, ancient and modern. Unfortunately, the prospective readers showed a complete lack of interest in this offer, so the authoress-publisher decided the cause might be that she was offering such high-class fare too cheaply. So a new prospectus was issued advertising instead 'The Collected Works of Mlle Lenormand, revised and enriched with unpublished manuscripts, commentaries and biographical notes on the French Revolution and the actors in that political drama'. The whole would consist of 5 quarto-paged volumes and of 80 octavo-paged volumes, all for 975 francs.

As the cost of printing such an edition would require a great deal of capital Mlle Lenormand wrote to all the booksellers in France asking them to agree to place advance orders. Here is the letter she sent to Messrs Trublet and Wurtz of 77 rue de Bourbon, Paris:

> As I have informed you, gentlemen, my Diaries are historic documents. For over thirty years, I have occupied a unique position as counsellor and confidante to those who have played important parts in public affairs. This has enabled me to learn all the facts concerning our Revolution and its causes. My revelations will enable readers to say: 'The authoress writes with authority about what she has herself seen and heard—she is not romanticizing—she is essentially truthful and trustworthy.' . . . I ask you, gentlemen, therefore to support me as best as you can by placing a large order to meet the requirements of your extensive clientèle.
>
> As for terms they will be very reasonable as in the past: a special discount of 10% up to ten dozen; over ten dozen, 12%; and over 15 dozen, 15%. Orders can be sent in now. You stand to gain by doing so.

But it seems the booksellers were not attracted by the sensational revelations she promised, and publication of her

Collected Works was postponed until an indefinite later date. So instead the sibyl published in October 1824 *L'Ange protecteur de la France au tombeau de Louis XVIII*, barely a month after that monarch's death. Such an event was too good an opportunity to miss, and she eagerly grasped it.

The angel of peace appears before the royal tomb and reels off verses in honour of the deceased, quoting exact predictions Mlle Lenormand claimed to have made in the past, but she is somewhat nebulous about the future, and sprinkles her effusions lavishly with exclamation and question marks.

> An extraordinary event will take place on the banks of the Tagus. . . . Will the troubles of Spain be over ? No! Saturn has not yet struck all his blows! Alliances will appear to reunite two divided branches! . . . Great events could astonish Europe. The star of the East is in good aspect for Poland and Greece. . . . The key of the Mediterranean—will it be seized by the eagle!!! Memorable happenings in Prussia. Germany promises herself wonders. Oh, Belgium, should you not fear the awakening of the lion ? Superb Rome, will you be humiliated ?
>
> Oh, France, happy France, you could rescue your neighbour! Your new king, Charles X, will surpass all you may expect!! He possesses the clemency of Augustus and the virtues of Marcus Aurelius!!!

Two years later, in 1826, she brought out further valedictory verses to mark the death the previous year of her former client, the Tsar, who defeated Napoleon, *L'Ombre immortelle de Catherine II au tombeau d'Alexandre Ier*. The critics disapproved of this, as they had of her other works. One sneered that she wrote like a cook and spoke like a coachman, and yet was still earning 20 000 francs a year from her '*sottes paroles*'. He ended, 'What can one say about the credulous dupes who each day consult her ?'

Her waiting-room now was furnished with a few chairs, a large sofa, two clocks, a round table of citrus-wood on which copies of her books were displayed, and some fifty pictures completely covered the walls. In a prominent position hung her portrait painted by Isaby, which was exhibited in the Paris Salon of 1825. This showed her seated, dressed in green velvet, with Bichonne at her feet, and resting her left arm on a pedestal table bearing a crystal and a book.

Opposite this a plaster bust of her, crowned with a laurel wreath, stood on a fluted marble column, the pedestal of which bore the inscription

Quand près d'elle de Delphe, on cherche une prêtresse
On entend toujours la voix de la sagesse.

ACHILLE LEONNAS.

Among the other paintings were ones of an enormous sphinx, a winged Mercury, Louis XVI and XVIII, Charles X, the Child Jesus, and a large one of the sibyl herself, pointing her index finger at a Nine of Diamonds as she gazed at a young army officer standing before her. This was a representation of her foretelling his arrest to General Charles de La Bédoyère, who was executed by a firing-squad in 1815.

The faithful Flammermont, the former baker-journeyman, dressed in black, received clients and ushered them in turn into the consulting-room. In her later years Mlle Lenormand saw consultants seated in a large grease-stained armchair in her bedroom, of which the maple-wood furniture had been intended for the Duchesse de Berry, who had ordered it in 1828 and who failed to take delivery, with the result that the fortune-teller had acquired it for 2 800 francs.

Laferrière, the actor, in his reminiscences published in 1874, gave a description of her appearance when he visited her in the early 1830s:

> Imagine an ugly little woman so stout that it made her look vulgar, wearing a dark velvet dress with slashed sleeves. On her head, which sank between her shoulders and which was remarkable only on account of her piercing eyes, she wore a kind of turban of matching velvet that made me think of Madame de Staël. Round its edges were coquettishly

> arranged silky blonde corkscrew curls. The gray locks of the old witch escaped behind her ears from under this transformation and straggled down her nape. I found it rather sad and grotesque.

The sibyl always asked her visitors the same question: 'What are the date and place of your birth—your Christian names—your favourite animal and flower?'

The worldly wise Welshman, Captain Gronow, who visited her in the 1830s under an assumed name, records in his reminiscences how impressed he was by what she foretold to him. 'She informed me that I was *un militaire*, that I should be twice married and have several children and foretold many other events which have also come to pass, though I did not at the time believe one word.'

The young Sicilian, Count Hector Lucchesi-Palli, who became Caroline de Berry's second husband, stopped in Paris for a few days in 1829. One morning he happened to be passing the Tuileries when she drove out, and he joined in the cheering from the crowd gathered outside. That afternoon he visited Mlle Lenormand, who said to him, 'You are young and not planning to get married, yet within two years you *will* be married—to the lady you met this very day and cheered when her carriage passed you.' The prophecy came about.

Marie, Comtesse d'Agoult, when faced with the choice between giving up a life in Parisian society or Franz Liszt, with whom she had fallen in love, consulted a close friend, the novelist Eugène Sue, who knew his way about the underworld of Paris, and he recommended a visit to Lenormand.

In her *Mémoires* Marie wrote that she visited her on 23rd June 1834 'in a very dark, dirty, stuffy room in the rue de Tournon, to which some rather childish devices gave an atmosphere of necromancy'. She mentions how the seeress had predicted a throne for Josephine, and how the fulfilment of that prediction had won for her the confidence of the leading sovereigns of Europe, so that at the Congress of Aix-la-Chapelle Alexander I of Russia often consulted her and took what she said seriously. Marie also says that the Duke of Wellington called on Mlle Lenormand in 1818 in order to find out who had tried to assassinate him.

> I paid a few francs extra for what she called 'the big pack'. She began to shuffle the cards and stealthily threw me a quick, piercing look. . . . 'Your destiny', she told me, 'will take a completely new course two or three years from now. What seems to you absolutely impossible today will come to pass. You will change your way of life entirely, and later even your name to one that will become famous not only in France but in Europe. You will leave your country for Italy, where you will be honoured. You will love a man who will make a sensation in the world and whose name will be remembered. You will incur the enmity of two women who will try to harm you in every possible way. But have faith: you will triumph over everything. You will live to a ripe old age surrounded by loyal friends, and exert a wide influence for good. Heed your dreams, for they will warn you of danger. Be wary of your imagination: it gets easily excited and will lead you into many perils. . . . Your intelligence will make you many enemies, and your kindness will be misunderstood.' This prophecy came true almost to the letter.

Like so many fortune-tellers, Mlle Lenormand failed to foretell correctly the date of her own death, having written in the *Souvenirs prophétiques* that she would live to be 108; on page 43 of *Souvenirs de la Belgique* this changed to 123, and on page 299 of the same book to 115. A favourite saying of hers was 'A raven in the morning means sorrow; a raven at night, despair.' She was 71 when she died on 25th June 1843, in the garden of her house in the rue de la Santé after a stroke brought on, so claimed *Le Charivari*, through seeing a pigeon flash in and out of her bedroom window, which short-sightedly she mistook for a raven.

All Paris flocked to the Requiem Mass two days later in the Église Saint Jacques du Haut-Pas, which was draped in white. At 11.30 a.m. there arrived before the great door the hearse drawn by four caparisoned horses, followed by crowds of women and over a hundred mourners with large wax candles in their hands. After the service the first-class funeral cortège went to Père Lachaise cemetery. Prominent among the mourners was the Foreign Minister, François Guizot, whom she had helped when he was poor and unknown. A willingness to aid with money anyone in need was in fact her chief virtue, and the reason why she left less than had been expected, 120 000 francs.

Jules Janin, the French literary and dramatic critic, wrote in the *Journal des Débats* on 3rd July 1843:

> The death of this woman shatters another link we had with the worm-eaten empire of Napoleon. After having crowned him, she dethroned him with as little ceremony as if she had predicted to a valet that he would lose his job within a week. For these reasons, Mlle Lenormand already held her place in the drama of modern times, whilst awaiting history's final judgment. Looking well ahead, who can say that an aureole of recognition will not be placed round the head of this magician and that future generations will not regard the Emperor Napoleon and her with equal admiration and warmth on account of her having spurred him to fame with the words of Shakespeare's witch: 'All hail, Macbeth, that shall be king hereafter!'

1 ◄ 2 ▲ 3 ▼

7 'Cheiro'

'Cheiro' was born on 1st November 1866, at Bray, County Wicklow, and his birth certificate gave his names as William John Warner. His father claimed to have traced his ancestry back to Rollo, first Duke of Normandy, whose descendant, Robert Fitzhamon, founded Tewkesbury Abbey (where Cheiro's ashes now repose). The son in view of this later changed his name by deed poll to Louis le Warner Hamon, ennobling himself at the same time. When he had become famous his entry in *Who's Who* showed him as the son of 'Count William de Hamon'.

This most successful of modern fortune-tellers much admired Cagliostro, whom he regarded as a great mystic, refusing to believe that he was in any way a charlatan. There were certain similarities between the two men. They both styled themselves Counts, took imposing new names and had exceptional hypnotic powers. On the other hand, while the one dressed and often behaved like a mountebank, the other had the appearance and manners of an elegant diplomat. Mme Blavatsky, however, was certain that Count Louis Hamon was the reincarnation of Cagliostro.

Hamon himself believed in reincarnation. When asked by a friend, Major Cross, whether he had any recollections of his former lives he replied that he decidedly did have, but it was something he did not wish to talk about. 'People think it savours too much of the imaginative side of life, so I keep my visions to myself', he said.

For his early days, one has to rely on what he wrote in his autobiographical writings, which were obviously romanticized

---

1 Cheiro

2 Cheiro's Indian waiting-room, London

3 The house at 7416 North Vista Street, West Hollywood, where Cheiro died on 8th October 1936. The photograph shows the house as it appears today. It is now reputed to be haunted

accounts to give him the appropriate aura of mystery for his work as a palmist. His French mother, born Marguerite Dumas and of Greek descent on the distaff side, was fascinated by the occult, and, he claimed, gave him all the books she had on the subject for his tenth birthday. As a result, a year later he so upset his conventional father by an essay on the lines of the hand that he was packed off to boarding school with the intention of being trained for the Church, as the disapproving parent considered it was all for which his character fitted him.

But, unrepentant, he went on poring over books on palmistry. One day his form-master surprised him doing this. However, instead of reprimanding the boy, the old man (who was reputed to be a misogynist) challenged him to read his own hand, which the other did, giving accurate details of a love affair that had ended in tragedy. Astonished and impressed, the master then became his strange pupil's friend. 'Many a difficult exercise he let me off,' wrote Hamon later, 'and many an old Greek and Latin book on hands he translated for my benefit.'

In a lecture delivered in London on 25th April 1912, and reported next day in *The Times*, Count Louis Hamon told his audience why he did not go into the Church. It was the end of term, and he had passed the examinations which would have taken him to the university. On the morning of prize-giving day the headmaster noticed that he looked extremely pale, and inquired the reason. He replied that the night before he had dreamt that when at four o'clock the next day he was about to go up to receive a prize an usher had handed him a letter which had just arrived. He recognized the handwriting on the envelope as that of his father, then he was overcome by a feeling that it contained bad news.

The headmaster had laughed, and talked of overwork. But when the youth did that afternoon return to his seat with his prize an usher handed him a letter. It was from Louis's parent, saying that he had been ruined by an unfortunate land speculation and that the lad would have to leave school and start earning his living as best he could. He decided to try his luck in London.

Later, in his *Confessions*, Hamon wrote that in the train from Liverpool he read another book on his pet subject, bought at a station stall. The other occupant of the compartment, a distinguished-looking man, noticed the title on the cover and half humorously suggested that his companion should attempt to read his palm.

The stranger had a well-marked Line of Destiny, indicating great qualities of leadership. 'But why does it fade out suddenly?' he demanded.

Young Hamon answered, 'Oh, well—another Napoleon sent to St Helena, I suppose.'

'And what will be my Waterloo?'

'A woman, without a doubt. You can see for yourself how your Line of Heart breaks that of Destiny just below the point where it fades out.'

The older traveller laughed and retorted that this was most unlikely, as his life was dedicated to a cause, giving him no time for women. Then before they parted he handed Louis a card which read 'Charles Stewart Parnell'.

It was some years later that the Irish leader fell in love with Katherine O'Shea and was cited in the divorce case that led to his downfall.

The prospect of a routine clerical job in an office, however, did not appeal to the youth when he reached London, so, acting on an impulse, he spent what money his father had given him to go by cargo ship to Bombay. Here on arrival he became friendly with a Brahmin, 'a member of the Joshi caste, which had 'practised palmistry for centuries in the north-west province'. They read each other's hands, and the priest offered to help him develop his occult gift, but said that it would mean passing several months in preparation, which would include a fast of seven months, seven days and seven hours. Then he would have to achieve dissociation of consciousness by spending some time in a trance, from which, the Brahmin warned him, he might not recover. But, undeterred by this, young Hamon agreed to undergo this initiation, so they travelled together up into the mountains, where Louis first fasted. After this had ended the Brahmin offered to show him all that was happening to his people at home. They went further up. A flat slab of rock was found, on which a black liquid was poured, and soon he saw all that his friends and relations were doing, even to the antics of his dog.

Weak as he was from the long fast, he decided after this revelation to risk going through with the trance ordeal. His Brahmin friend took him to an ancient Hindu temple carved from the rock in the face of a mountain. Far underground they reached a huge marble statue of Shiva, the head of which glowed in the darkness of the cavern. The illumination came from a hole pierced upward through the rock to the daylight above. Then, as he lost consciousness, waves of light seemed to surge in and engulf him. The last sense to go was sight. Now in his astral body he was free to roam outside the temple. He was told later that he had been in a state of coma for seven days. When life came back to his physical body he found that sight was the last sense to return, and was for a time stricken with the fear that he was blind. But he saw again little by little, and made a vow that ever afterwards he would help the blind all he could.

He was allowed to examine an ancient book which was one of the jealously guarded treasures of the Brahmins with whom he was now living. It was of enormous size, made of human skin, and contained hundreds of well-drawn illustrations of hands, with records of how, when and where this or that mark was proved correct.

> It was written in some red liquid which age had failed to spoil or fade. The effect of these vivid red letters on the pages of dull yellow skin was most remarkable. By some compound, probably made of herbs, each page was glazed, as it were by varnish. The outer covers alone showed the signs of wear and decay.

It was apparently written in three sections. The first part belonged to 'the earliest language and dated so far back that very few of the Brahmins even could read or decipher it'.

Palmistry had been studied for three thousand years, centuries before Christ, among the Hindus and in China, and then by the Chaldeans and Egyptians, but it is to the days of Greek civilization that we owe its present form. Anaxagoras taught and practised it in 423 B.C. Hispanus discovered on an altar dedicated to Hermes a book on cheiromancy, written in gold letters, which he sent as a present to Alexander the Great as 'a study worthy of the attention of an elevated and enquiring mind'.

Regarded as a valid science by such as Aristotle, Pliny, Paracelsus and Albertus Magnus, it fell into disrepute in the Middle Ages when the Church denounced it as a form of sorcery and witchcraft, and branded all palmists as Satan's sons. Nevertheless, two major works on it were printed in medieval times, *Die Kunst Ciromanta* in 1475 and the *Cyromantia Aristotelis* in 1490—the latter is now in the British Museum.

Louis Hamon was later to claim that the seventh verse of Chapter XXXVII of the Book of Job was purposely mistranslated by the ecclesiastics and other scholars responsible for the Authorised Version of the Bible because it gave divine approval to palmistry. He pointed out that a correct translation ought to read, 'God placed signs and marks on the hands of all the sons of men so that all men might know their works'. The Authorised Version of this is, 'He sealeth up the hand of every man; that all men may know his work'.

The sceptic will argue that the creases and lines on which the palmist bases his predictions are simply 'lines of flexor' caused by the action of the hand when folding to form a fist. If this were so one might expect the pattern of such marks to remain fixed in the hands of those pursuing the same occupation, but close study over a period has revealed that they often change their design.

When asked how one can possibly gauge a person's future by reading the lines on his or her hand chirologists usually advance the following arguments. They say that tendencies such as eloquence, anger and affection are shown by movements of the hand. These are coarse or fine, and so produce large and small creases or lines on the palm. Creases and lines therefore bear a definite relation to movements, and so to tendencies. There are four well-marked creases or lines on every hand, found by experience to bear a definite relation to the tendencies of affection, mental capacity, length of life and mental bent.

Now Sir Charles Bell, the eminent anatomist, has proved that every part of the brain is in touch with the nerves of the hand, and that the lines on the palm are more particularly connected with nerves from the brain to the hand than any other portion of the body.

Suppose, says the defender of palmistry, that certain tracts of brain cells are, incredible though it may seem, affected by coming events and made to vibrate. The vibrations excited in these cells cannot awaken the activity of the cells engaged on reasoning processes that adjoin them, but merely cause further vibrations in them—these being transmitted and marked on the palms of the hands by creases of different shapes.

Such is the theory of most palmists, and, according to them, the left hand is how you are born and the right hand what you make yourself or acquire.

After living for three years in India, Hamon heard that he had inherited a considerable sum of money from a relative and returned to London, where he proceeded to indulge in a hobby of collecting impressions of hands of all types of individuals, visiting hospitals, asylums and even prisons for the purpose. This involved him in a murder committed in the East End. A blood-stained hand-mark on the door of the house concerned led a detective on the case to call on him to ask if he could make anything out of the impression.

When Hamon compared the lines shown on this with those on the dead man's hands he became convinced that the print could not have been his, but as there was a striking similarity in some of the markings he reached the conclusion that the person responsible was a close relative. This led to the arrest and subsequent confession of the man's illegitimate son, whose existence had not up until then been suspected.

London life proved such a contrast to that he had led in India, and so jangled on his nerves, that Hamon now joined an expedition leaving to explore ruined temples at El Karnak and the Valley of the Tombs of the Kings. While there he became friendly with a guide who claimed to be descended from an ancient temple priest, and who gave him a mummified hand bearing a gold ring which he said was that of Princess Makitaten, youngest daughter of the Pharaoh Akhenaten, whose first wife was Nefertiti and who broke the power of the priests in Thebes and made Tel-el-Amarna his new capital. After his death the Princess is supposed to have raised an army to try to crush a rebellion of the Thebans incited by the priests. But she was defeated and captured, and the latter hacked off her hand, embalmed it and displayed it in a temple at Karnak as a warning to anyone who might seek to overthrow them.

'Going on as if a person inspired, he said to me that on my return to London I would find I had lost everything. I would then start to earn my living as a teacher of occult studies.' There was a curse on the hand that had been only partly fulfilled. This was that sooner or later it would be exhibited in all the principal countries of the world until after the end of a great war the lost tomb of King Tutankhamun was discovered. Hamon was the person chosen to carry out this latter part of the curse. In less than a year he would begin his wanderings and would carry the hand with him. On the eve of the lost tomb's discovery, the hand would endeavour to get free from his custody and the 'Ka', or spirit, imprisoned in it would return to its own. Until then the hand would protect him from all danger, if he in return promised to keep it always with him. Hamon promised.

He claimed that on returning to England he found the predictions being fulfilled, each in turn. His solicitor had embezzled his inheritance and had committed suicide. He tried, with scant success, to earn a living as a free-lance journalist. Then he met a Jewish civil servant whose palm he had read while in Cairo, and who declared that what he had foretold had already come about. Learning of his financial trouble, the man offered to set him up in business as a palmist on the signing of an agreement surrendering half his earnings for twelve years.

The backer wanted Hamon to adopt the name of Solomon for professional purposes, but it did not appeal to him. Then he wrote:

> One night in a dream the curious name of Cheiro, spelling itself in Greek and English, appeared to stand out in gold letters before me. I realised that 'cheir' was the Greek root for the word 'hand' and that Cheiro would therefore mean 'the knowledge or wisdom of the hand'. I did not hesitate for a moment. The next morning I had a large brass plate made with the words, 'Cheiro. Hours: 11 to 6', engraved upon it and had it placed on the street door of my rooms in Bond Street.

His first client was Arthur James Balfour, later a Conservative Prime Minister, and then President of the Society for Psychical Research, who was sufficiently impressed with Hamon's reading to recommend him to his friends. Before long people were climbing the narrow, steep staircase all day to the palmist's rooms, which in order to create the appropriate atmosphere he furnished in Indian fashion.

Women were attracted from the first by the tall, broad-shouldered, handsome and distinguished-looking young man. They were fascinated by his magnetic eyes, which seemed dark but were really blue, and his deep voice with its slight Irish accent. As an interviewer, Miss Ina Oxenford, was to write seven years later in *The Palmist* for November 1897, 'His manner is sympathetic, he appears to imply, "You are misunderstood, I understand you".' She waited in 'a quaintly draped room with curiosities of many kinds from many nations' and on a carved teak table were volumes containing prints of the hands of celebrities who had consulted him.

> After a brief interval Cheiro came and took me into a room hung with Indian and Burmese curtains and containing only a table and two chairs. On the table was a small cushion and a reading glass, and a most curious pointer, consisting of two serpents twisted to form a pencil with which to indicate the lines. He holds the hand and traces with the pointer the direction of the various lines, reading their meaning, as he goes, and is careful to explain exactly where he sees the different events.

He rarely touched his clients' hands with his own. When he did he would put down the pointer, take the consultant gently by the wrist and stare over his or her head into the shadows. Then, according to a medium friend of his, Edith Halford Nelson, he would no longer be studying their palms but seeking clairvoyance through contact with their vibrations.

Cheiro once wrote that it was always his rule to reveal events of the early life and give dates or years when such and such a thing occurred. He realized that accuracy about the past gave his consultants confidence in what he might have to say regarding the future.

In order to impress the society people with whom he was soon mixing he called himself Count Leigh de Hamong. It was not till some ten years later that he changed this again to Count Louis Hamon on going to live in Paris. Before long he became so well known that he was the subject of an article in a London evening paper. The journalist mentioned that fortune-telling was still illegal, and the civil servant, who was nearing retirement age, began to fear that if the police prosecuted Cheiro he himself might be involved in the court proceedings and lose his pension, so he tore up his agreement, leaving the other his own master.

In his *Confessions* Hamon stated that he eventually received a visit from a police inspector who drew his attention to

> the Act of Henry VIII whereby any person or persons found guilty of practising Palmistry, Astrology, Witchcraft, or all such works of the devil is hereby deemed a rogue and vaga-

> bond to be sentenced to lose all his goods and possessions, to stand for one year in the Pillory and to be expelled from the country, or to be imprisoned for life.

Either Cheiro's recollection of the incident or the inspector's knowledge of the law must have been at fault. The position up to 1735 was that any form of fortune-telling was a capital offence, then by the Witchcraft Act of that year earlier Acts were repealed and for the future

> any person proved to have pretended to exercise or use any kind of witchcraft, sorcery, inchantment or conjuration, or undertake to tell fortunes or pretend from his or her skill or knowledge in any occult or crafty science to discover where or in what manner any goods or chattels, supposed to have been stolen or lost, may be found, every person, so offending, being thereof lawfully convicted on indictment or information, is to be imprisoned for a year, to stand once every three months during that period upon the market day there and openly in the pillory by the space of one hour, and to find security for his or her good behaviour.

This Act was in its turn repealed by the Vagrancy Act of 1824, which provided that

> every person pretending or professing to tell fortunes, or using any subtle craft, means or device, by palmistry or otherwise, to deceive and impose on any of His Majesty's subjects, shall be deemed a rogue and a vagabond and may be imprisoned for three months with hard labour.

Such was in fact the law when the inspector called on Cheiro and said that if he closed down by the following Saturday no further action would be taken.

Hamon claimed that never did he work harder than during that week. When at about six o'clock on the Saturday evening he was about to leave his rooms, an unexpected latecomer, a Mrs Walter Palmer, asked if he could come that evening at 9.30 to her house in Brook Street to read the hands of her guests. It proved a fortunate assignment, for there besides giving readings to Sir Henry Irving and his son, Laurence, he met an influential lawyer, Sir George Lewis, thanks to whose efforts the police withdrew their notice of closure, and from then onward he never received any interference from them.

Later that year Cheiro was consulted by Oscar Wilde after a dinner party given by the celebrated Blanche Roosevelt. So that he might not know who his consultants were, he sat behind a curtain. A pair of rather fat hands were pushed through holes in it. He was struck by the difference in the markings on the left and right palms, and told the stranger that the left denoted hereditary tendencies, while the right showed developed or attained characteristics, and that as we use the left side of the brain the nerves cross and go to the right hand, so that it consequently revealed the true nature and development of the individual.

Hamon went on that the left hand before him had promised the most unusual destiny of brilliance and uninterrupted success, which was completely broken and ruined at a certain date in the right.

> Almost forgetting myself for a moment, I summed up all by saying: 'The left hand is the hand of a king, but the right that of a king who will send himself into exile'.
>
> The owner of the hand did not laugh. 'At what date?' he asked rather quietly.
>
> 'A few years from now, at about your fortieth year.'

Cheiro learned later that he had been speaking to Oscar Wilde, who came to see him again just before his trial to inquire if the break in his Line of Fate was still there. 'I told him it was, but that surely his Destiny could not be broken. He was very, very quiet, but in a far-off voice he said: "My good friend, you know well Fate does not keep road-menders on her highways".

In early 1893 Hamon became so ill through overwork that he spent nearly three months in a private nursing home in Devonshire Street. He had given readings to some six thousand persons in the previous year, and after recovering his health decided to visit the United States. He sailed on the *Paris*, and on arrival in New York rented a fine apartment on Fifth Avenue, but found that to make himself known as a palmist, since he lacked letters of introduction and friends, was difficult. He was seriously thinking of returning to London when one afternoon a very determined woman journalist called and told him that she had been sent by the *New York World* to propose a test to him. If he accepted and were successful he would receive tremendous publicity in that Sunday's paper, but if he failed or refused he might as well take the next steamer back to England.

Cheiro asked the nature of the test, and was informed by the reporter that she had brought with her a number of hand-prints on paper. Without knowing whose they were, and without asking a single question, he was to study them and dictate his readings to her. He agreed to do this. His very nervousness, he wrote later, helped to make him succeed. 'My brain screwed up to such a pitch seemed to drink in every line and formation and made mental pictures of the owners in such a way that I was able to describe their characteristics as if I had known them personally.'

When he came to the fifth impression he paused and said to the woman that there was something so abnormal about this hand that he must refuse to read it unless she brought him the written consent of the individual concerned. The journalist assured him her editor held such permission from all whose prints he was examining. Hamon then pointed out that the lines shown on the left palm were normal, while those on that of the right were in every way abnormal with the line of head twisted out of its place, closing in against the heart-line under the base of the third finger.

> Judging from these, [Hamon dictated] this man undoubtedly commenced his career in a normal way. He is even likely to have been a religious kind of man in his early years, probably a Sunday-school teacher. Then later he became in-

> terested in science or medicine. His character slowly and steadily changed under the urge to acquire wealth at any cost, until finally he decided to murder for money, which he did. As he enters his forty-fourth year, he will be found out, arrested, tried and sentenced to death. It will then be proved that for years he has used his mentality and whatever profession he has followed to obtain money by crime and has stopped at nothing to achieve his ends. Though this man will be condemned to death, yet his hands show that he will escape this fate and live on for years—but in prison.

When Cheiro had concluded his readings the woman journalist left without revealing whether or not he had been correct. She simply told him that he would know the result in the following Sunday's *World*. He hardly slept that Saturday night. Then at 9 a.m. on 26th November 1893 he was roused by his servant who told him excitedly that there were over a hundred people sitting on the stairs waiting to consult him. In the man's hand was the *World* and the entire front page was devoted to the interview, relating how Cheiro had described with uncanny accuracy the characters and lives of among others the Mayor of New York, the District Attorney, Ella Wheeler Wilcox the poetess, Lillian Russell the prima donna, Reginald de Koven the composer, and of forty-four-year-old Dr Meyer from Chicago who had recently been arrested on suspicion of having used his position as a medical man to poison rich patients whom he had insured for large sums.

'Americans are like no other people in the world,' wrote Cheiro. 'When they take an idea into their heads, they do not waste time in putting it into execution.' This was why, only a short while after reading the newspaper report, so many were queueing outside to see him. He went out and told them it was Sunday and that they must return next day. 'I believe I rose in their eyes by my very refusal. . . . All day long callers were similarly informed and when Monday came my Secretary had to book appointments for nearly two months in advance.'

Later, following a sensational trial, Dr Meyer was sentenced to die in the electric chair, and all appeals failed. A week before the date fixed for the execution he requested Hamon through his lawyers to visit him in his cell at Sing Sing prison. The broken man reminded the palmist of the reading that had appeared in the *World*, and asked whether he still believed in the prediction's complete fulfilment. Cheiro examined the other's right hand and found that his line of life still showed no sign of any break, and so he left the Doctor with the hope that some miracle would yet occur to save him.

The days passed with no news to relieve the tension. Then at midnight, a few hours before Meyer was due to die, Hamon suddenly heard boys rushing through the streets shouting 'Special Edition'. He read across the front page of the paper he bought 'MEYER ESCAPES THE CHAIR—SUPREME COURT FINDS FLAW IN INDICTMENT'. Fifteen years later the reprieved murderer died peacefully in a prison hospital.

Hamon soon became as famous in America as in Europe. In Washington President Cleveland and many distinguished statesmen consulted him. Mrs Leiter a Chicago millionaire's wife, called and placed the print of a right hand before him. It was that of her daughter, she explained, adding the date and time of Mary's birth. 'I believe you are an impostor, but do your best—or worst!' she challenged.

He prophesied that the girl would marry a man from another country and then lead the life of a queen in the East, but that she would die young. The mother laughed and left. Within a few years Mary Leiter became Lord Curzon's wife and later Vicereine of India, and as foretold her life was short.

Colonel Robert Ingersoll, a famous New York lawyer and cynic, said to his friends after a reading 'I may not believe in God, man or the devil—but I believe in Cheiro'.

Samuel L. Clemens, better known as 'Mark Twain', submitted his hands to the palmist for comment, and before he left wrote in the Visitors' Book, 'Cheiro has exposed my character with humiliating accuracy. I ought not to confess this accuracy, still I am moved to do so.'

The humorist told Hamon that he thought it possible the

past might leave its mark, and by considering the length and shape of the fingers and thumb, the texture of skin and nails and their colour, a person's character and occupation might be deduced, but he did not understand how the future could be foreshadowed by observing lines of flexor and the shorter and finer lines and measuring where breaks and intersecting occurred.

Cheiro argued in reply that the subconscious mind might know in advance what we shall attempt and where we shall fail, that nothing in the world was left to blind chance and that our very failures were as necessary to our development as were our successes. Then, seeing that he was making no headway, he showed the other the impressions of a mother's left and right hands and compared them with those of five of her children's, until they came to one where the right hand of the child almost exactly tallied with the markings on the mother's right hand.

He told Twain that every occurrence in the girl's life repeated, even to dates, what had happened in the mother's, although twenty years separated them in time. Both had married, had five children, been widowed, and suffered from identical illnesses, all at the same ages. So, he concluded, if one had known the events of the mother's life and had seen that the same markings appeared in the child's hands, one could have predicted the events that would take place in that girl's future life.

A baby an hour old, Cheiro said on another occasion, has lines that tell its future—'lines that could they speak would even tell its burden of heredity, the fate that perhaps its mother made for it, and that later she would give her life to unmake if it were possible'.

Hamon went on a long and immensely successful lecture tour of the States, and was even invited to speak in many churches; on one occasion he had an audience of over two thousand at a Methodist educational gathering in Florida. In Boston he held classes, and ten leading physicians enrolled themselves as his pupils to learn how diseases could be indicated by lines and formation of hands. In recent times, the researches of the Galton Laboratory in London have reached similar conclusions: some thirty congenital disorders have been linked with certain markings on the palm, many of which are to be seen before the diseases occur. Doctors at a hospital in Osaka, Japan, started in 1967 to collect prints of the hands of all patients. After an exhaustive study of some two hundred thousand of these they found diagnostic meaning in the course taken by lines, when they were chained, had little hair-lines clinging to them, where they were broken or were interrupted by islands and so on. Most extraordinary of all, this has enabled them to predict some of the diseases from which patients were likely to suffer, and when this would happen. Statements made by Cheiro in his books on palmistry have been found to be true, such as that a narrow island in the centre of a sloping line of head generally indicates some brain illness, that an island on the line of life indicates bad health at the age represented by the position where it is situated, and that if this line is broken on both hands it generally signifies death.

Hamon was stimulated at first by his spectacular success in America. But as time passed he tired, as he puts it, of the 'pets of American society who came to me in hundreds, and whose chief concern was "When shall I have more money?" and "When shall I be free to marry again?" ' So in 1894 he returned to England, where that summer he received a mysterious summons to the High Courts of Justice. Three years previously 'a very exacting and apparently severe elderly gentleman dressed in tweeds like some country squire' had consulted him. Cheiro had predicted that in 1894 his interlocutor would reach the summit of whatever was his ambition.

The visitor, who had obviously come under an assumed name, then said somewhat mockingly, 'And now, sir, as you have gone so far, you may as well make a guess at the exact date of this wonderful event'. The other replied that according to his system of numerology the day should be any one of those days which by addition made the figure of a '1' in the month of

July 1894, such as the 1st (1+0), 10th (1+0), 19th (1+9) or 28th (2+8), but he thought it would be the 19th.

Before the stranger left Cheiro asked him for impressions of his hands, and was told that he should have these on one of the dates mentioned, provided the prediction came about. Then on the morning of 19th July 1894 a messenger called at 108 New Bond Street and without any explanation informed Hamon that his attendance was required at twelve o'clock that day at the High Courts of Justice.

He waited in a room at the back of one of the Courts for nearly an hour, then the door opened and the Lord Chief Justice appeared in his robes of office. Cheiro did not recognize his former client until the imposing figure said, 'I am willing to keep my promise—you can have impressions of my hands now'. After Hamon had taken them the judge wrote by the side of the print of the right hand 'Russell of Killowen' with the date, 19th July 1894, and said, 'You see, this is the first day I have put on these robes as Lord Chief Justice of England —your date was exact, though how you did it I cannot imagine.'

If it is difficult for sceptics to believe in palmistry, it is even more so for them to accept that numerology is credible in its assumptions.

On Sunday, 13th December 1936, Dr Cosmo Lang, then Archbishop of Canterbury, broadcasting in a BBC religious service, said, 'On the eleventh day of December two hundred and forty-eight years ago, King James II fled from Whitehall. By a strange coincidence, on the eleventh of December, 1936, King Edward VIII went out into exile.'

The supporter of numerology will point out even stranger coincidences. For example, take those occurring in the lives of the American presidents Lincoln and Kennedy, both of whose names contain seven letters, both of whom were assassinated on the fifth day of the week, by John Wilkes Booth and Lee Harvey Oswald respectively, each with fifteen letters in their names, the one born in 1839 and the other in 1939. Lincoln and Kennedy both had Vice-Presidents named Johnson:

Andrew John, born in 1808, and Lyndon in 1908; even the first Christian names of these Vice-Presidents contain an identical number of letters, six.

Three Presidents were inaugurated in the 1860s and three in the 1960s, and the first was shot dead in each decade, while the names of the last in both instances, Ulysses Simpson Grant and Richard Milhous Nixon, correspond as regards numbers of letters, seven-seven-five.

Even curiouser are the coincidences that Lincoln's secretary was called Kennedy and one of Kennedy's Lincoln, while Lincoln was assassinated in Ford's Theatre and Kennedy in a Lincoln automobile!

King Edward VII was very superstitious, and as Prince of Wales he consulted Cheiro in the Belgrave Square house of the American society hostess Lady Arthur Paget. The fortune-teller told the monarch that the numbers 6 and 9 were the most important in his life.

The Prince pointed out that they would come together when he was sixty-nine, and commented, 'As you say they are the keynotes of my life, I suppose that must be the end'. Later, as King Edward VII, he was to die in his sixty-ninth year.

This was the beginning of a long association with the future King, who on one occasion presented Hamon with the birth particulars of five persons, whose identities he did not disclose, and asked him to work out their astrological charts. Afterwards he revealed that they were the Kaiser, the Tsar of Russia and three members of the British Royal Family.

Many years before the Prince succeeded to the throne, Cheiro foretold that his Coronation would take place in August 1902. When in due course this event was planned for the June of that year and had to be postponed owing to his illness, Queen Alexandra sent for Hamon and reminded him he had once impressed her husband with his prophecy that Edward would not die until his sixty-ninth year. She asked the fortune-teller to do all he could to convince the sick man he would get better.

Cheiro recorded that he was taken into the royal bedroom,

where he found the King very weak, so, summoning all his will-power, he drew the invalid's attention to the earlier prediction and stressed that he still believed the Coronation would take place that August. They were then only at the end of June, and he was certain complete recovery was imminent.

The monarch replied, 'I am almost forced to believe you. Every other date you gave me turned out correctly. I jotted them down on that.' He indicated a sheet of paper on the bedside table. 'Tell me, which date then in August would be the best one to fix for the Coronation?'

Cheiro suggested the ninth, which was the King's strongest 'fadic number'. He had been born on 9th November. Hamon wrote:

> That month in occult studies was regarded as the House of the Nine, or the House of Mars negative, which was why his name would go down to posterity as Edward the Peacemaker. The month of August was called the Royal House of Leo the Lion, therefore August 9 would be the best date he could choose.

The next day Queen Alexandra sent Hamon a message: his words had so cheered her husband that he was showing signs of rapid improvement, and had given orders for the Coronation to be fixed for 9th August.

Another monarch who consulted Hamon was Leopold II of the Belgians, son of Queen Victoria's favourite uncle, who was informed that '9' was his key numeral and that 1909 would be his fatal year. Cheiro also said that his death would be caused by serious trouble with his digestive system and internal organs. Leopold died on 17th December in the year mentioned, the official bulletin giving the cause as 'the complete breakdown of the digestive organs and intestinal obstruction'.

As already mentioned, Hamon at Edward VII's request worked out for him the horoscopes of a number of persons without giving him any clues as to whom they were. About a year later, a stranger called on him one afternoon and, producing a sheet of paper covered with Cheiro's own handwriting, asked him to explain his reasons for saying:

> Whoever the man is that these numbers and birth date represent will be haunted all his life by the horrors of war and bloodshed. He will do his utmost to prevent them, but his destiny is so intimately associated with such things that his name will be bound up with some of the most far-reaching and bloodiest wars in history, and in the end, about 1917, he will lose all he loves most by sword or strife in one form or another, and he himself will meet a violent death.

As the anonymous caller listened intently to Cheiro's explanation he made notes, paid the usual fee and left. In late 1904, when in St Petersburg, the palmist was taken to dine with the Tsar in his Summer Palace, and recognized him as the stranger who visited the Bond Street consulting room. Afterwards, the Tsar asked Hamon to work out the charts of two other persons, which he did. Both gave similar indications that 1917 would be 'overwhelmed by dark and sinister influences indicating the end of the Romanoff dynasty'.

Later during that visit to St Petersburg Gregori Rasputin came to consult Cheiro one January afternoon in 1905. According to Cheiro, it was a stormy interview. The monk suddenly roared when the palmist was looking at his hands, 'I know the Future—you do not; my Future is to redeem the People, and save the Emperor from himself'.

When, somewhat nonplussed, Hamon asked if he wanted to be told anything about what lay ahead, he retorted that he would laugh at whatever was said. It was his divinely appointed destiny to be the Saviour of Russia, and he was the master of his own fate. Cheiro wondered whether the man was mad, yet the dirty, thick, coarse hand had inscribed on it an extraordinary future. He told him that he would wield enormous power over others, but it would be a power for evil. Did he want to know more?

'Yes, yes!' Rasputin exclaimed impatiently, then, correcting himself, he added grandly, 'But, of course, I knew all this before. I am a prophet, and a greater one than you. I know all things. But what of the Future?'

Hamon hesitated before replying, 'I foresee for you a violent end within a palace. You will be menaced by poison, by knife, and by bullet. Finally I see the icy waters of the Neva closing above you.'

The consultation then closed with Rasputin shouting furiously in Russian, 'Who are you who can predict my end? I can never die. I am the Saviour of my people. I am the Protector of the Tsar. I am greater than the Tsar.'

Hamon commented that Rasputin attempted from the first moment to hypnotize him, and that it was only his own knowledge of how to prevent this that saved him. Instead of looking into the other's eyes, he concentrated his attention on a point between the monk's eyebrows, with the result that he failed in his intent.

In 1894 Herbert Kitchener, then Sirdar of the Egyptian Army and in his forty-fourth year, had returned to England over the Abbas Affair. His determined behaviour was soon justified by the course of events. He was made a KCMG, went back to Egypt with more authority than before, and shortly afterwards successfully concluded the Sudanese Campaign.

It was a time of crisis for him, with his future career at risk. This was possibly why he decided to consult Cheiro, who called on him by appointment at the War Office on 21st July 1894, and took an impression of his right hand. After studying it, the palmist said that the other's military responsibilities would be at their most onerous in 1914, and that when he reached his sixty-sixth year he would be in great danger of death in the month of June 'caused by storm or disaster at sea'.

Kitchener then revealed that some years earlier, using an assumed name, he had visited Cheiro, who had warned that water would be his worst enemy, with the result that he had made himself an expert swimmer. When Hamon left Kitchener said, 'As, of course, you believe in thought transference and that sort of thing, who knows if I won't send you some sign, if it should happen that water claims me at the last'.

That the victor of Khartoum did not forget the prediction is proved by a report published in London newspapers on 19th June 1915, that when he came to the British Front he met at Dunkirk Commandant de Balancourt, to whom he mentioned that a 'Jack Johnson' had dropped not far from him. 'That did not alarm me,' the Field-Marshal declared, 'because I know I shall die at sea'.

At 8 p.m. on Monday evening, 5th June 1916, Hamon was sitting in the lounge of his country house talking to friends when they were startled by the sound of something crashing down in the *north* end of the room. He found that a large oak shield painted with the United Kingdom's arms had fallen, breaking in half. At the same time Lord Kitchener probably died in the disaster to H.M.S. *Hampshire* in the North Sea when it struck a mine on the way to Russia.

Cheiro reproduced in his books on palmistry some impressions of hands of the famous who consulted him, as proof that his fulfilled predictions were indicated by palm-lines and markings. That of Lord Kitchener's shows the line of voyage or Travel breaking the line of fate at what Hamon estimated would be about the sixty-sixth year of the Field-Marshal's life.

In 1900, when in Rome, Cheiro was summoned to the Quirinal Palace by King Humbert I, who had become very concerned about his future ever since his near-assassination three years earlier. He asked the palmist to tell him frankly what the lines on his hand indicated would happen. The other, after studying them, replied that all the signs portended sudden death in three months' time. (This came about when at Monza on 29th July that year the King was killed by the anarchist Bresci.)

Cheiro went from Rome to Paris where he told friends in diplomatic circles about his prediction and added that if it were fulfilled there would shortly afterwards be an attempt to murder the Shah of Persia, who was then visiting the famous Exhibition as a guest of the French President. The Grand Vizier, hearing this, called on Cheiro, who confirmed that he felt the Shah's life was in peril. Consequently the Vizier arranged for a strong police guard to shield his master, and it was owing to this protection that Salson the anarchist failed to assassinate the Persian ruler.

The morning after the attack the Grand Vizier visited Cheiro to convey the Shah's thanks for having been alerted in advance, and requesting him to call at five o'clock on the following afternoon at the Palais des Souverains to read his hands.

At the consultation an interpreter translated what Cheiro said. The Shah was unimpressed, and commented that all he had heard could have been inspired by what the palmist might have read in books about Persian affairs. He would test his powers in a better way. Cheiro must know how an earlier King of Persia, Cyrus, put the powers of the oracles of ancient Greece on trial. He would subject him to a somewhat similar test. 'Tell me', he demanded, 'exactly what is happening in Teheran at this moment. A cable will be sent there at once to prove the truth or not of your statement.'

According to Hamon, he asked the Shah for some object he carried on his person and was given a silk handkerchief, which Cheiro then clasped and, closing his eyes, concentrated with all his force of will.

> For a few seconds I found my mental canvas a hopeless blank. Then, suddenly, a picture formed with startling distinctness before my inward sight. Opening my eyes and looking the Shah full in the face, I said in French: 'Your Majesty, grave events are happening in your capital, at this hour. The Governor of the city has been thrown into gaol by the mob, on account of serious food riots that have been taking place for several days. He is in danger of becoming a victim of the people's rage against the price of bread and wheat.'

This infuriated his Imperial Majesty, and Hamon was hurried out by a trembling Grand Vizier. But a few days later the palmist was summoned back to the Palais, where an impressed and most affable Shah showed him a telegram from

Teheran confirming his clairvoyance.

Sir Ernest Shackleton, the famous explorer, believed that Cheiro learned more from the appearances of his clients than from the lines on their palms. So he arranged for a friend to make an appointment for Mr X—'a famous tenor'—requesting that no windows be left open lest he caught cold. Then Shackleton disguised himself with curly wig, short pointed false beard, and Quartier Latin black cape and went to the Bond Street consulting-room. He spoke with an Italian accent, and carried a large roll of music, which he placed very deliberately on the table beside him.

But to his surprise he soon found that the fortune-teller was not taken in by the subterfuge and, on examining his visitor's hands, said that they revealed him to be 'a born leader of men, one who courted danger', and who was 'planning one of the most hazardous enterprises of his life'.

Shackleton could not refrain from asking whether it would be successful.

Hamon replied, 'Only in the way that you will escape losing your life while engaged in it. After that, you will carry out another enterprise exactly similar, and it is while engaged in this second one that then, I fear, you will lose your life, in or about your forty-eighth year.'

The other commented that it sounded as though he was in for an eventful, risky time, and when the palmist replied that it was just such a life as would suit Shackleton the explorer, the visitor removed his disguise and declared that, as Hamon evidently did not learn these things from outward appearances, he might as well reveal his real identity.

As foretold, Sir Ernest Shackleton never returned from his second expedition to the Antarctic and died in South Georgia on 5th January 1922 a few weeks before his forty-eighth birthday.

In 1896 Cheiro brought to his rooms for experiments with clients a 'Divinometer', an invention of a French scientist, Professor d'Odiardi. This, it was alleged, recorded on a chart the movement of the brain without any personal contact. The person to be tested had to stand within a foot or two of the instrument, but someone with a strong will could influence the needle at a distance of from ten to twenty feet. So long as the brain was normal the needle would record its movement, but those who were addicted to drugs or alcohol made the apparatus work very slowly, and an idiot had no power to deflect the needle at all. Such were the machine's claimed powers.

In his book *Language of the Hand* Hamon devotes a chapter to this invention, which he described as a 'register of cerebral force first used by the Professor in the Notting Hill Gate Hospital. He states that on one occasion a man was standing in front of the machine criticizing its action when some other visitors arrived and one of them mentioned that the shares of the South African Chartered Company had fallen steeply in value. No one knew that the other man was a large holder of these shares, but at the moment 'the drop was mentioned his emotion caused the indicator in the machine to move rapidly, and register one of the highest numbers that has been recorded by it'.

According to Cheiro, people had tested the 'Divinometer' in every conceivable manner. It had been examined by the Académie des Sciences in Paris. 'The greatest unbelievers in this machine have tried in every way to prove that the needle was moved by other agency but this unknown force radiating from the body, but one and all have in the end admitted that the action of the needle was due to a force given off by the person tested.'

Eighty years have passed since Savary d'Odiardi invented his apparatus, and scientists now accept that the brain produces a measurable electric charge. Harold Burr of Yale has developed an instrument sensitive enough to detect this, while Paval Gulyaiev of Leningrad University's more advanced equipment can chart a brain-induced electric field at some distance from the body.

Edith Halford Nelson, the young actress who acted as a medium for Hamon at séances, wrote that he was no saint, neither did he wish to be thought one.

It was because he was a man of the world with immense experience that men and women came to him with their life problems, knowing that they would obtain from him not only an extraordinary sympathy and understanding, but also practical advice.

His life was many times endangered by the love-affairs of his clients, and also by his own. The fact that he was a dead shot, an expert at ju-jitsu, and even thought to possess some strange and unknown means of defence, did not prevent a jealous husband from stabbing him twice in the side, inflicting wounds from which he suffered the rest of his life.

The lines in his own hands signified, Hamon once wrote, that he would not be married till late in life. In 1899 he was still a bachelor when he was cited as a co-respondent by the husband of a woman client who had become infatuated with him. He asked Sir Edward Marshall Hall to defend him, but was able to prove his innocence, and the petitioner withdrew his charges, apologized and paid all costs and expenses. One outcome was that in the August of the same year Hall himself consulted Cheiro and when in November 1924 he heard that the palmist was writing his reminiscences he sent a copy of the notes he had jotted down at the time of the interview. Cheiro had said:

> I see something so vividly that I feel bound to tell you of it. . . . I see you standing on the balcony of what looks like a large country house with a garden below and big trees all in front. But the strange thing is, that the grounds seem lit up with coloured lamps—what makes it still stranger is that there are thousands of people trampling down the flower-beds and looking up at the balcony, and you are apparently trying to speak or actually speaking. There are several people on the balcony, men and women, and the faces of the crowd are very white in the strong light. Beside you on your left is a woman, much shorter than you are, waving a white pocket handkerchief in her left hand and the people below

are shouting. That is what I see, but what it means is more than I can tell you.

Sir Edward enclosed with this a detailed account of how some sixteen months later this prevision came about. In August he was asked to stand for Southport at the next election. He intended to decline, but in the train fell asleep, and on waking found what seemed an endless line of trucks running on a parallel line in the same direction as they were going. At last they overtook them and ran abreast of the engine drawing them. Sir Edward goes on:

And there in big gold letters on it was this name, 'SOUTHPORT'. That such a name should be on what I thought was a G.W.R. engine struck me as very curious and, being a little superstitious, I began to think. It seemed to me a direct omen, and when I got to Chester, I sent a wire to say I would stand for the constituency.

The polling took place on 11th October 1900. The betting was 10:1 against Sir Edward. After two recounts, the result was a narrow victory for him by 209 votes. Before formally announcing the figure, the Returning Officer asked that no one present should signal who had won to the crowd outside by waving coloured handkerchiefs. Then Marshall Hall went with him and others on to a balcony where he had never been before. He continues:

When I got outside, I very nearly fell over the low parapet in front, for there before me and below me was the exact reproduction of Cheiro's prevision. There was what looked like a big country house, there were the big trees all lit up, there were the thousands of people with their upturned faces showing white in the brilliant electric light of the arc-lamps, and there the flower-beds being trampled down by their feet.

And then a most weird thing happened. I recognised the scene in a moment, and equally instantaneously I re-

> membered the other detail, and almost chuckled when I thought that that at any rate could not be reproduced, but turning around I saw standing beside me my wife, who was waving a white pocket-handkerchief in her left hand. She had anticipated the instructions of the Returning Officer literally and did not think that a white handkerchief came within the prohibition of red and blue.

Together with this account of the fulfilled prediction, Sir Edward enclosed a note saying that he had just been studying the deductions drawn by Cheiro from the lines on his hand in August 1899, and adding, 'I find throughout they have proved to be wonderfully true'.

Mrs Nelson claimed that there were two sides to Hamon's character, and this is confirmed by what he himself has written. In his *Language of the Hand* he included a photograph of his own right hand as an example of what is called 'the double line of head'. He states that the mentality indicated by each of these lines is in apparent contradiction to the other. The lower line closely joined to the line of life denotes an extremely sensitive, artistic and imaginative nature. The upper line rising on the Mount of Jupiter and running nearly straight across the palm shows self-confidence, ambition, power to dominate others and a level-headed, practical way of looking at life.

On Cheiro's left hand there was no sign whatever of any upper head-line, and he alleged that it began to appear when he was about thirty. Then, he wrote, being forced by circumstances to lecture and speak in public, he made a supreme effort to overcome his extreme sensitiveness as denoted by the lower head-line, with the result that the upper line commenced to develop, and in a few years became the dominant one on his right hand.

He developed, too, an insatiable appetite for travel, often vanished for months to explore India, China and Russia. He acted as a Press correspondent during the Sino-Japanese War of 1894–5 and the Russo-Japanese War of 1904–5. In the

Palmist's Review for June 1899 reference was made to rumours that 'Count Leigh de Hamong is giving up business in consequence of the ill-repute into which his science is being brought by blackmailers and other questionable characters. Again it is asserted that a handsome legacy has been left him by some unknown relative.' A reporter from the *Review* had called on him at 108 New Bond Street, and had been told that

> for some time past he has been in failing health, and for this reason alone the present season will be his last in London for some years to come. After August, 1899, he will travel to New York to deliver a course of lectures. From thence he will go to Paris to lecture at the *Exposition* of 1900. After that, as he quaintly puts it, he will write books with which to inflict mankind.

The *Review* next mentioned Cheiro in its issue for October 1900, stating that he was enjoying great success in Paris and that his 'latest conquest' was the Shah of Persia, who had bestowed on him the Order of the Lion and the Sun in recognition of his services in saving the potentate from assassination through his warning. Then in March 1901 one reads that 'an offer of territorial proprietorship in the pleasant land of France proved too tempting to be resisted and with his laurels still fresh upon him, Cheiro retires to rural seclusion and the cultivation of his own vines and fir trees in the sunshine of his adopted country'.

But it was impossible for him really to rusticate, tired as he must have been after reading some nineteen thousand hands to date. Enthusiastically supporting the policy of close friendship with France now to be pursued by Queen Victoria's successor, King Edward VII, he founded that year and also edited *L'Entente Cordiale*, an illustrated monthly published both in English and in French. He was able to cheer the sick monarch with news of this when the following June he went to London at Queen Alexandra's request to reassure her husband that he would recover and be crowned in August as earlier predicted.

In 1900 Hamon had bought for £1 000 a Parisian paper catering for Americans in Europe, the *American Register*. This had been in existence since 1868, but was languishing. The new owner-editor revitalized it with up-to-the-minute details of transatlantic society's comings and goings, gossip and useful hints. This success spurred him into taking an increasing interest in business. Under the style of Hamong et Cie of Reims he made and sold his excellent 'Royal Imperial Champagne' which he served in the mansion he bought in the rue du Bois de Boulogne where an impressive little army of liveried servants waited on the royalty, statesmen and *beau monde* who were his guests. He had offices in New York and St Petersburg as well as in Paris and London.

Then in 1910 the crash came. On 10th June a receiving order was made in London against him, and on 5th August he was adjudged bankrupt, followed by his public examination on 20th September in the King's Bench Division of the High Court of Justice. He was described as 'of 32 Piccadilly Circus, W.1., lately trading as Hamon and Co. of Gracechurch Street, E.C.3. His liabilities amounted to £43 966 and his assets at no more than £10.

It was revealed that in January 1908 he had sold the *American Register* to a company of his own formation for £20 000 in fully paid shares, when he was appointed managing director at an annual salary of £500, which post he had now resigned on account of these proceedings. In 1905 he had begun business as Hamon and Co. at 8 place de l'Opéra, Paris, with a branch office at 59 and 60 Gracechurch Street. In Paris the business was conducted under what is known in England as a limited partnership. He provided £2 000 capital and was joined by three other persons who contributed £14 000. According to French law, it was necessary that one member of the firm should make himself liable for its debts. He accepted that responsibility, and the liability of the other members was limited to the extent of their contributions.

The business in Paris was managed and controlled by a

Mr Loewry, and consisted chiefly in the flotation of companies and the placing of shares. There was also a banking branch. The first year's trading produced a profit of £6 000, but subsequently heavy losses were incurred during the financial panic of 1907, and the concern was closed down at that year's end, together with a financial paper, *La Gazette Financière*, that had been started in connection with it and had cost about £14 000.

The bankrupt said that the greater part of his indebtedness was in respect of money advanced to enable him to discharge the liabilities of Hamon and Co. He had expected that a large profit would have been made through a concession which he had obtained from the Russian Government for the running of automobiles from Tiflis to Vladikaffcasse, shortening the journey by two days, but this could not be operated owing to the unsettled state of Russia. The company's debts in London and Paris had amounted to £72 000, and he had succeeded in paying them, with the exception of about £4 000 in Paris. He now possessed no interest in the company which had acquired the *American Register*.

On 12th January 1911 Hamon's discharge from bankruptcy was suspended for 2 years, 6 months, on the grounds that his assets had realized only 4 shillings. Then, on 2nd May 1913, he was granted an earlier discharge on payment of £50.

This was an unfortunate time for Louis Hamon. In France a series of political scandals had rocked the country, and in April 1911, one Frantz Théodore Hamon, who was in control of the accounts of the Ministry of Foreign Affairs, was arrested, charged with corruption, then sent for trial. In the United States Louis was at first confused with this civil servant, and so when Cheiro died in 1936 this resulted in a leading American paper stating incorrectly in its obituary notice that he had been sentenced in Paris to serve thirteen months in gaol for fraud. If he had been alive, of course, he could have obtained heavy damages for libel.

Back in London, he went to live at Devonshire House, 15 Marylebone Road. Edith Halford Nelson wrote in *Out of the Silence* that during his absence another palmist, believing he had retired, adopted the name of 'Cheiro', was involved in a shady transaction and came out of prison just then, after serving a long sentence. She asserts that the real Cheiro had the greatest difficulty in establishing his identity with the public and even some friends.

Twelve years previously Lily Langtry had consulted him anonymously, wearing a heavy black veil. When he was so burdened with trouble, it came as a pleasant surprise for him to receive a letter from her dated 15th April 1911, and addressed '28 Regent's Court, Hanover Gate, London, N.W.1.' Calling him 'My dear Cheiro', she wrote:

> I have heard that you have returned to England and I think it is only fair to tell you how very accurate your remarks were in my case. . . . You told me that I would not be accompanied by my husband to America, although I had planned my tour there expressly for that purpose. I could not see how your words could come true, but the Boer War broke out and events happened exactly as you said they would.
>
> You foretold a scandal for me in the States. . . . In this I again doubted your accuracy, as I was taking an excellent company and a play that had been a great London success. But you were right again, for I reached America during a political campaign, and the play in question, 'The Degenerates' was dubbed on account of the title immoral by those who were glad to seize on anything to further their party interests, but, be that as it may, I had all the trouble and scandal which you had indicated, being in some cases hounded from town to town.
>
> But perhaps the most curious incident was the following. You told me that about the following month of July, I would have an accident in connection with a horse that would cause a shock to my nervous system which would take me some time to get over. This happened when my favourite racing mare, Maluma, ridden by Tod Sloan, broke her shoulder in the race for the Liverpool Cup and had to be killed. . . .
>
> These are only the things that stand out more clearly than

> others in the years that have passed since I last saw you, but in even minor details you were equally true in all you said.

She ended, 'Believe me, very truly yours. Lillie De Bathe'.

An oft-quoted prophecy of Cheiro's was the one he made to the famous editor W. T. Stead, who was opposed to the Boer War, and whose office was smashed by a London mob on account of this. As a result he suffered from a phobia that he would die through mob violence. He kept consulting Hamon about this. The latter wrote on 21st June 1911, assuring him that as far as he could judge there was no likelihood of such a fate occurring. He had gone over the impression of his hands, taken many years earlier, also the more recent notes he had made, and

> judging from them and from your date of birth in the Sign of Cancer, otherwise known as the First House of Water, in my humble opinion, any danger of violent death to you must be by water and nothing else. Very critical and dangerous for you should be April, 1912, especially about the middle of the month. So don't travel by water then if you can help it. If you do, you will be liable to meet with such danger to your life that the very worst may happen. I know I am not wrong about this 'water' danger; I only hope I am, or at least that you won't be travelling somewhere about that period.

Cheiro's prediction was fulfilled. Stead ignored the warning, and was drowned in the disaster to the *Titanic* on her first voyage to New York on 15th April 1912.

At least nineteen people had premonitions of the sinking of the *Titanic* within a fortnight of the disaster. Some fourteen years earlier Morgan Robertson, a former sailor, who had taken up the writing of sea stories, sat one evening in his study on 24th Street in New York City, unable to get any inspiration. Then he found himself falling into a trance-like state in which, through a sort of fog in mid-Atlantic, he glimpsed the largest liner he had ever seen, with a vast number of people on its decks. He counted only twenty-four lifebelts, and made out the letters THE TITAN. He reckoned she was moving at a speed of 25 knots. He heard the words 'unsinkable' and 'April' being spoken, then foghorns sounding. Next he noticed that the ship was bearing down on an iceberg.

Using what he had experienced in this condition, he wrote a short story, 'The Wreck of the Titan', telling of the disaster that overtook 'the largest craft afloat, as it hurled itself at an iceberg' and of 'nearly 3 000 voices, raised in agonized screams'. He wrote this in 1898, thirteen years before the *Titanic* was built. *Titanic* was the largest ship in the world, 46 000 tons, and sank on her maiden voyage with about 2 200 passengers aboard, some 1 500 being drowned—and hardly any lifebelts available, as foreseen by Robertson. The strange thing about the latter was that he received no education and believed that 'an astral writing partner' took over when he started typing his stories.

Louis Hamon did not marry until he was fifty-four, and this was to Mrs Mena Dixon Hartland in 1920. Edith Halford Nelson wrote that until then he was too capricious to allow himself to be held for long by any woman. His taste in them, she claimed, was as changeable as his affection and varied from the Junoesque beauty of a certain Edwardian hostess to the sinuous snake-like grace of Mata Hari, dancer and spy. Mrs Nelson was told by her brother, Major Halford Thompson, a well-known police officer, that Hamon sometimes worked for the British Secret Service.

This was possibly how he became involved with Mata Hari. He did not love her, but it seems he was attracted by her perverse charm. He told her that her life would reach its climax about October 1917. Then she would be in great danger of violent death. Several writers have mentioned how she went to her execution at Versailles confident that it had been prearranged for blank cartridges to be substituted for real ones in the rifles of the firing-squad. Such accounts describe how one of Mata Hari's lovers, of unknown identity, visited her shortly before she went from her cell, and how he made her believe that this had been done. She was to pretend to collapse, then she would be laid in a coffin and driven to the convent of the nuns who had accompanied her to the execution-trench. According to Mrs Nelson, this mysterious visitor was Hamon. He could not save her life, so he removed the horror of her execution, and was the cause of her dying with such courage.

All who knew Cheiro said that he had strong hypnotic powers. He also when attacked never hesitated to hit back hard. Once at a country-house party, an arrogant Society beauty was deliberately rude to him.

The conversation, according to those who were present, went as follows. She said, 'You think because you are handsome, you have all the women at your feet. You are an impostor, a charlatan. I suppose you think you could bring me to your feet?'

Hamon smiled with confident charm and replied, 'I don't *think* anything about it. I *know* it.'

'How dare you!' She was furious.

'You have called me an impostor, a charlatan. That's not very pleasant, not even polite. But why should we quarrel—won't you apologise?'

'Certainly not!' she shouted.

He stared at her. 'Very well, then at midnight you will come here in this room and kneel at my feet.'

'Me kneel at your feet—*me*! The man's mad!'

'Yes, at midnight you will come and kneel at my feet,' he repeated.

She laughed. 'At midnight I shall be asleep in my bed. I am going there now. Goodnight, everyone, I leave you to the amusing company of this *charlatan*.'

When she had flounced off Louis Hamon invited the others to be in the room at five minutes to twelve to witness what he expected to happen. They all agreed to come back then. Just before midnight he set the door open and asked them on no account to make a sound. Then he switched off all the lights, so that the only illumination came from the fire-glow.

As the hour struck the woman appeared wearing only her nightgown and, making for Hamon, knelt at his feet, then, raising her arms, lowered them and her head till they almost touched the carpet, like a slave acknowledging its master. He said, 'Go—back—to your bed. Go—back—to your bed.'

Like an automaton, she obeyed.

Cheiro told his fellow-guests that he would leave early in the morning in order to spare Lady X the humiliation of meeting him again. He assured them that she would have no recollection of what had transpired.

Cheiro had another opportunity for employing his hypnotic powers one night in New York when he and a woman secretary were held up by a man with a gun. Having just ended a lecture tour, he had a large sum of money on him. As the assailant aimed the weapon Hamon's hand shot out on a level with the fellow's face. The revolver dropped on to the sidewalk, but his arm remained stiffly outstretched. Cheiro retrieved the revolver and strolled on.

The would-be robber stumbled behind, begging him to let his arm become normal again. For a while Hamon moved heedlessly on, but presently he paused and, swinging round, said, 'If I give you back the use of your arm, will you give up this life of crime?' The man swore he would reform, and his arm then slipped down to his side.

That the already mentioned predictions of Cheiro, based mostly on his readings of the hands of the famous, were made before fulfilment has been well authenticated by convincing documentary evidence. In some cases it may be argued that the persons concerned were scared into dying at the times foretold, but that still leaves us with some impressive prognostications that cannot be so explained away.

In 1925 Cheiro foretold the treaty made in the following spring between Soviet Russia and Germany, the General Strike of May 1926, the breaking out of civil war in China and its effects on British interests, the extraordinary number of fires that destroyed large private mansions all over England that year, and the earthquake that occurred in the Channel

Islands in July 1926.

He wrote that during 1927, 1928 and 1929, 'Italy will seize important positions in the Mediterranean and Africa and will hold them by force of arms. . . . She will become one of the most militant of the European nations, and will keep the War Cauldron for several years at fever heat.'

In his *World Predictions*, published in 1927, Cheiro stated, 'The planetary influences governing King George V will be unfavourable for him personally between 1928 and 1930. I foresee in those years a critical time and a period of deep anxiety for the Royal Family.' This proved correct, for between November 1928 and the summer of 1930 the King was dangerously ill with pneumonia and inflammation of the lungs and bronchi.

Hamon continued:

> The portents are not favourable for the prosperity of England or for the Royal Family with the exception of the Duke of York. In his case it is remarkable that the regal sign of Jupiter increases in power as the years advance, which, as I have explained, was also the case of his Royal father, before there was any likelihood of his coming to the throne.

In 1891 Cheiro, at the beginning of his career, had made the then unlikely prediction that the future George V would become King. Here in 1927 he is predicting that his son, the Duke of York, would ascend the throne, which was to happen in 1936.

Of the Prince of Wales, later Edward VIII, he asserted:

> His astrological chart shows perplexing and baffling influences that most unquestionably point to changes likely to take place greatly affecting the throne of England. . . . It is well within the range of possibility owing to the peculiar planetary influences to which he is subjected, that he will fall a victim to a devastating love affair. If he does, I predict that the Prince will give up everything even the chance of being crowned, rather than lose the object of his affection.

Cheiro made a remarkable long-range forecast for the latter part of this century:

> The influence of Communism will spread like an infective fever through all countries, the most fantastic doctrines will be openly preached and absorbed by all classes. Rich men will give away their wealth and gladly become poor; kings will break bread with workers and workers will dictate to kings, sons and daughters of the highest will become Socialists, and the lands they inherit they will give to the people.
>
> Even the Church will have revolution within itself. Strange creeds will be preached from all pulpits.
>
> For a time Religion will save itself from catastrophe by abolishing her Bishops' palaces, her gilded ceremonials, and her alliance with Monarchs.

The Jews would return to Palestine and call their state Israel. He goes on:

> As foreshadowed in Ezekiel, Chapter XXXVIII, the great battle of Armageddon will be fought on the plains of Palestine. It is clearly set out for all those who may choose to read that that conflict will be a life and death struggle for the contending armies fighting in Palestine. It describes how the people of the North by which Russia is evidently indicated will descend into that country with allies drawn from Persia, Ethiopia, Libya and many other people.

In his new *World Predictions*, published in 1931, Cheiro foretold a world war before the end of the decade.

> England will be attacked in all her Mohammedan possessions. She will give India her freedom, but religious warfare will rend that country from end to end until it becomes equally divided between the Mohammedan and the followers of Buddha. Italy and Germany will at the same period be at war with France. . . . The United States will be engaged in war with Japan and will not take part until later in the

European carnage. . . . In Ireland there will be civil war between the North and South.

When it comes to personal occult experiences Cheiro claimed to have had we have to rely almost entirely on his word. Some of the stories published in his books are too fantastic for credibility. One feels that the truth has been somewhat embellished, and this is especially so when one is reading about the mummy's hand given him as a mysterious talisman in his youth. It was supposed to protect him, which appears to have happened on at least two occasions.

Once a man concealed in his suite in a Chicago hotel tried to rob him during the night. The intruder had already grasped his quarry's watch and wallet lying on the bedside table when his hand in the dark touched that of the mummy. With a frightened gasp, he dropped everything and fled.

Another time, when Cheiro was travelling in South America the hotel caught fire. People rushed from their rooms, and so did he. As they crowded into the elevator he suddenly remembered that he had left behind the Princess's hand in his room. He got out, let the others descend without him and ran back to collect the relic. As he did so the rope of the elevator burned and gave way it fell with a crash, everyone in it was killed.

During the First World War Hamon lived in Ireland where, he wrote, he was engaged in converting peat into coal by a special process he had himself invented.

In 1922, when Lord Carnarvon was in Egypt at the head of the expedition which discovered the tomb of King Tutankhamun, Hamon, still in Ireland, was becoming increasingly concerned over the hand of Princess Makitaten, which, it will be remembered, he had been given by a guide in Egypt at the beginning of his career. The fingers, which had always been rigid as iron, had become supple and soft.

One morning, in the autumn of that year he claimed, he started back with horror. Small drops of what looked like blood were glistening on the knuckles, larger drops were oozing from the fingertips. He called in an English chemist employed at the factory and said: 'Have you ever heard of a mummy's hand or any part of a mummy showing signs of bleeding after having been embalmed for over two thousand years?' He showed him the hand lying on the cushion. 'You will remember that when you came here in 1920 it was as hard as if carved out of ebony.' He asked him to take it into the laboratory to analyse some of the globules under the microscope, and give his opinion.

After a few hours the chemist reported that there could be no doubt it was human blood that was oozing from the fingers. He added that the only thing he could do to stop the bleeding and restore the hand to its former state was to dip it in a solution of pitch and shellac. Hamon held a sworn affidavit from the man confirming these findings, and also one from the manager of the factory who witnessed his laboratory tests.

It was a disturbed part of Ireland and one night, when the furniture had been sent off for the Hamons' return to England and nothing remained in the drawing-room but the hand, four men forced their way into the house.

As they switched on the lights the ring of Egyptian gold attracted the leader's attention. He snatched up the hand, but dropped it at once on seeing his own covered with blood. With a cry of fear he rushed out, followed by his companions, and the Hamons were left in peace.

A few nights later, as they could not take the hand with them on account of its condition, they decided to light a large fire in the chimney of the hall and cremate the relic Louis had carried with him in his thirty years' wanderings.

He recalled the Egyptian guide's words that before the discovery of Tutankhamun's lost tomb the hand would endeavour to get free from his custody, and the 'Ka' or spirit imprisoned in it would return to its own.

He realized that by accident the night on which they had decided to cremate the hand was Hallowe'en. While waiting for the fire to burn up, as the night was clear and warm, they walked up and down the garden. When they re-entered, close on midnight, he says they noticed that the servants had left the dining-room windows open, with a supper on the table, following the quaint Irish custom of bidding welcome to the spirits of the departed on that one night of the year.

Before committing the hand to the flames, Hamon's wife repeated a verse from the Egyptian *Book of the Dead.*

> Thy flesh have I given unto thee,
> Thy bones have I kept for thee,
> Thy members have I collected,
> Thou art set in order;
> Thou seest the gods,
> Thou settest out on thy way,
> Thine hand reaches beyond the horizon
> And unto the holy place where thou wouldst be.

As she ended Louis opened the heart of the fire and slipped into the flames the ebony stand, the velvet cushion and the hand.

According to him, they waited until only the red glow of the fire and ashes remained before thinking of retiring. Then they started to mount the stairs.

'The night was warm and calm, there was not enough breeze to move the leaves on the trees. Yet at the doors of the outer porch a noise like a whirlwind seemed to force them open, and to our horror we saw the oak doors of the inner hall yielding to some pressure behind them.'

They feared that this was another raid from armed men. But instead, far out in the glass porch where a large passion flower formed an arch of green leaves, something was taking shape.

> As this undefined form slowly moved towards the inside door, it appeared to gather more substance. Then suddenly, in the deeper shadow of the hall, it assumed both shape and figure, until we actually saw before us the form of a woman....
>
> It was a very beautiful and remarkable face that finally came towards us.... The head-dress appeared like leaves of

> beaten gold formed like the wings of beetles. . . . In the centre of the forehead was a golden asp, the emblem of Egyptian royalty. . . .
>
> The figure reached the fireplace where the dying embers were still glowing. For a moment it appeared inclining towards where the fire had been, then faced us again with both hands clasped together as if in a moment of ecstasy.
>
> For a second her lips seemed to move, we thought she was going to speak. Her eyes looked into ours. Then throwing her head back, she lifted her hands slowly in the form of an arch over her head, and bowing towards where we stood, the figure glided backward through the hall and out into the porch where the form had first appeared.
>
> As if hypnotised we followed—we could not help ourselves. Like frightened children awakened from some dream, we stood at the porch of that lonely house we were soon to leave. It was no use trying to go to our rooms. We knew we could not sleep.

With the dawn, Cheiro continues in his fantastic story, their courage returned and they raked out the ashes of the fire and, finding the calcined bones of the hand, carefully gathered them together, vowing as they did so that they would some day take them back to Egypt and place them in one of the tombs in the Valley of the Kings.

The last thing they found was the ring of Egyptian gold that had always been on the first finger of the mummified hand. It was untarnished by the fire. Cheiro rubbed the ashes from it. He kept it for the rest of his life.

One evening some weeks later, back in London, Louis Hamon and his wife were discussing the discovery of the tomb of King Tutankhamun by the expedition headed by Lord Carnarvon. Suddenly, he claimed, the figure of Princess Makitaten appeared again, and under her influence he found himself automatically writing, 'Lord Carnarvon not to enter tomb. Disobey at peril. If ignored would suffer sickness—not recover—death would claim him in Egypt.'

As Carnarvon had been a client of his, Cheiro immediately sent him a letter with the warning. But Howard Carter, the archaeologist who had discovered the tomb, was determined to enter the Sepulchral Chamber, and this entry took place on 24th February 1923. The rest of the young King laid there some 3 265 years previously was thus disturbed, with, as is well known, fatal results for most of those responsible.

The death of Lord Carnarvon shortly afterwards was followed by a panic among collectors of Egyptian antiquities. The *Daily Express* for 7th April 1923 reported, 'All over the country people are sending their treasures to the British Museum. The avalanche of parcels containing mummies' shrivelled hands and feet and other relics from the ancient tombs arriving by every post has caused storage problems.'

In 1930 Cheiro went to live in Hollywood with the intention of writing for the films. He wrote a screen play about Cagliostro but it was never made. Where, however, he had great success was foretelling the future for the stars. Lillian Gish, Mary Pickford and Erich von Stroheim were among those who later acknowledged that his predictions had been fulfilled. A great impression was caused by his describing in advance the manner and time of the death of Norma Shearer's husband, Irving Thalberg.

He started a school of metaphysics, where he taught his methods of divination until he died on 8th October 1936. He left instructions that his funeral should be very simple, but his many friends in the film community carried out his wishes in their own way. He lay in state on a bed of roses, his favourite flowers. 'I Hear You Calling Me' was sung by Count John McCormack at the service.

Extraordinary stories circulated as to what occurred in the house towards Hamon's end. Howard Dangerfield, his constant companion for several years, wrote:

> Doors were opened and shut, footsteps were heard coming up the stairs, yet no one could be seen there. His favourite Alsatian began the terrible death-wail of the wolf. The footsteps paused now at the door of the bedroom, but when the door was opened there was no one to be seen, yet those footsteps were heard to advance towards his bed.

Mrs Edith Phelan, the brisk, efficient English nurse who attended Hamon, told the Press:

> The whole house was filled with an overpowering fragrance of flowers. There were none in the room and none outside, yet we all smelled the fragrance.
>
> I was sitting at the head of the stairs except at the last moment. They were deserted and yet they creaked as though an army of people were coming and going. I cannot deny the evidence of my senses, yet I cannot believe them.
>
> I am a registered nurse. I have seen hundreds of people die and I don't believe in spooks. I came to this house four days before my patient died and I did not even know his name.
>
> When doctors called me about midnight I noticed he was sinking. I told his wife he couldn't last long. They were just asking me how long when the clock struck one—my wrist-watch showed 12.15.
>
> Twice again at about ten minute intervals the clock struck one.

The house in which Hamon died had been rented by him from its owners, the famous Talmadge sisters, and was at 7417 Hollywood Boulevard. A friend of mine, Mrs Margret Busse, went in search of it for me in March 1976, and found that the whole place was surrounded by an old brick wall with a new entrance on the side, so that it has now become 7416 North Vista Street. The large, rustic-looking house is pleasantly situated amid trees on rising ground and is built of wood. In the garden is an elephant tree that Cheiro planted. The property is owned and occupied by a writer, Ken Luber, and his family, and they say that the house is definitely haunted. There are strange noises at times and 'plenty of apparitions, single and different people'.

▲
1

2 ►

Karl E. Krafft

Nostradamus
vê o futuro da Europa

1 9 4 1

8 Krafft—'Hitler's Astrologer'

Ever since the early 1930s there was a popular belief in Germany that Hitler owed his extraordinary run of successes to the advice he received from astrologers. Later this spread to other countries. The *Daily Mail* in 1939 twice mentioned this—first that he employed one permanently, then that he had five. The *Gazette de Lausanne* in April that year also alleged that he kept several at Berchtesgaden, and that the reason his coups took place in March was because that was the month when the stars were most favourable for him.

Walter Schellenberg, who was in charge of counter-espionage in the Reich Central Security Office, states in his *Memoiren* that Hitler was extremely interested in astrology till Hess's flight to Scotland, following which he became completely hostile to it. One of the Führer's private secretaries from 1933 to 1945, Fraülein Schröder, has written that as far as she was aware Hitler did not consult astrologers, and scoffed at the idea that the stars could affect one's fate. The only prediction that had impressed him was Frau Elsbeth Ebertin's. She was the well-known fortune-teller who had foretold in her annual almanack for 1924 his rise to power.

When the war was going against him Hitler may have found solace in his horoscope, according to what his Minister of Finance, Count Schwerin von Krosigk, wrote in his unpublished diary, which was used by Professor Trevor-Roper in his book *The Last Days of Hitler*. Two horoscopes were in Himmler's custody, the horoscope of the Führer drawn up on 30th January 1933, and that of the Weimar Republic dated 9th November 1918. The documents were fetched and

---

1 Karl Ernst Krafft as a young man in London. *By courtesy of Ellic Howe*

2 Cover of Portuguese edition of Krafft's *Comment Nostradamus a-t-il entrevu l'avenir de l'Europe?*, originally published in French in 1941 by Goebbels's Propaganda Ministry. *British Library*

examined and, according to von Krosigk,

> an astonishing fact came to light. Both horoscopes had predicted the outbreak of war in 1939, the victories till 1941, and then the series of defeats culminating in the worst disasters in the early months of 1945, especially in the first half of April. There was to be an overwhelming victory for us in the second half of April, stagnation till August, and in August peace. After which there would be a difficult time for Germany for three years; but from 1948 she would rise to greatness again. Next day, Goebbels sent me the horoscopes. I could not fathom everything in them; but in the subjoined interpretation newly drawn up, I found it all; and now I am eagerly awaiting the second half of April.

What Krosigk does not mention is that in Hitler's horoscope Neptune was at the cusp, the beginning degree of the twelfth field of his chart in April, and Neptune was his 'death significance'. This could mean his own death, of course, although that event was not likely to occur before Saturn was at an angle of 180 degrees to Hitler's Moon position, which would be the case on 1st May. It might be regarded as the death of an enemy. An astrologer named Wolff was consulted, and he diplomatically decided that the aspect meant the death of Hitler's worst enemy.

On Friday, April 13, Goebbels heard of the death of President Roosevelt and, Professor Trevor-Roper tells us, phoned Hitler to congratulate him. 'It is written in the stars,' he cried, 'the second half of April will be the turning point for us. It is the turning point!'

But the 'interpretation newly drawn up' of the horoscopes to which Krosigk refers proved wrong, for within a fortnight both Hitler and Goebbels had taken their lives, which makes one suspect that it had been specially prepared to raise morale. An impartial interpreter would have concluded that the Führer was likely to die about 1st May, as in fact happened.

In 1935 there arrived in England a partly-Jewish refugee from Nazi Germany, who was also of Hungarian descent. This was the late gifted and highly intelligent Ludwig von Wohl, born in Berlin, where he had spent most of his life up until then, first earning his living as a writer and later as a professional astrologer. Now calling himself Louis de Wohl, he was soon making a living again from both callings, and in 1940 he was introduced to Virgil Tilea, the Romanian Minister in London. It was to prove for de Wohl perhaps the most fortunate contact in his life.

In the spring of 1937 Tilea had been introduced in Zürich to a young Swiss astrologer, Karl Ernst Krafft, who offered to cast his horoscope. He reluctantly accepted, and was startled when the other told him about a past occurrence in his life of which nobody else knew. A year later, when they again met, Tilea asked the astrologer if he would consent to take part in a test to prove his powers, and when the other agreed he handed him photocopies of two specimens of handwriting and the dates, times and places of the writers' births. No indication of any kind was given as to their identities. In less than a week he received back readings for both. Regarding the first, Krafft wrote that he thought 'X' had a schizoid personality, which from his own experience was often so with people of Jewish extraction. He felt that the man was unlikely to be still alive by the end of November 1938. For 'Y', he foretold that he was a person of importance and eminence, but would lose everything in September 1940.

'X' hid the identity of Corneliu Codreanu, leader of the Rumanian Fascists, whose mother was a Jewess, and who, after being arrested and accused of high treason, tried to escape and was shot dead in the attempt on the last day of November in 1938. 'Y' was King Carol of Romania, who was forced to abdicate on 6th September 1940.

Tilea was so impressed with the fulfilment of both predictions that he asked Krafft to draw up his own astrological chart. This was probably in December 1938. For some reason or other Krafft seems to have taken a considerable time over this, and a year later, three months after the outbreak of the Second World War, he wrote to Tilea to say that he was still working on the horoscope but needed the dates of birth of both parents and of his wife. This was because he believed that a chart needed to be studied in conjunction with those of one's nearest relatives for it to be accurately interpreted.

In the following month Krafft began working for the German Propaganda Ministry in Berlin, as we shall learn later, and letters sent abroad by him had to be read first by his immediate chief, Dr Fesel, who was employed in Himmler's RSHA. In mid-February, 1940, Tilea wrote from Bucharest giving the requested information, and his letter was forwarded from Krafft's Swiss address to Berlin. The Rumanian received back in due course a twelve-page typed letter in which Krafft apologized for the delay in answering. It was because he had moved to the German capital, where he had been working on a new edition of Nostradamus's prophecies for a society connected with a Government department. It would be privately printed, with commentary by himself, and would prove that the 'Seer of Salon' had genuine prophetic gifts. He would send M. Tilea a copy.

With the additional information received, he planned to work out a new interpretation of his correspondent's natal chart, using an entirely new technique that he himself had recently discovered. Most of the lengthy letter, however, consisted of rather obvious propaganda aimed at influencing Romania to support the Germans. This made the recipient highly suspicious that Krafft must now be employed by the leading Nazis. M. Tilea had read a confidential report in which his country's representative in Berlin had stated that Hitler believed in astrology, and Krafft's reference to his being involved in preparing a new edition of Nostradamus, with commentary, made him suspect that the interpretations would be slanted in Germany's favour.

Shortly afterwards, pausing in Zürich on his way to London, Tilea discussed the matter with Dr Franklin Bircher of the Bircher–Benner clinic, who had originally introduced him to Krafft, and learned that he had concluded that the man was advising Hitler.

Back in London, Virgil Tilea happened to be introduced to

Louis de Wohl, and, hearing that he was an astrologer and had practised in Berlin, he told him about Krafft. Wohl responded by asserting that he was certain Hitler consulted astrologers and followed their advice. His interest had started, he alleged, when the occultist who called himself Rudolf Freiherr von Sebottendorff had warned Hitler that if he attempted a putsch in November 1923 he would end in prison. Hitler had ignored the prediction, which had been fulfilled. As a result of this experience the Führer had made a close study of the occult, and had resolved to seek the assistance of astrologers of proven ability to help him attain all his ambitions.

In his book, *The Stars of War and Peace*, published in 1952, de Wohl wrote that in 1935 he was approached by a member of the National Socialist Party, who it appears was recruiting astrologers for a central bureau where they would employ their gifts to further the Nazi cause. Louis de Wohl claimed that he gave a noncommittal reply, and heard no more, as shortly afterwards he left Germany for good.

He stated in his book that when Tilea told him what he suspected Krafft was doing he himself suggested the following. If having first the Führer's birth data and that of the top-ranking Nazis, including military and naval commanders, he were to cast their horoscopes he would immediately know what kind of advice the Führer was currently receiving, and be able to inform the appropriate British Intelligence departments. He said he stressed that it was of no moment whatsoever whether or not the British Foreign Office and top military men believed in astrology. What mattered was that Hitler certainly did, and was guided by the advice he so received. According to de Wohl, he so impressed Tilea with these arguments that the latter agreed to give him some introductions.

But, according to Ellic Howe, author of that brilliantly researched book *Urania's Children: the Strange World of the Astrologers*, he was told by M. Tilea that it was the latter who reasoned on these lines, and 'furthermore, a good many weeks passed before de Wohl became personally involved in the

"Tilea Plan".'

Mr Howe makes a cogent comment on the whole scheme. He points out

> As far as so-called predictive techniques are concerned, an astrologer has a choice of up to half a dozen more or less well-known methods. The fact that none of them has a strictly scientific basis is beside the point. . . . Logically, then, it would be necessary for an astrologer working in London to use the same predictive method as his counterpart in Berlin.

Louis de Wohl was astute enough, however, later to claim that he knew which method Hitler's astrologer used. By then he (and others) had created the legend that this man was Karl Ernst Krafft. But, as Ellic Howe so definitely proves in his book—published in 1967, and the authoritative work on the whole subject—not only did Krafft never succeed in meeting Hitler, but the latter never employed any astrologer or occultist.

An interview with Louis de Wohl, under the heading of 'Strangest Battle of the War', was published in the London *Sunday Graphic* on 9th November 1947, in which Krafft's name was incorrectly spelt. De Wohl was purported to have told the reporter, 'In Britain one of my best clients was an old customer of Karl Klafft (*sic*), Hitler's pet astrologer. From him I learned Klafft's technique. I knew what his advice to Hitler would be long before he was summoned by the Führer.' As Mr Howe says, the 'old customer' could have been only M. Tilea, who certainly could not have explained Krafft's technique.

Once he heard of the Romanian Minister's plan, Louis de Wohl enthusiastically supported it, saying that if it could be arranged with British Intelligence he would make the same astrological calculations as Krafft and let them know what kind of advice Hitler was receiving. M. Tilea then proceeded to introduce Louis to influential people. His big chance came when over port after dinner at the Spanish Embassy he spoke for an hour to Lord Halifax, then Foreign Secretary, concerning what he knew about Hitler's horoscope, and convincingly answered all questions. He claimed that the dates of every major move by the German leader were chosen by him after astrological advice.

In *The Stars of War and Peace* de Wohl wrote that very soon he was introduced to a general and an admiral, but that as neither the War Office nor the Admiralty could employ an astrologer he was put on the payroll of the Special Operations Executive. In a suite at Grosvenor House, rented and furnished at the SOE's expense and called the 'Psychological Research Bureau', he busied himself preparing astrological reports on German generals and admirals for dispatch to Military and Naval Intelligence, indicating where the next attack might be expected on the grounds that the German officer there in command had favourable aspects. It would appear that no one took this counsel in earnest.

Sir Charles Hambro, Louis's chief, came to the conclusion that he could be most usefully employed in psychological warfare, and sent him for that purpose to the United States, where Dr Goebbels was already at work, contributing articles and letters through his paid agents to the most widely circulated magazines specializing in the occult. These asserted that all planetary aspects made a German victory certain. So it was planned that de Wohl should visit the States in the guise of a private astrologer and popularize in every way he could the belief that according to the stars Germany must lose the war.

He began his campaign in New York, where he stated that Hitler's horoscope showed the planet Neptune in the house of death, and that this implied his days were numbered. A few weeks later he received unexpected support from a Cairo astrologer whose prediction received wide publicity in the Arab world. This was that 'a red planet will appear on the eastern horizon four months hence, which means that an uncrowned emperor will die, and that man is Hitler'.

De Wohl was most successful when he attended the national convention of the American Federation of Scientific Astrologers at Cleveland, Ohio, in August 1941. Lecturing on Napoleon and Hitler and comparing their astrological charts, he completely held his audience. Both had the same Saturn position, which meant that the latter would fall from power within a few years. Although he could not have known of Eva Braun's existence, he said that Hitler had a mistress who would die a violent death, which was in itself a remarkable prediction, as was his next one. The Russian campaign had just opened, and, according to de Wohl, it was the first major action of Hitler's that could not possibly have been countersigned by any astrologer, as all the signs in the sky pointed to eventual disaster.

When asked who Hitler's astrologers were he confined his reply to saying they were the best in the world, and included Karl E. Krafft of Switzerland. He asserted that Hitler had his astrologers' conclusions verified by the Geopolitical Institute in Munich, and explained that geopolitics was 'an extremely clever combination of history, geography, military strategy and astrology, with the latter science functioning as the time-keeper. Professor Karl Haushofer, who conducted it, 'was said to control a staff of two thousand strategists, physicists, meteorologists, engineers and economists who checked the information that Hess supplied through spies and other agents for Hitler's "strategic Index".' The truth was that Haushofer ran the Institute with one assistant and a typist.

De Wohl went on that this Institute had told Hitler that it was always best to strike at a country when the malefic planets, Saturn and Uranus, were in the zodiacal sign ruling the nation to be attacked. Saturn and Uranus would be in Gemini, the sign ruling the United States until the late spring of 1942. Therefore, if Hitler took astrological advice he must not invade the States till then. The Institute had also told the Führer that for success to continue to be his the war must always be fought on foreign soil.

The lecturer told his by now admiring and impressed audience of 'scientific astrologers' that he believed the Germans would use Brazil as their base for the coming onslaught on

North America. 'Brazil is ruled by Virgo,' he pointed out, 'and therefore she, too, will be under the hostile influences of Saturn and Uranus from the late spring of 1942 onward. America has always been subject to grave events when Uranus transits Gemini.'

During his American visit de Wohl also prepared astrological charts of those on whom Hitler was most dependent, and then told all the American journalists he met about any adverse aspects to which these people would be exposed.

Back in England, de Wohl worked on a free-lance basis for Sefton Delmer's secret 'black' section in Political Warfare Executive, writing the text for faked issues of *Der Zenit*, the German astrological magazine, which were smuggled into Germany so that copies fell into the hands of members of the armed forces. The issue dated April 1943, for example, was actually printed about three months later, by which time Delmer had received details from the Admiralty of the dates on which U-boats had been destroyed in the interim. This would make the remaining crews in German ports believe that the astrological correspondent of *Der Zenit* possessed genuine prophetic powers.

Delmer wrote in his *Black Boomerang*:

> My respect for the sage's mystic integrity, however, did not preclude me from ante-dating some numbers of *Zenit* in order to include astoundingly accurate forecasts of events which had in fact already taken place. Thus Hitler's defeats at Alamein and Stalingrad were astrologically foreseen in a *Zenit* number which bore the date June, 1942, but had in fact been printed in March, 1943. I felt that this little subterfuge would add weight to other predictions which were concerned with developments far ahead of the date when our German customers would first find it lying around.

There was, for example, an oblique attack on Himmler: 'The *Reichsführer* of the SS is now coming to a period when his cosmic constellations bode no good'.

Soon it was known in London that Dr Goebbels had earlier (1940–1) prepared and distributed faked Nostradamus quatrains. Sefton Delmer counter-attacked with *Nostradamus prophezeit den Kriegsverlauf* ('Nostradamus prophesies the Course of the War'), which was supposed to have for author a Dr Bruno Winkler of Weimar, and which contained fifty spurious quatrains cleverly couched in archaic French and with German translations, and allegedly based on a non-existent manuscript in a collection at Ratisbon. All this was largely the work of de Wohl. The translation of one quatrain read: 'Hister who won more victories in his wars than was good for him; six will kill him in the night. Naked, surprised without his armour, he dies.'

This was actually quatrain 30 of *Century III* with 'Hister' substituted for 'Celuy' at the beginning. This verse in the late sixteenth century had been interpreted as describing the fate of Montgomery, who had accidentally killed King Henri II of France while jousting. The booklet was a masterpiece of the faker's art. Bearing the imprint of the occult and astrological publishers, Regulus Verlag of Görlitz, its 124 pages printed on the thinnest paper weighed under an ounce.

After the War Louis de Wohl made a great deal of money from articles published all over the world, which were exaggerated accounts of his own wartime activities and which necessitated the continuation of the myth that Krafft was Hitler's astrologer. In the *Sunday Graphic* interview already mentioned he maintained that he knew in advance, through working closely to Krafft's formula, that it was obvious he would be advising Hitler to act.

> The Führer took that advice and swept into France. . . . After Dunkirk, for the first time Hitler's belief in his Chief Astrologer was shaken and from then on he began to rely more and more on his own intuition. This intuition became the unknown factor in my calculations. Up to the last, Hitler believed in astrology, and the demand for my reports never ceased. More than once, we forestalled some of Hitler's tactically unpredictable motives.

But, according to what Ellic Howe was told by Miss 'I', a former senior secretary at the Special Operations Executive, although de Wohl went on for some time sending astrological reports on German generals and admirals to the Admiralty and the War Office, with the intention that they should be forwarned where the next attack was coming from, no one took them at all seriously.

In the summer of 1943 he helped to prepare the text of a letter addressed to a Dutch friend of Krafft's in which the latter was made to say that according to his latest astrological calculations Germany was certain to lose the War and Hitler to die a violent death. The intention was that this should fall into the hands of the Gestapo, leading to Krafft's arrest and the Führer's loss of the astrologer on whose services he so much depended. What the SOE did not know was that Krafft had been in a concentration camp since early that year.

The ironic side of the Krafft legend is that it was the height of his ambition to become Hitler's personal astrologer, while in reality the Führer never employed or consulted one and in fact disapproved of occultists.

The writer responsible for revealing the facts in detail for the first time about Krafft is Mr Ellic Howe, to whose admirably documented book, *Urania's Children*, reference has already been made. He spent several years in research, travelled widely, interviewed scores of people, patiently cutting his way through the lurid jungle of fiction round the pathetic truth.

Karl Ernst Krafft was born on 10th May 1900, in Basle. The hotel there bearing his surname was built and owned by his German grandfather. His solid, thick-set father was a brewery director in the town, and his German mother he once compared to an irresponsible volcano. At school he excelled at mathematics, then went to study science in 1919 at Basle University. Very soon after this his only sister died, of which he had foreknowledge in a dream recorded at the time in his diary. The bereavement so upset him that he read every book on spiritualism and occultism in the University library.

Called up for military service at the age of twenty, he obtained an early release on account of ill-health. While in the army he persuaded some fellow-conscripts to take part in telepathic experiments, and he was startled on finding that he could transmit messages to them from a distance.

Those who knew him at this time have described him as a pale-faced, sharp-featured gnome with brilliant, deep-set, piercing eyes. All were impressed by the latter, though apparently he had hardly any sight in one of them. Countess Keyserling wrote in English to Ellic Howe, 'There was some flame burning in him, but a cold fire, like one of those dancing lights one reads about in books, which lead people astray in a swamp'. He was undoubtedly a complicated character. Howe thinks that he was probably schizophrenic.

In November 1920 he went to continue his studies at the university in Geneva, where he led a solitary life, practising yoga exercises in a loin-cloth in the bedroom of his lodgings, while at the university his course of studies was erratic and aimless.

Then he became interested in investigating astrology on a scientific basis, and embarked on a prodigious project which entailed spending long hours for months at the Geneva registry of births and deaths, copying particulars of members of the same families as far back as 1820, assisted by his landlord's young son, and next casting their horoscopes to prove his theory that people were not born under chance planetary constellations but under ones that bore a significant similarity to those of others in their own family.

Following this, he investigated the possibility of what he termed 'cosmic influences on human temperament' and decided to study the natal charts of persons with the same calling. From biographical dictionaries he obtained the relevant details for some 2 800 musicians, cast their horoscopes, and then laboriously analysed the data thus gained. When he had completed all this research he had accumulated some 60 000 numbered comments to support his claim that there was a definite link between the planetary positions at birth and musical talent.

Lastly, he investigated in similar fashion the question as to whether there were cosmic influences on human physiology, and as a result claimed to have proved that death was not fortuitous, that celestial configurations at birth determined a person's physique, natural tendencies, strengths and weaknesses, that during one's life successive planetary transits affect physical development, either encouraging, enfeebling or finally destroying it.

These conclusions and others were published in 1923 in Krafft's pamphlet *Les influences cosmiques sur l'individu humain*, and in 1939 were advanced again, supported by the analysed details of his lengthy researches in his *Traité d'Astro-Biologie*. Professor Liebmann Hersch, who had taught him statistical mathematics at Geneva University, went through his papers in 1923 and checked his findings and announced himself convinced. At a seminar the Professor permitted Krafft to read a paper on *Cosmic Influences on the Human Individual* and stated afterwards, 'If there is a rational explanation of the relationship between cosmic and biological phenomena, the proof offered by Monsieur Krafft's statistics should be considered as conclusive'.

The professors of botany and astronomy, however, were severely critical, the one describing his theory as complete nonsense and the other urging him not to squander any more of his time on such absurdities. A Basle mathematician then scrutinized his massive dossier and admitted that both material and method appeared faultless, but what he could not comprehend was 'how a Gauss or a Helmholtz could have overlooked such important facts'. His conclusion was that Krafft's results were founded upon some sort of self-deception that was not easy to detect.

Karl was not depressed by the two professors' disapproval, especially as they had not troubled to examine his papers. The fact that two authorities had found no flaws in his statistical procedures was sufficient to encourage him into believing that he must in time be regarded as a great scientist, founder of 'Cosmobiology'.

After the War a French statistician, Michel Gauquelin, attempted to repeat Krafft's investigations, with mostly negative results, and showed that his statistical techniques were antiquated and deceptive, but later, using his own advanced techniques that have not since been faulted, Gauquelin reached similar conclusions to his Swiss predecessor.

When Karl returned home from Geneva full of enthusiasm, and stories of the acclaim his discoveries had made in academic circles, his previously hostile and down-to-earth father was impressed in spite of himself, but this soon changed to exasperated dismay when he learned that the young 'genius' had come back without a degree and that the authorities had rejected his application to be allowed to submit a Ph.D. thesis on 'Cosmobiology'.

There were angry scenes with the elder Krafft, who demanded that Karl should start earning his own living in a bank or insurance office, or read for a degree in economics or law. At last the obstinate son persuaded his parent to let him go to London to study statistical techniques at University College, where brilliant Karl Pearson, Galton Professor of Eugenics, attracted biostatisticians from every country to his department. But Krafft returned to Switzerland after six months complaining that Pearson was a 'convinced Darwinite', too prejudiced to try to understand the documentary evidence he had submitted to him.

It was July 1924, and Krafft senior had just retired and was too busy moving to a small villa close to the Lake of Geneva to engage in another battle until he had settled in his new home. Meanwhile, Karl devoted his days once more to copying several thousand dates of births and deaths, first at the registry in Basle and then at Geneva, where those in charge, tiring of his perpetual presence, angered him by imposing a charge of two francs per hour.

The elder Krafft's retirement had reduced his means, and he soon prodded Karl into working first part-time at the International Students' Union in Geneva, then as an assistant in a shop specializing in theosophical books. At his parents'

Villa Rose life for him became increasingly acrimonious, and he later told a friend that the great thing about the place was that it had 'five exits, not counting the chimneys'.

At last, in January 1926, his father announced that as he was not earning enough money 'to pay for the water in his soup' he must take a post with prospects. So it had been arranged with a banker friend, Oscar Guhl, who also owned the 'Globus' department store and the Orell Füssli publishing house, for Karl to be trained by the latter for management duties. He would receive a nominal salary and would have to live on this in Zürich, with no further financial assistance from home.

There were hysterical outbursts from the 25-year-old son, but eventually he went off to his new job. However, he made a great success of it, to his father's astonishment and relief. This was probably because he felt that if he made progress with a publishing firm it might lead to their printing a book by him on 'Cosmobiology'. In the autumn he was promoted to deputy manager, and the following January was able to inform a friend that he had replaced an old director and now occupied his room. It was his 'wide culture and mercurial adaptability' that had helped him in business.

But jealousy among his older colleagues at his rapid promotion, his dictatorial attitude and lack of tact led to Guhl transferring him to his bank. The latter's son-in-law, Hans Mahler, who was in charge of the 'Globus' department store, had learned of Krafft's earlier researches and also that when he had first come to Zürich he had supplemented his small salary by casting horoscopes with impressive accuracy.

The 'Globus' chief now began using Krafft's services on a part-time basis. Mahler had a progressive outlook and was willing to try any techniques, however unconventional, that might result in his recruiting top-quality staff and placing them in the positions for which their capabilities best suited them.

At the bank, too, Krafft soon became similarly engaged, not only with employees but also in advising whether or not in borderline cases to advance loans to clients.

Mahler wrote to Ellic Howe in 1962:

> He became increasingly involved in personnel selection on the basis of graphological analysis, combined with astrological predictions based on natal horoscopes. I gladly acknowledged that almost without exception the character analyses he prepared at that time of people with whom I am still acquainted have proved to be fundamentally correct. . . .
>
> He also did some economic forecasting and in this connection used his knowledge of 'planetary cycles', rhythms and the like. Thus from a knowledge of the past he tried to predict the future. In many cases, his market forecasts were correct, but there were some 'misses', which were nevertheless unavoidable. These 'misses' used to puzzle him. However, I told him that I sincerely hoped that no one would ever succeed in obtaining an accurate knowledge of either his own destiny or that of the world at large, because if life's course could be accurately predetermined, it simply would not be worth living.

In 1928 a French publishing house brought out Krafft's short book *Influences solaires et lunaires sur la naissance humaine*, and a Leipzig firm his *Astro-Physiologie*, which established his reputation in German astrological circles.

By 1931 he had lost interest in 'Cosmobiology' and his new objective was to replace, as Ellic Howe aptly puts it, 'the unsatisfactory, indeed intellectually unacceptable nature of the old astrological Tradition' with something better. This took him many years to evolve, and proved to be a bewildering hotch-potch of astrology and metaphysics which he labelled 'Typocosmy'. It was 'the General Alphabet of the World of Phenomena' and a 'universal' system that could be used for horoscope delineation, and was a considerable improvement on conventional astrology. Once more he was certain that he had made a discovery of historic significance.

Krafft had also become extremely powerful behind the scenes at 'Globus'. Whether or not one was given employment, received advancement in the firm or a rise could be decided by his character-assessments. Because he was invariably proved correct, and because it was known that he employed astrology in arriving at his conclusions, he was called 'the magician'.

In mid-March, 1932, he came so intoxicated with his own importance that he told Mahler that one of the directors (whose private life he had been investigating without authority) should be asked to resign, and that he himself should replace him. This led to Mahler's giving him notice, with a modest sum of money as compensation. Krafft then lost his self-control and so screamed and raved that he had to be taken to a private nursing-home. When after a few days he had calmed down he left Zürich, as he felt he had lost face through the episode. He made his way to Paris, where he obtained work as a part-time psychological adviser to the Printemps department store.

In January 1933 his father died and he inherited some money. He had evolved certain complicated theories based on the influence of cosmic phenomena on the stock market that had involved monumental research — for example, into American railway share prices between 1831 and 1932, and German wheat prices between 1800 and 1930. He claimed to have discovered a definite relationship between cosmic cycles and economic fluctuations. Unfortunately, when he tried to make money out of these theories by playing the stock market he lost most of his legacy.

Besides his duties at the Printemps, Krafft had begun lecturing to small groups, and had also become intensely interested in Nostradamus's prophecies, on the interpretation of which he contributed several articles to the leading German occult periodical, *Zenit*.

In 1935 he went to lecture on his Typocosmy at the annual astrological congresses held in Wernigerode in Germany and at Brussels. Théodore Chapellier, the Belgian astrologer, gave Ellic Howe a vivid description of Krafft's appearance at the latter. 'He made a theatrical entry, agitatedly and yet nonchalantly. One beheld a slim, short, dark-haired young man with a pale, sharp-featured face and ecstatic, virulent eyes. A sort of Spanish cape was loosely draped on his shoulders and he wore a monocle. His audience was not impressed.'

Naturally, this lack of appreciation among the Latins irritated Krafft. They could understand only what was clearly and concisely expressed, he complained to a friend. The Germans alone could grasp the essence of Typocosmy. 'Thus in the near and distant future I count more and more upon a growing understanding in the German-speaking countries.'

On 7th May 1937 Krafft married Anna von der Koppel at Zürich. He was now earning a living visiting a few towns in Southern Germany and Switzerland giving lectures, followed by private consultations for horoscope interpretation and sometimes personal psychological treatment.

During August 1937 he wrote to a friend asking him to recommend some isolated place in the Black Forest, 'somewhere that has not been corroded by civilization', and was recommended to Urberg. The place appealed so much to the Kraffts that they spent most of their time there up until 1939, while he worked on a book, which he called the *Traité d'Astro-Biologie*, and which he had printed at his own expense in Brussels. He noted that his first consignment of bound copies arrived at 2.40 p.m. on 20th July 1939, probably so as to cast a horoscope for the book's chances of large sales. It could not, of course, have been published at a more unpropitious time.

Krafft was in Urberg when Great Britain and France declared war on Germany on 3rd September, and he decided to remain there. From letters to friends it is clear that he had fallen for Nazi propaganda, and was now violently anti-Swiss because he had never been accepted at his own valuation in his homeland.

Dr Gollner, a Stuttgart psychiatrist interested in astrology, and who visited Krafft at Urberg, wrote in 1961 to Ellic Howe, 'Krafft completely and wholeheartedly believed in the powerful Uranian [magical] force that linked his own horoscope with the Uranus-laden quality of the ruling Fascist hierarchy in Germany and reckoned that it would be this force that would carry him to the top.'

Karl had an acquaintance in Dr Heinrich Fesel, a junior member of Section VII of the Reichssicherheitshauptamt (Head Office for State Security), which was that part of

Himmler's secret intelligence service that investigated strange cults and occultism. He wrote to Fesel offering his services, and the latter consulted his superiors, who no doubt thought that the applicant might make a useful agent to send back later to Switzerland on some mission. As a result, Fesel met him near Urberg and arranged to pay him monthly 500 marks in return for his free-lance services, writing papers containing any information he considered might be useful to Germany, political and economic, as well as astrological predictions.

The first reports submitted by Krafft commented on the war with Poland, and forecast war in the west. Then on 2nd November Dr Fesel was startled to receive a sheet of paper from him in which he stated that the Führer's astrological aspects showed that his life would be in danger between 7th and 10th November and added, 'There is a possibility of an attempt of assassination through the use of explosive material'.

Fesel kept the memorandum, but did not pass on its contents, as there was a ban on all predictions concerning Hitler. Then, on the evening of the 8th, when the annual celebration of the 1923 Putsch took place at Munich, a bomb hidden behind a pillar on the rostrum exploded, only a few minutes after the Führer had left earlier than originally planned.

When the news broke next day Krafft decided that here was an opportunity he must not miss to further his position, so he immediately sent a telegram to Rudolf Hess drawing attention to the fact that he had predicted the assassination attempt in a letter to Dr Fesel, six days beforehand. He warned that Hitler would still be in danger for the next few days. The wire was seen by Hitler and Goebbels soon after it arrived, and the same day the Gestapo arrested Krafft. After close interrogation in Berlin, he satisfied them that he was not involved in the attempt on the Führer's life, and was released.

Karl had come into the limelight with his correct prediction just when Dr Goebbels had become aware of the possibilities of using Nostradamus's prophecies for psychological warfare.

One evening Frau Goebbels had been reading in bed a seventeen-year-old book, *Mysterien von Sonne und Seele* by

Dr H. H. Kritzinger, in which there was a chapter on Nostradamus which mentioned how a German commentator, C. Loog, in a book published in 1921, had interpreted quatrain 57 of *Centuries III* as meaning that in 1939 there would be major crises in both Britain and Poland. She was so excited that she roused her husband and made him read it.

Within a few days four other people drew Goebbels's attention to this prophecy, with the result that he sent for Dr Kritzinger. When Ellic Howe questioned the latter he described what happened at the Propaganda Ministry on 4th December 1939. It appeared it was the manner in which the prophecy had been fulfilled that had impressed Goebbels. He could see a host of psychological warfare possibilities, and obviously supposed that any Nostradamus expert would be able to provide him with further propaganda material for circulation outside Germany. Would Dr Kritzinger work through Nostradamus for him?

The visitor explained that he was fully occupied as director of a scientific research institute. Goebbels then asked whom he could recommend as the best available Nostradamus specialist, so he suggested Loog, but as the latter when approached declined the assignment Dr Kritzinger at last mentioned Krafft.

As a result the latter was summoned to Berlin for discussions. He did not see Goebbels, and was interviewed instead by Dr Fesel. He was told the sort of Nostradamus material that he would be expected to provide, and that he might be asked to undertake some kind of intelligence work in the Low Countries.

In January 1940 Karl Ernst Krafft started work for the Propaganda Ministry under Dr Fesel's supervision. His ego was flattered when at a party Dr Hans Frank, the Governor-General of Poland, introduced him as 'the man who accurately predicted the attempt on the Führer's life'. During the course of the evening he was asked to speak about Nostradamus's prophecies, and afterwards he displayed a chart showing the astrological aspects that he considered would aid Germany during 1940. He ended by warning that for final victory to be certain the war must be over by early 1943.

The first results of Krafft's work proved to be 299 copies of a photolithographic reproduction of the 1568 edition of the *Centuries*, with a commentary in the form of a 32-page pamphlet in a pocket inside the cover. The original typescript had come to over two hundred pages, and made a number of astonishing deductions, such as the imminent invasion of Holland and Belgium by the German armed forces. But the security people objected, and ruthlessly censored it, with the result that all that was left was an innocuous essay on the difficulties of interpreting the quatrains.

It is puzzling why the propaganda authorities should even have allowed the copies to be produced. Ellic Howe points out that for the purposes of psychological warfare it would have sufficed to allow their tame editor to supply his own interpretations of an appropriate selection from the thousand available quatrains, and then have them adapted or rewritten by a hack propaganda writer who would certainly not have shown Krafft's reverent interest in Nostradamus. However, Howe states, if Krafft required a bait to make the task attractive the concession that he should have a book to show for his pains was psychologically a sound move.

The bait must have worked, for Walter Schellenberg writes in his memoirs that in mid-May, about the time the German armies were crossing the Belgian frontier near Sedan, he was instructed to collaborate with the Propaganda Ministry in the production of material for dissemination in France. He mentions leaflets containing appropriately threatening quatrains from the *Centuries* that were dropped from aircraft.

Nostradamus was made to predict that south-east France would not be affected by the hostilities, and Schellenberg claimed that the civilian population accordingly took to the roads in that direction, thus leaving the approaches to Paris and the Channel ports less congested when the German armies began to move.

In early 1941 Krafft's book, *Comment Nostradamus a-t-il*

entrevu l'Avenir de l'Europe?, was published in German-occupied Brussels, while preparations were in progress to invade England. It was just over 200 pages long, and contained interpretations of forty quatrains. Krafft had had some heated disagreements with Dr Wilmanns of the Foreign Office, who had supervised the preparation of the work, and who had wanted him to make certain comments more definitely in Germany's favour. Krafft thought that to do so would be to arouse suspicions, so to end the dispute the quatrains in question were omitted.

Commentators in more recent years have regarded the following as referring to the controversy in Britain over her entry into the Common Market:

Dedans les isles si horrible tumulte
Rien on n'orra qu'une bellique brigue
Tant grand sera des predateurs l'insulte
Qu'on se viendra ranger a la grande ligue.

(II, 100)

Within the Isles there will be such horrible tumult
That nothing shall be heard but the clashing of factions,
So great shall be the insult of the Robbers
That everyone shall join the great league.

Krafft's interpretation of this was: 'Within the British Isles there will be such a state of chaos that nothing shall be heard but total war. The injuries that these pirates have inflicted upon the nations in the past will have been so great that all Europe will unite to put an end to their predatory behaviour.'

The volume contained a statement to the effect that translations into German, English, Spanish and Rumanian were in preparation, but Ellic Howe during his researches failed to find any printed copies in these languages, though he did discover a Portuguese translation that was brought out under the title of *Nostradamus vê o futuro da Europe* by Ediçioes Alma, a firm of publishers that were secretly controlled by the German Embassy in Lisbon. A copy of this is in the British Museum Library.

On 10th May 1941 Rudolf Hess flew to Scotland, hoping to see the Duke of Hamilton and through him Winston Churchill and to negotiate a peace with Germany. He did this because his astrological advisers had told him that from the end of April 1941 Hitler's aspects were bad and that from then onwards Germany's chances of winning the war would deteriorate.

The Nazis explained the defection by saying that Hess had become mentally deranged through consorting with astrologers. On 9th June all engaged in such pursuits, including occultists, were arrested and put in concentration camps. Their homes were searched and their books and papers confiscated. Three days later two members of the Gestapo called on Krafft and took him away to the Alexanderplatz police prison in Berlin for interrogation. It soon became clear that, as a Swiss national who had come to live in Germany at the beginning of the war, it was suspected he might be a British agent. It took a year to convince the Gestapo that he was not a spy.

Twelve days after Hess's flight to Scotland an article entitled 'Astrology in Hitler's Service' had appeared in *Die Zeitung*, a weekly whose readership consisted of émigré Germans and Austrians in Britain. In it, the author, Walter Tscheppik, wrote that the Führer kept his personal astrologer at Berchtesgaden, and that until recently this had been Krafft, who, however, had disappeared and was believed to have been murdered. He had been succeeded by Rudolf Assietz, 'a young man of whom it is only known that he has daemonic dark eyes and black hair brushed back over his head'.

This was published on 22nd May, and Krafft was not arrested until 12th June, so the article appears based on rumour rather than fact. It was on 13th June the following year that he was released and taken to a branch of the Kommandantenstrasse, where he was told that he was to work on the preparation and interpretation of horoscopes of British, American and Russian generals, admirals and statesmen.

Herr F. G. Goerner, another astrologer who assisted Krafft, told Ellic Howe that they were shown the chart of Field-

Marshal Montgomery, who was born on 17th November 1887, while Rommel was born at almost exactly the same time as Montgomery on 15th November 1891—both under Scorpio, the lucky-in-war sign. Krafft commented, 'Well, this man's chart is certainly stronger than Rommel's.'

It is interesting to note that shortly before this Goebbels had written in his diary for 19th May 1942 that a plan had been drawn up demonstrating how they could enlist the aid of the occult in their propaganda. 'We are really getting somewhere. The Americans and English fall easily for that type of thing. We are therefore pressing into our service all the experts we can find on occult prophecies . . . Nostradamus must once again submit to being quoted.'

After two months Krafft and Goerner were transferred to a squalid building in the Köpenickerstrasse. The former was depressed by the move. When his wife saw Herr Ehrhardt of the Reichssicherheitshauptamt and said she was surprised that he had been engaged to do astrological work, as she thought it had been completely forbidden in Germany, the other replied that this was so. 'We don't want any astrology in Germany. His stuff is being used for propaganda purposes.'

Ellic Howe believes that it was the realization his sole function was to provide astrological fodder for processing by propaganda hacks which had a demoralizing effect on Krafft and brought on a nervous breakdown. He had always been talkative; now he became silent and withdrawn. Even when, after ten weeks, they were transferred to better quarters in the Lützowstrasse his condition did not improve. He developed a persecution mania, and wrote a letter to a senior official accusing him of trying to find a pretext for incarcerating him in a concentration camp. It was humiliating for a man of his reputation to be asked to provide commonplace astrological predictions, but he would make one that would very shortly come true: British bombs would rain down on the Propaganda Ministry, punishing them for their scurvy treatment of him.

Frau Krafft went to see the man to whom this letter had been sent and begged him not to take any notice of it, but the fellow told her curtly that his department had no further use for her husband's services.

On 12th February 1943 Krafft was taken to an underground cell in the Lehrterstrasse prison. Fifty prisoners were confined in a space scarcely large enough for a quarter of that number. Three weeks later he caught typhus. No sooner had he recovered than he was removed to the concentration camp at Oranienburg, where he was so ill that he had to be admitted to the infirmary. Another Swiss prisoner, Jacques Farjon, who met him later, described his impressions in a German newspaper. He wrote, 'His expression was remarkable. It had magnetic strength. Beneath a large intelligent forehead his deep-set eyes burned with an inner fire—two dark eyes that held you and did not leave you, peering at you and seeming to penetrate your most secret thoughts.'

Nearly two years later, on 8th January 1945, Krafft died while he was being transferred to the dread Buchenwald camp.

As Ellic Howe says, the lesson to be learnt from the Krafft story is how astrological beliefs, preoccupations and ambitions can dominate a human life, and, in Krafft's case, ultimately destroy it.

9 *Some Seeresses—and Premonitions Bureaux*

Apart from the priestesses employed in the oracles of ancient Greece, my choice has included only one woman. This is due to the sad fact that in the past a male-dominated society made it difficult for the daughters of Eve to rise to any eminence. When they displayed any prophetic gifts they might, were they members of religious orders and predicted in a way that did not offend the ecclesiastical establishment, hope for beatification or even canonization when dead. But if they offended their superiors or were in secular life, then they would most likely be denounced as devil-possessed witches, suffer persecution and a terrible death, which is what happened to France's great patriot and prophetess, Joan of Arc. It is true that she was canonized, but it took nearly five hundred years before that happened.

But with emancipation women have excelled in every field, and in the past hundred years many of them have made their names as successful practitioners in precognition all over the world.

Since Mlle Lenormand, probably the most successful of French fortune-tellers was Anne Victoire Savary, better known as Madame de Thèbes, who published an almanac every year containing her predictions. In the issue that appeared on 1st January 1899 she foretold the death of President Félix Faure within two months, and he obediently died on 16th February that year. Then in 1905 she wrote, 'The future of Belgium is extraordinarily sad. . . . This land will set all Europe in flames.' In 1913 she went into more detail:

Jeane Dixon. *By courtesy of William Morrow & Co. Inc., New York*

> I see in the hands of distinguished Italians I have studied signs of a war of unprecedented violence. . . . When it comes, Germany will have desired it; but after that neither Prussia nor the Hohenzollerns will keep their former dominating position. As I have repeatedly emphasized, the days of the Kaiser are numbered, and after him great changes will take place in Germany. I speak of his reign, not of the days of his life.

In the almanack for the same year, she also said. 'The Prince who awaits the Imperial throne shall not reign'. Then in 1914 she stated, 'The tragedy in the Imperial House of Austria, which was foretold a year ago, will come to pass. No one is able to ward off destiny.' Her prophecies came to fruition—on 28th July, when the Archduke Francis Ferdinand was assinated at Sarajevo—on 4th August when Great Britain declared war against Germany—and four years later in 1918, when the Kaiser abdicated and the rule of the Hohenzollerns ended.

Madame de Thèbes, who was a palmist as well as an astrologer, also drew attention before the outbreak of the 1914 war to the many hands of Englishmen she had seen bearing indications of violent deaths and wounds, including loss of life through drowning. The number of them was so striking that she believed Britain would be involved in a great war.

Sir Osbert Sitwell, without actually mentioning her by name, wrote in his book *Great Morning*, published in 1948, that 'nearly all the brother-officers' of his own age had visited in the first half of 1914 'a celebrated palmist of the period whom, I remember it was said, Mr. Winston Churchill used sometimes to consult'. In each case, just when she had started to read the outstretched hand, she had flung it from her, exclaiming, 'I don't understand it! It's the same thing again! After two or three months, the line of life stops short and I can read nothing.' Sir Osbert stated that the officers concerned were later killed in the War.

Eileen Quelch in *Perfect Darling*, her biography of George Cornwallis-West, Churchill's stepfather, mentions how years previously in the nineties the future Sir Winston as a young man spent two guineas on a palm reading from Cheiro's rival, the remarkable Mrs Robinson, and was impressed by her 'strange skill' but could not agree to have his 'hand published to the world' in her book, *The Graven Palm.* Randolph Churchill in his life of his father records how in 1899 on return from abroad he again consulted Mrs Robinson, 'who had claimed to see favourable omens in his hands'. It was she whom Oscar Wilde called 'the Sibyl of Mortimer Street' and who told him in July 1894, 'I see a very brilliant life for you up to a certain point, then I see a wall. Beyond the wall I see nothing.'

Frau Elsbeth Ebertin was the first woman in Germany to achieve fame as a professional astrologer. It was in 1917 that she started to publish yearly her almanac, *Ein Blick in die Zukunft*, 'a glance into the future'. This proved better written and, more important, more accurate, than most similar publications, with the result that her reputation grew.

In the spring of 1923 she was preparing the script for her 1924 volume when she received a letter from a woman living in Munich, who was an ardent supporter of Hitler and his new National Socialist German Workers' Party which was just beginning to come to the fore. The correspondent gave details of Hitler's birth and wrote that she would like to learn what Frau Ebertin thought his future would be. The latter cast Hitler's horoscope and included her findings in the almanack for the coming year, without mentioning him by name. This read:

> A man of action born on 20 April 1889, with Sun in 29° Aries at the time of his birth can expose himself to personal danger by excessively uncautious action and could very likely trigger off an uncontrollable crisis. His constellations show that this man is to be taken very seriously indeed. He is destined to play a 'Führer-role' in future battles. It seems that the man I have in mind, with this strong Aries influence, is destined to sacrifice himself for the German nation, also to face up to all circumstances with audacity and courage, even when it is a matter of life and death, and to

> give an impulse which will burst forth quite suddenly to a German Freedom Movement. But I will not anticipate destiny. Time will show, but the present state of affairs, at the time I write this, naturally cannot last.

The opening reference about exposing himself to personal danger by excessively uncautious action and triggering off an uncontrollable crisis was fulfilled when in early November, 1923, Hitler's *Putsch* in a Munich beer cellar was followed by a march led by himself, Goering and other supporters, some of whom were killed when the police fired on them. Hitler's shoulder was broken in the affray. He was later arrested, sentenced and imprisoned, and spent the time writing part of *Mein Kampf*.

Frau Ebertin made the most of her Hitler prediction at the time of his trial by writing in collaboration with a journalist, L. Hoffmann, and publishing a best-selling book *Sternenwandel und Weltgeschehen* ('The Stars in their Courses and World Events').

It appears that her warning was shown before November 1923 to Hitler, who commented irritably, 'What on earth have women and the stars got to do with me?' Frau Ebertin went to one of his meetings and told Hoffmann that when speaking on the platform he seemed to her 'a man possessed, like a medium, the unconscious tool of higher powers'. She predicted 'that recent events will not only give this movement inner strength, but external strength as well'.

Frau Ebertin was killed in an air raid on Freiburg im Breisgau in November 1944. Nearly twenty years later, writing in *Kosmobiologie*, her son, Reinhold Ebertin, wrote:

> My mother saw the crisis coming, for she knew the horoscopes of many people living in the neighbouring houses. However, if she had left, it would have caused a terrible turmoil and she would have been picked up by the Gestapo because people were saying: 'So long as Frau Ebertin is here nothing very much can happen to us!'

Bulgaria has its own State-sponsored seeress in a blind peasant woman, Vanga Dimitrova. Those anxious to consult her would wait for hours in the yard outside her cottage, refusing to leave until she had given them a reading. Sometimes she gave over fifty a day, with the result that she had a nervous breakdown, so the Government took her under its protection in 1965. All applications for appointments have to be submitted first through a committee so that she is not overworked. Bulgarians are charged ten leva for a consultation and foreigners sixty, while the State pays her four hundred a month, which is her salary as 'Assistant Professor'. Mr K. Q. F. Manning, British Cultural Attaché at Sofia, informed me that this title 'was apparently given in recognition of the scientific significance and validity of her unusual gifts'.

Tests have been conducted with her by Dr Georgi Lozanov of the Institute of Suggestology in the Bulgarian capital. Once a year questionnaires are posted to her clients asking them to report on the accuracy or otherwise of her predictions. Her average score to date has been over 80% correct, and she is regularly consulted by leading Bulgarian personalities, including, it is said, the head of the Government. Soviet parapsychologists seeking a scientific explanation for her gifts have studied the energy fields around her, but have reached no positive conclusions.

Hungary's most noted woman fortune-teller this century was probably Boriska Silbiger, who in 1934 predicted that a Nazi leader would be killed by his friends and that a king whose name began with an 'A' would be murdered. On 30th June Ernst Roehm was shot on Hitler's orders, and on 9th October King Alexander I of Yugoslavia was assassinated at Marseilles. In December 1935, she foretold that during the coming year 'the king of a great empire would die'. He would be succeeded by his eldest son. 'But the reign of this successor will not last twelve months, whereafter he will renounce the throne.' King George V of Great Britain died on 20th January 1936, and was succeeded by his eldest son, the Prince of Wales, who became King Edward VIII and abdicated on 10th

December 1936.

Evangeline Adams, descendant of John Quincy Adams, sixth President of the United States, shocked upper-crust Bostonian society, among whom she had been brought up, by starting to tell fortunes professionally. When her own horoscope advised her to move to New York she did so on 16th March 1899, but was refused accommodation by a staid Fifth Avenue hotel owned by a family friend, when it was learned that she wished to receive clients in her room.

Warren E. Leland, proprietor of the Windsor Hotel on 8th Avenue, proved much more broadminded in his outlook, and while her suite was being made ready she rewarded him by casting his horoscope. She was alarmed to find that he was threatened by the worst possible combination of planets, and warned that a terrible disaster would overtake him on the morrow.

However, Leland, whose hobby was speculating on Wall Street, only laughed and retorted, 'Tomorrow's a public holiday. Stocks can't go down'. But the new arrival proved right when next day, during the St Patrick's Day Parade the hotel was burnt down and (small consolation to Leland) she at least lost her luggage in the blaze.

All the New York newspapers featured the fulfilment of the grim prediction, and the publicity helped to establish her as a professional astrologer. She proved remarkably correct with her forecasts and her clients included King Edward VII, Enrico Caruso, Mary Pickford and the millionaire J. P. Morgan, who regarded her as the best of all his financial advisers.

In 1914 someone newly in charge at police headquarters in New York disapproved of fortune-telling and had her arrested and charged. She decided to conduct her own defence, and arrived in court with a pile of authoritative tomes on astrology. She explained to the judge how a chart was prepared, and offered to prove the truth of astrology by casting a horoscope given any birth data he might care to provide.

He agreed to do this, supplying the particulars pertaining to a 'Mr. X'. She consulted an ephemeris and table of houses, filled in the blank parts of a chart and commenced her analysis. The judge listened intently. When she had ended he commented, 'Evangeline Adams, you understand my son better than I do. You have raised astrology to the dignity of an exact science. The case is dismissed.'

After such a compliment and such an acquittal, her consulting-rooms in Carnegie Hall were besieged by would-be clients, and the Press named her 'America's female Nostradamus'. As a result of her victory New York today is one of the few states where it is legal to advertise and charge fees for astrological advice and horoscopes.

In 1930 she became the first astrologer in the world to have her own radio programme broadcasting three times a week. Soon she was receiving 4 000 orders a day for her sun-sign forecast pamphlets. Apart from accurate predictions, much of her success was due to her sympathetic and soothing way of speaking over the air to the lonely, the frustrated and the bereaved who wrote to her. She died on 10th November 1932, having, unlike most seers and seeresses, given the date of her own death. This was in a way fortunate for her, as shortly afterwards the Federal Radio Commission banned all fortune-tellers from broadcasting stations in the United States owing to the plethora of astrologers who, encouraged by her pioneering breakthrough, were pouring out their cosmic claptrap to the annoyance of the witch-hunting class.

The Duchess of Windsor tells in her memoirs how in 1926 at the time of her first divorce she was persuaded to consult a New York woman astrologer, known as Evangeline Adams's favourite pupil, who predicted Wallis would have two more marriages in her life and eventually die unexpectedly and in an unusual place. Between the ages of forty and fifty, she would exercise 'considerable power of some kind'. The last fascinated her, and she asked what kind.

'The aura is not clear', the astrologer replied. 'But the power will be considerable. You will become a famous woman.' When the other inquired whether such power would be connected with a job the fortune-teller shook her head. 'Absolutely not. There is nothing to suggest an association with a business career. The indications are all strongly in the opposite direction. You will lead a woman's life, marrying, divorcing, marrying again, with several serious emotional crises. The power that is to come to you will be related to a man.'

The future Duchess had just tried to earn her own living as a travelling saleswoman in tubular scaffolding which had ended disastrously during the training course through her poor arithmetic. The astrologer's words, it would seem, made her abandon attempting a business career, marry Ernest Simpson instead and go to live in London.

Perhaps the most talked of prediction this century was that of Mrs Jeane Dixon, who foretold John F. Kennedy's assassination—and to Franklin D. Roosevelt his four election victories. When in November 1944 the latter questioned, 'How long have I left?' her answer was: 'Six months or less'. On 12th April 1945 he died. She told him at the same interview, 'China will go Communist and become our greatest trouble. Africa will be our next biggest worry in the foreign field.'

Her first forecast concerning the American Presidency occurred while she was still at school, when she said Herbert Hoover would be elected. Harry S. Truman could not believe it possible when she informed him during the Second World War that he would soon become President and hold the office for two terms. Her next correct prophecy came with Dwight Eisenhower's win in 1952.

When in 1945 Sir Winston Churchill was in America she warned him that if he called an early election he would be defeated. He disregarded her advice, went to the country that June and lost. She had also said that he would be Prime Minister again within six years, which, of course, occurred.

It was in June 1947 that she accurately predicted Mahatma Gandhi would be murdered on 30th January 1948. Eight years later, when questioned by Nehru as to who would succeed him as Indian Prime Minister, she told him that within eight years a man whose name commenced with 'S' would do so. This proved to be Lal Bahadur Shastri. Much earlier, in 1946, she had prophesied India's partition, and the very date when it would take place in 1947.

When the American Ambassador to Russia, Joseph E. Davies, asked her what she foresaw happening in that country she replied that Malenkov would be peacefully succeeded within two years by 'a man with an oval-shaped head, wavy gray hair, a little goatee and greenish eyes', which proved to be an excellent description of Marshal Bulganin, and that he in his turn would soon be replaced by 'a short, bald-headed man', which was an apt pen picture of Khrushchev. The latter would win prestige through the sending up of 'a silken ball into outer space, which would circle the globe and return to the USSR'. This turned out to be the first sputnik satellite, launched in 1957.

Dag Hammarskjöld died when his plane crashed on 18th September 1961. A few months previously Mrs Dixon had warned a friend, Eleanor Bumgardner, 'Whatever you do this summer—don't fly in the same plane with Dag Hammarskjöld in mid-September, for this plane will crash and he will be killed.' Soon after this prediction was fulfilled, she made another startling one—that Marilyn Monroe would take her life 'within the year', which occurred through an overdose of sleeping tablets.

In 1956 an interview with Mrs Dixon appeared in the American magazine *Parade*. She told the writer, Jack Anderson, that four years earlier on a drizzly rainy morning she went into St Matthew's Cathedral in Washington for her morning devotion. She experienced a feeling of expectancy as if something momentous was going to happen.

> I remember standing in front of the statue of the Virgin Mary when suddenly the White House appeared before me in dazzling brightness. Coming out of a haze, the numerals 1–9–6–0 formed above the roof. An ominous black cloud appeared, covering the numbers, and dripped slowly into the White House. . . .
>
> Then I looked down and saw a young man, tall and blue-

eyed, crowned with a shock of thick brown hair, quietly standing in front of the main door. I was still staring at him when a voice came out of nowhere, telling me softly that this young man, a Democrat, to be elected as President in 1960, would be assassinated while in office.

Following Kennedy's election she had another vision, this time of his coffin being carried out of the White House menaced by black clouds. In October 1963 she told the psychiatrist Dr F. R. Riesemann and the journalist Ruth Montgomery of a vision in which the vice-presidential plaque was removed from Lyndon Johnson's door. The man responsible for doing this had a two-syllable name with five or six letters. She said, 'The second letter was definitely an 's' and the first looked like an 'O'. The last letter ended with a little curve that went straight up.' The name of Kennedy's assassin was, of course, Lee Oswald.

From the beginning of November, 1963, Jeane Dixon was obsessed with the belief that the President was going to be shot. She informed a friend, Mrs Harley Cope, and other well-known personalities in Washington of this feeling that was growing daily stronger. Then, on the Tuesday of the assassination week, she saw in another vision John F. Kennedy being shot in the head. On the fatal Friday when she sat down for breakfast she suddenly exclaimed, 'This is the day it will happen.'

Mrs Dixon also foretold the assassination of Robert Kennedy. She says that in this case she picked up 'the thoughts of the plotters by telepathy'. She predicted the Watergate scandal, and in 1975 telephoned King Faisal of Saudi Arabia to warn him that his life was in danger. A month later he too was assassinated.

Regarding the future, she forecasts a woman President in the White House, possibly 'at the same time as the comet'. The latter will disrupt Russia's plans for world conquest. This refers to Halley's comet, due to return in 1985.

On a short visit to London in mid-February, 1976, Jeane

made a number of startling prophecies in the *Sun* newspaper. Harold Wilson when he left office would be knighted and would remain as an M.P. in the House of Commons. Should he resign before the end of 1978, then there was a strong possibility that following a General Election Mrs Thatcher would become the next Prime Minister, but only for a short while. Should he not retire by then, she would never occupy No. 10. Mrs Dixon believed that Eric Varley would 'leap into the spotlight' and have a 'tremendous triumph', probably in 1978. She foresees Sir Geoffrey Howe, the Conservative Shadow Chancellor, eventually attaining the Premiership. By the end of this century there will be so many parties in the House of Commons that no Government will ever have a majority, with the result that the military will be forced to intervene to restore order.

As regards the Royal Family, Prince Charles's marriage will be a late one to a British bride, and 'he will never rest too easily with the duties of Kingship' and might 'consider giving them up entirely as the years go by'. But he will 'certainly do a splendid job as King'. Prince Andrew's performance of 'the roles assigned to him in government will win the respect of those who do not favour the monarchy'. Probably in the period from 1988 to 1990 he will reach 'fantastic heights', and may even assume the Crown from his brother.

For the Shah of Iran, Mrs Dixon foresees a gloomy future. In 1977 a revolution will drive him abroad, due to the machinations of a foreign Power. But after living in seclusion for a time he will once again 'stride into the world spotlight'.

Jeanne Gardner, the housewife of West Virginia, is another much-discussed American seeress. She claims to be told what is going to happen by a voice which is calm when the prediction is a happy one and which cries when it is tragic.

She says she knew a year beforehand that Robert Kennedy would be murdered. On Sunday, 2nd June 1968, she travelled to Washington where the annual booksellers' convention was being held in the Shoreham Hotel. She hoped to persuade Mrs Bea Moore of Simon and Schuster, the publishers, to bring out a book about her life and prophecies.

She rested that evening in her hotel. Next morning she was about to set off when the Voice spoke and told her to write down a message in her journal, which she did. It was to the effect that Kennedy would be assassinated early on 5th June in a 'galley' by a short, swarthy man. The message ended with the words 'Sirhan–Sirhan'.

Mrs Gardner was extremely upset, and hurried to the convention, where she told sceptical Mrs Moore what had happened and half dragged her back to the other hotel to point out to her what she had written down at the Voice's dictation.

Mrs Moore flew back to New York on the evening of Tuesday, 4th June, leaving behind a desperately worried Jeanne Gardner, who paced her bedroom in growing apprehension and then found herself racing to the crowded suite in the Shoreham Hotel, where she startled the booksellers and publishers' sales people by announcing that Robert Kennedy would be murdered in a kitchen in the early hours of the coming day. Then she made her way back to the other hotel and went to bed.

Something made her wake at 3 a.m. She switched on the bedside radio and heard an agitated man's voice giving the news that she had been fearfully expecting. There were so many witnesses to what she had predicted that there can be no doubt as to its authenticity.

Another American who predicted the murder of Robert Kennedy was Alan Vaughan, who sent a letter to the Central Premonitions Registry from Germany in May 1968 to this effect. In 1970 he also recorded that Nixon would be re-elected, and that there would be trouble and 'possibly scandal in his second term'.

In early 1963 Jeanne Gardner claims in her book *A Grain of Mustard*, published in 1969, that she had heard her Voice warn that John F. Kennedy would be assassinated. Then in August that year it called out 'Oswald', but she did not understand at the time what this meant.

According to Mrs Gardner, both her mother and her

grandmother used to hear the same Voice prophesying, and sometimes she herself together with an aunt and uncle will carry on a conversation with it. She claims that when they are far apart the Voice will speak a few words to each which separately do not make sense, but put together clearly foretell some event.

In 1947 a group of British doctors and psychiatrists began a series of experiments. They agreed that immediately they woke up in the mornings for six days a week they would write down their dreams in as great detail as possible and then post off the record to the Jung Institute in Zürich. If they felt that what they had dreamed the previous night was of special significance they were to lodge an account of it with a bank so that the date and time of the dreams could be established.

Some of the dreams thus collected from all over the world seemed to give foreknowledge of major events such as atomic-bomb tests and aircraft disasters. Soon it was found that, while the dream of one member of the organization might vaguely foretell some calamity, if all the dreams recorded and received from all over the world were carefully considered quite an impressive pool of information might be assembled, giving a strong indication of what one could expect to happen.

For example, on 2nd and 3rd September 1954 Dr Alice Buck, the psychiatrist responsible for the commencement of this investigation, dreamed of an impending aircraft disaster in which the time of 3 a.m. seemed important. At 3.40 a.m. on 4th September a KLM Constellation airliner crashed within sight of Shannon Airport. Meanwhile, during the night just before this catastrophe another member of the research unit had dreamed of a small number of men and women battling on a journey against severe climatic conditions. These people appeared to be passing through a ford when the water engulfed them. The dreamer summed it up by saying that it was like Christian and Faithful going through the River of Death.

This dream is remarkable when one compares it with the following description of the disaster in a newspaper.

Men and women died yesterday, trapped in darkness in the cabin of a crashed airliner slowly filled with the muddy waters of the river Shannon. One man had clung for 3 hours to the tail of the almost submerged airliner waiting for rescue. The plane crashed at 3.40 a.m., but it was not until nearly 2½ hours later that a warning was given to the airport by the Second Officer who swam to a mudflat and then crawled painfully through two miles of mud and slime. The first rescue party arrived 3½ hours after the crash.

On 12th March 1954 another participant in this project, a governess, dreamed of a bird like a duck on the ground amid tropical vegetation. Immediately she awoke she drew a picture of what she had seen. In this drawing the duck looked exactly like the outline of a modern airliner. That same night, Dr Alice Buck in London awoke with a feeling of great distress. Next day there was the Constellation crash in Singapore with the loss of 33 lives.

These investigators came to the conclusion that any connection between the dreamer and the persons likely to be involved in a disaster might produce a warning dream. For this reason, after the Comets had been grounded following the Elba disaster of 10th January 1954 Dr Buck decided to travel herself in the first plane directly the service was resumed on 23rd March.

But from the beginning of February correspondence describing dreams increasingly suggested that some new calamity was impending. Dr Buck therefore did not proceed with her plan to travel on the Comet. At the start of April the dreams became more specific, giving details of site, altitude, cause, number of passengers and amount of wreckage likely to be found in the next Comet crash, which occurred, as predicted, off Naples on 8th April with a death roll of 26. All these details had been sent in advance to the Ministry of Transport and Civil Aviation, but no action was taken by them in the matter. The officials there were startled and embarrassed when the disaster occurred exactly as predicted in the solid-looking document on 'pre-accident detection for aircraft' which they had disregarded.

A somewhat similar project began in late 1966 through the efforts of the late Dr J. C. Barker, the psychiatrist and authority on Morbid Periodicity. Over many years he had investigated hundreds of cases where patients had willed themselves to disease and death, and in his book *Scared to Death* he discussed cases of persons dying at the exact time predicted by fortune-tellers, and suggested that some of them had literally frightened themselves to death as the fatal day approached. He pointed out that the endocrine glands were involved in cases of mental disturbance arising from fortune-telling.

Dr Barker also suggested that possibly precognition does not go much beyond Dr Maurice Nicholl's elaboration upon Jung's theory of synchronisms. He was struck, as many of us are by the way one is suddenly besieged with repetitions of the same notion. The idea itself may be quite trivial, but within a day or two we can find ourselves meeting two different men with the same unusual surname. He writes, 'A premonition may be nothing more than a special case of synchronism and in fact the order of events may be quite immaterial'.

On the morning of 21st October 1966 a huge coal-tip on the mountain-side above the Welsh mining village of Aberfan suddenly started to slide down, ravaging almost everything in its way, including Pantglas Infants and Junior School which it buried beneath its avalanche of black slurry, killing 128 children. Houses too were pulverized, and 16 adults lost their lives.

Dr Barker, who was then a consultant at Shelton Hospital, Shrewsbury, travelled to Aberfan to try to help in the rescue operations. The thought then occurred to him that dream premonitions of the tragedy might have been experienced by some people. He consequently contacted Peter Fairley, Science Editor of the London *Evening Standard*, and persuaded him to publish an appeal inviting letters from their readers giving particulars of any such precognition.

Seventy-six replies were received: sixty of these could be regarded as containing sufficient correct details of the event to merit Dr Barker's investigating them further. He found that twenty-two were supported by statements from one to four persons to whom the dreams had been described before fulfilment, while two had been written down immediately on awaking.

Possibly the most impressive account came from Mrs Grace Engleton of Sidcup, Kent, who wrote on 30th October 1966:

> I have never been to Wales nor do I possess a television set. On the night of Friday, October 14, I had a vivid horrible dream of a terrible disaster in a coal mining village. It was in a valley with a big building filled with young children. Mountains of coal and water were rushing down upon the valley, burying the building. The screams of those children were so vivid that I screamed myself. It all happened so quickly. Then everything went black. I have had many dreams and premonitions which have come true.

Her statement was confirmed by her neighbour, Mrs Rollings, whose letter read:

> Mrs Engleton told me about her dream on Monday, October 17. She said she was standing on a kind of mountain and saw what looked like coal come sliding down into a valley on to a lot of children. . . . She said she heard the children screaming and she screamed with them.

Mrs Engleton's dream, it will be noted, occurred a week before the disaster, and she told it to Mrs Rollings three days later.

In an article published in the *Medical News-Tribune* of 20th January 1967 Dr Barker wrote, 'While analysing the letters, I realized that the time had surely come to call a halt to attempts to prove or disprove precognition. We should instead set about trying to harness and utilize it with a view to preventing future disasters.'

The previous month in December 1966 at Barker's suggestion Peter Fairley had agreed for one year from 1st January

1967 to operate a Premonitions Bureau from the *Evening Standard* offices and to invite the public to send in their experiences. At the end of the first twelve months 469 predictions of natural disasters, political events, etc., were recorded, and Mr Fairley, reporting in his paper on 11th March 1968, stated that he believed the Bureau had received in advance of the events foretold eighteen genuine examples of precognition.

Seven of the eighteen came from two people, Miss Lorna Middleton, a 53-year-old ballet and piano teacher of Edmonton, and five from Mr Alan Hencher, a 44-year-old Post Office switchboard operator, of Dagenham. General conclusions were that there was an almost equal distribution of premonitions between the sexes, that more than half came in dreams and most of the remainder in 'visions' before the eyes.

Mr Hencher on 21st March 1967 predicted in considerable detail an early-morning air crash in mountains in which 123 or 124 people would be involved. On 20th April a Britannia crashed into a hill in Cyprus, killing 124.

On 22nd April he foresaw a train accident involving a narrow-gauge railway with flat-sided, wooden coaches and wooden seats for passengers. On 31st May a 'Tom Thumb' miniature train crashed at Scarborough, injuring seven.

On 1st May he foretold an air disaster in the near future in which more than 60 people would die—including children—but from which there would be several miraculous escapes. He made a special point about the tail fin. Peter Fairley wrote that the details Mr Hencher gave tallied well with the Stockport air disaster on 4th June when 72 people, 10 of them children, were killed. The tail fin stood out vividly from the wreckage and there were some incredible escapes.

As a result of the success of the experiment, the Bureau was kept open for another year to amass more material and observe certain people more closely. In 1968 Dr Barker died and operations were taken over by Peter Fairley himself, who in February 1969 moved to the offices of the *T.V. Times* at 247 Tottenham Court Road, London, W.1., and took the Bureau there with him. He has continued to run it with the assistance of his secretary, Mrs Preston. In February 1976 he told me that since 1969 between 1 000 and 1 500 letters containing premonitions had been received by him each year, but that disappointingly no significant cases of precognition had resulted.

Such pioneering activities in this field have led to similar ones in the United States, where Robert Nelson founded the Central Premonitions Bureau in June 1968. By the end of the first year 600 premonitions had been sent in, and this rose to a total of 2 000 by May 1971. On 23rd June 1969 a letter came from a woman living in Pennsylvania stating, 'There is to be an explosion and fire on the water. . . . Ted Kennedy appears to be involved. . . . An accident brought about by carelessness.' A month later he was involved in the accident to his car at Chappaquiddick.

A woman living in Bridgeport, Connecticut, had a feeling on 17th August 1970 that President Nasser would die as a result of a heart attack. As the days passed this feeling grew so strong that on 21st September, she wrote to the Bureau about it. A week later, on 28th September Nasser died suddenly. This woman mentioned that she received her premonitions when reading the newspapers, and that they occurred in the form of answers to questions raised in news articles.

When the outbreak of a Second World War grew increasingly likely in 1939 the editor of the British occult monthly *Prediction* also tried to gain foreknowledge by consulting a number of people, in this case mediums and astrologers. That February he arranged a special séance with Miss Geraldine Cummins, the internationally reputed automatic writer, and her guide declared that there would be no war that year.

In the April number James Leigh, an expert numerologist pointed out that the figures 1–9–3–9 added up to 22, which was a most powerful force for good in cementing international friendship, and therefore he reached the same conclusion as Miss Cummins.

The following month an article appeared in the sam

periodical headed 'Peace Assured for Ten Years', in which Frank T. Blake, President of the Spiritualists' National Union, wrote, 'I am certain there will be no war in which the British Empire will be engaged within the next decade'.

Then in June R. H. Naylor, the *Sunday Express*'s celebrated astrologer, assured the journal's readers, 'No, Hitler will not lead Germany into war'.

Even in the September issue, which was printed before war broke out on the 3rd of that month, the editor, supported by a cross-section of astrologers and mediums, insisted that there would be no war for the next few years. Then the following month he was faced with the problem of explaining what went wrong. He did so by quoting the distinguished psychic researcher, H. F. Saltmarsh, who had once written that a prophecy may be overridden by human intervention.

The actual passage to which he was referring occurs in Saltmarsh's book *Foreknowledge*, wherein he stated that after long investigation of cases suggesting precognition he had concluded that

> there is a future which is now determined by the present and past, but that it is not inexorably fixed and unalterable—it is, to some extent at least, plastic, and can be modified by actions which we, as beings of some degree of freedom of choice, initiate in the present.

St Thomas Aquinas had somewhat similarly concluded in the thirteenth century that there were two kinds of prophecy: that given in a vision which was inflexible, and that subject to changing conditions which the prophet had not anticipated intellectually.

Most modern astrologers assert that the stars impel but do not compel, and if one takes the view that the future is not inexorably fixed prediction can be regarded as no more than an indication of what is likely to happen. Should the universe function only according to those rules of cause and effect of which we are aware, then it ensues that the causes of everything that will occur in the future exist now. A brain sufficiently responsive to be affected by these causative influences through the known senses—and any others of which we are at present ignorant—ought to be able, like a highly developed form of computer, to classify and interpret them so as to foretell their likely ultimate effects.

Many theories have been advanced to try to explain the enigma of time and render credible precognition, but unfortunately all are based on assumptions, and so the great debate continues. One thing, however, is certain: mankind being incurably curious, there will always be an affluent future for those who foretell it.

Select Bibliography

1 THE PYTHIA OF DELPHI

For quotations from Greek historians and philosophers the following editions have been used:

DIODORUS SICULUS: *Bibliotheca historica*, text by L. Dindorf (1866–68) revised by F. Vogel (1888–93).

HERODOTUS: *The History*, translation by George Rowlinson (1858–60).

PAUSANIAS: *Description of Hellas*, text with translation and commentary by J. G. Frazer (1898).

PLATO: *Dialogues*, translation by Benjamin Jowett (1871).

PLUTARCH: *Lives* (Nicias), with commentary by H. Holden (1881–98).
Moralia, edition by G. Bernadakis in the Teubner series (1881–96).

For further reading, the following are recommended:

FARNELL, L. R.: *Cults of the Greek States* (London, 1896–1909).

FLACELIERE, ROBERT, trans. D. Garman: *Greek Oracles* (Elek, London, 1965).

GLOTZ, G.: *The Greek City and Its Institutions* (Kegan Paul, London, 1929).

GUTHRIE, W. K. C.: *The Greeks and their Gods* (Methuen, London, 1950).

HALLIDAY, W. R.: *Greek Divination* (Macmillan, London, 1913).

HAYS, D. A.: *Greek Culture* (New York, 1925).

LIVINGSTONE, SIR R. W.: *Greek Ideals and Modern Life* (Oxford University Press, London, 1935).

MOORE, C. H.: *The Religious Thought of the Greeks* (Harvard University Press, 1916; Humphrey Milford, London, 1917).

NILSSON, N. M. P., trans. F. J. Fielden: *A History of Greek Religion* (Humphrey Milford, London, 1925).

PARKE, H. W.: *A History of the Delphic Oracle* (Basil Blackwell, Oxford, 1939).

SARGEAUNT, G. M.: *The Classical Spirit* (Bradford, 1936).

STEPHENS, K.: *The Greek Spirit* (New York, 1914).

TARN, W. W.: *Hellenistic Civilization* (E. Arnold, London, 1927).

ZIELINSKI, T.: *The Religion of Ancient Greece* (Oxford University Press, London, 1926).

2 NOSTRADAMUS

BARESTE, EUGÈNE: *Nostradamus* (Paris, 1840).

CHEETHAM, ERIKA: *The Prophecies of Nostradamus* (Spearman, London, 1973).

LAVER, JAMES: *Nostradamus* (London, 1952).

LE PELLETIER, ANATOLE: *Les Oracles de Michel de Nostredame* (Paris, 1867).

ROBERTS, HENRY C.: *The Prophecies of Nostradamus* (New York, 1940).

WARD, CHARLES A.: *Oracles of Nostradamus* (London, 1891).

Principal Early Editions

Les Prophéties de M. Michel de Nostradamus—Lyon, chez Macé Bonhomme, 1555. Contains Preface, Epistle to César, his son, Centuries I, II, III and IV (up to quatrain 53). Very rare.

Les Prophéties de M. Michel Nostradamus. Dont il y en a trois cens qui n'ont encore jamais esté imprimées. Lyon, chez Pierre Rigaud, 1558 and 1566.

Known as the *Edition Princeps*, a copy is in the Bibliothèque Nationale in Paris. Consists of two fascicules, one printed in 1558, containing Preface, Epistle, Centuries I–IV and VII (up to quatrain 42); the second, printed in 1566, containing an Epistle to Henri II and Centuries VIII–X in addition.

Les Prophèties de M. Michel Nostradamus. Lyon, chez Benoist Rigaud, 1568.

The True Prophecies or Prognostications of Michel Nostradamus. Translated and Commented by Theophilus de Garencières, London. Printed by Thomas Ratcliffe and Nathaniel Thompson, 1672.

3 DR DEE

The original notes for Dr Dee's Private Diary from 16th Jan. 1577 to 19th Jan. 1601 are in the Bodleian Library. In 1842 they were transcribed and printed for the Camden Society together with notes of nativities from 25th Aug. 1554. The 'Spirituall Diary' or *Liber Mysteriorum* is divided into separate books. The first five, dating from December 1581 to May 1583, are in the British Museum—Sloane MSS. 3188. The remaining twelve, ending on 23rd May 1587, were printed by Dr Meric Casaubon in *The True and Faithful Relation, or Book of Mysteries* in 1659. A translation of the *Hieroglyphic Monad* with a commentary by J. W. Hamilton-Jones was published by John M. Watkins of London in 1947.

DEACON, RICHARD: *John Dee* (Muller, London, 1968).

SMITH, CHARLOTTE FELL: *John Dee 1527–1608* (Constable, London, 1909).

WAITE, A. E.: *Lives of Alchemicall Philosophers* (Edinburgh, 1888).

4 THE BRAHAN SEER

HARVEY, WILLIAM: *Scottish Life and Character in Anecdote and Story* (Stirling, 1899).

MACKENZIE, ALEXANDER: *The Prophecies of the Brahan Seer* Stirling, 1899).

MILLS, HUGH: *Scenes and Legends of the North of Scotland* (Edinburgh, 1860).

5 CAGLIOSTRO

D'ALMERAS, H.: *Cagliostro, la Franc-Maçonnerie et l'Occultisme au XVIIIe siècle.* (Paris, 1904).

EVANS, H. R.: *Cagliostro and his Egyptian Rite of Freemasonry* (New York, 1930).

HARRISON, M.: *Count Cagliostro* (Chapman and Hall, London, 1942).

SCHUR, HARRY C.: *Mystic Rebels* (New York, 1949).

TROWBRIDGE, W. R. H.: *Cagliostro* (London, 1910).

ANONYMOUS: *The Life of Joseph Balsamo, commonly called Count Cagliostro. To which are added the particulars of his trial before the Inquisition. Translated from the original proceedings published at Rome by order of the Apostolic Chamber.* (P. Byrne, Dublin, 1792).

6 MLLE LENORMAND

DU BOIS, L. F.: *De Mlle. Lenormand* (Paris, 1843).

LENORMAND, MARIE-ANNE-ADELAIDE: *The Historical and Secret Memoirs of the Empress Josephine.* Translated from the French. (H. S. Nichols, London, 1895).
Les Souvenirs prophétiques d'une Sibylle sur les causes secrètes de son arrestation, le 11 décembre, 1809 (Paris, 1814).
La Sibylle au tombeau de Louis XVI (Paris, 1816).
Les Oracles Sibyllins (Paris, 1817).
La Sibylle au Congrès d'Aix-la-Chapelle (Paris, 1819).
Souvenirs de la Belgique (Paris, 1822).
L'ombre de Catherine II au tombeau d'Alexandre Ier (Paris, 1826).
L'ombre de Henri IV au palais d'Orléans (Paris, 1831).
Le petit homme rouge au château des Tuileries (Paris, 1831).

MARQUISET, A.: *La célèbre Mlle. Lenormand* (Paris, 1911).

7 'CHEIRO'

HAMON, COUNT LOUIS: *Confessions: memoirs of a modern seer* (Jarrolds, London, 1932).
Fate in the Making (Harper, New York, 1931).
Real Life Stories: sensational personal experiences (Herbert Jenkins, London, 1934).
Cheiro's Book of Numbers (Jenkins, 1935).
Language of the Hand (Jenkins, 1949).
World Predictions (London, 1928, 1931).
(etc.)

NELSON, EDITH H.: *Out of the Silence* (Rider, London, 1945).

8 KRAFFT

KRAFFT, KARL ERNST: *Traité d'astro-biologie* (Brussels, 1939).

HOWE, ELLIC: *Urania's Children: the Strange World of the Astrologers* (Wm Kimber, London, 1967).

9 SOME SEERESSES AND PREMONITION BUREAUX

BARKER, J. C.: *Scared to Death* (Muller, London, 1968).

BUCK, ALICE and PALMER, F. CLAUDE: *The Clothes of God* (Peter Owen, London, 1956).

DIXON, JEANE: *My Life and Prophecies* (New York, 1969; Frederick Muller, London, 1971).

GARDNER, JEANNE: *A Grain of Mustard* (New York, 1969).

MONTGOMERY, RUTH: *A Gift of Prophecy* (New York, 1966; Arthur Barker, London, 1966).

Index